Soldiers
and Society

Soldiers
and Society

THE EFFECTS OF MILITARY
SERVICE AND WAR ON
AMERICAN LIFE

Peter Karsten

GRASS ROOTS PERSPECTIVES ON AMERICAN HISTORY, NUMBER 1

GREENWOOD PRESS
WESTPORT, CONNECTICUT • LONDON, ENGLAND

Library of Congress Cataloging in Publication Data

Karsten, Peter.
      Soldiers and society.

      (Grass roots perspectives on American history ;
no. 1 ISSN 0148-771X)
Includes bibliographical references and index.
      1.   Sociology, Military—United States.   2.   Soldiers—United States.
3.   War and society.   I.   Title.
II.   Series: Grass roots perspectives on American
history ; no. 1.
U21.5.K37   301.5'93'0973   77-87972
ISBN 0-313-20056-4

Library of Congress Catalog Card Number: 77-87972
ISBN: 0-313-20056-4
ISSN: 0148-771X

First published in 1978

Greenwood Press, Inc.
51 Riverside Avenue, Westport, Connecticut 06880

Printed in the United States of America

10 9 8 7 6 5 4 3 2 1

For
Bonnie, Heather, Adam, and Amanda

Contents

Acknowledgments

The flaws and shortcomings contained in this book are, of course, my own, but some of the general design and the sources have been suggested by others, and in this regard I particularly want to thank John Chambers, Pat Merwin, Jeff Lewis, and Russ Owens. John Chambers initially agreed to join me in writing this book. His other research and writing commitments were unusually heavy, and he had to withdraw; but he made some useful suggestions, which I appreciate. He is in the enviable position of being free to identify with or disown this volume as he chooses. I also wish to thank Mac Coffman, Allan Millett, Don Rickey, William Gribbon, and the many scholars who responded to my round robin in 1974 for their good and thoughtful advice. All students of the military in society are indebted to Morris Janowitz, Charles Moskos, Kurt Lang, and other members of the Inter-University Seminar on Armed Forces and Society who have contributed to our understanding of the subject, and I want to acknowledge my own indebtedness. And finally I thank David Thelan, the series editor, for his patience and trust.

Soldiers
and Society

Introduction

In the past three centuries the United States has evolved from a localistic, basically agrarian set of loosely associated communities into a complex and relatively cosmopolitan industrial nation-state. In the process it has developed a sophisticated, highly centralized, machine-intensive "standing" military and has fought several large wars, and a larger number of smaller ones. Nearly half of its households are headed by veterans. Needless to say, the lives of a substantial number of foreign people have been affected in the process, but so have those of Americans, and in a variety of ways. The purpose of this book is to explore that variety.

Exploring the effects that military service and war have had on Americans is not an enterprise that I would claim to have pioneered. For many years writers have offered their views on what military service and combat do to or for those who serve, how military recruiting and expenditures affect the society and the economy, and how war affects the individual's psyche, his family, and his social institutions.[1] We have several studies of the effect that war has on articulate, well-educated intellectuals,[2] but only a few truly first-rate studies of its effect on "common folk." Much of what has been written is of limited value for our purposes, for most writers have failed to conduct systematic analyses. To be sure, impressionistic evidence of whatever point is being made is advanced. And some of this evidence is quite fascinating. But it is difficult to tell how representative the evidence provided actually is in many accounts that offer the "large view" of the question.[3]

Several scholarly studies of specific dimensions of the subject do exist and deserve our attention. Among these are the analyses by social scientists of World War II GIs, Jonathan Borus's study of the psychiatric consequences of combat experience, Peter Bourne's account of the physiological effects of such service, William Cockerham's analysis of Airborne training, Harley Browning's comparison of veteran and nonveteran income patterns, Nancy Phillips's and William Benton's analyses of postservice attitudes, Reuben Hill's study of servicemen's families, and Robert Havighurst's account of "a war-boom community."[4] But such studies are both few in number and, with the exception of Benton's, recent (in terms of the temporal character of the subject matter).

In order to provide the reader with a picture of the full sweep of the subject, of both its variety and its changing nature, in this book I have attempted a synthesis of the existing literature, and I have tried, at times, to go beyond it. As I see it, the task involves categorizing the various "effects," describing the key evolutionary developments and features of the military and war-making institutions that have produced these "effects," identifying the impulses behind the historical processes that generated these institutional changes, and assaying the record in order to provide truly illustrative materials for the reader.

Let us begin with our first task — that of categorizing the various ways in which military service and/or war may be said to affect individuals and society. Three general categories may be appropriate: physical injuries, alterations in socioeconomic or geographic status, and effects on value and personality formation.

Physical Injuries. Here we have in mind the losses of life or limb incurred by combatants and, increasingly, by noncombatants alike in wartime. Falling somewhat between this category and the second (alterations in socioeconomic status) are those losses to private and public property suffered in wartime — damage done to crops, cattle, buildings, roads, bridges, ships, trains, dams, power stations, factories, and places of employment. And falling somewhere between this and the last category (effects on personality formation) are matters such as psychiatric problems attributable to the stresses of combat, and drug addiction caused by experiences or injuries associated with military service and war.

Alterations in Socioeconomic or Geographic Status. Here we have in mind any differentials in the impact of both voluntary and "selective" military recruitment policies on the socioeconomic status of those affected, as well as any differentials in the income, occupation, or geographic mobility patterns of veterans and nonveterans after controlling for differential recruitment patterns. We have also in mind the impact of military expenditures and combat on various sectors of the economy and on available resources. Who pays for the military, and who benefits?

Effects on Value and Personality Formation. This category encompasses a number of potential consequences, some more lasting and substantial than, others. Attitudes, values, and personalities may be modified in permanent ways as a result of one's association with war or the military, or they may be adjusted only temporarily, enabling one to cope more effectively with trying circumstances that end when the service obligation, war, or occupation experience terminates. Moreover, one may reasonably distinguish between minor life style changes in habits, speech, or attire, and more significant alterations in values and behavior that flow from one's military or wartime experiences. The latter might include changes in one's personal, social, or political behavior—that is, changes in the degree to which one displays a propensity to offer violence and compulsion as solutions to problems, or changes in the degree to which one appears willing to obey orders and accept leadership. And, of course, someone might experience value modification whether or not he or she was actually in military uniform. Large-scale military preparations and the conditions of "total war" substantially affect the values and behavior of many nonmilitary persons.

In the American experience there is a considerable body of evidence that can be used to illustrate one or another dimension of these three impact categories. But there are some gaps in the record and some effects that Americans have not yet experienced to the same degree as many other societies. We know, for example, that military service and combat can stimulate egalitarian nationalistic and revolutionary impulses among those who serve. Forrest McDonald has offered evidence indicating that French veterans of the American War of Independence were in the vanguard of the movement in their homeland to abolish feudalism a decade later.[5] William Gutteridge offers a comparable argument regarding African anticolonialist veterans of World War II.[6] Others have written of the politization of veterans of World War I.[7] American soldiers, comparatively speaking, have thus far been less politicized by warfare than these veterans. John Helmer and David Cortwright provide evidence of the radicalization of some Vietnam veterans, and Pat Merwin and I can offer some confirmation of this (see Sources 172 and 183), but the degree of radicalization and the ultimate consequences of such radicalization must, to date, be regarded as modest when compared with that of France in 1792, Russia in 1917, or Algeria in the 1940s and 1950s.

Americans are atypical in another sense—they have suffered less from wars than have members of many other societies. One has only to consult Michel Roublev's analysis of the Mongol invasion of Russia, or Edward Spicer's account of the effect that Spanish, Mexican, and U.S. conquests have had on the Indians of the American Southwest to understand this. The experience of Southern Americans in the 1860s deserves noting (see Source 242), but it is hardly comparable; when one considers the fate of the losers in the civil wars in sixteenth-century France or twentieth-century Russia, Spain, Greece, or Cambodia, the Union's treatment of the Confederacy's soldiers and citizenry appears mild indeed. Given these qualifications, it is still fair to say that the consequences war and military service have had for Americans are quite comparable to their effects on other peoples. The specific historical context must always be considered (as indeed it will be). But one could reasonably say of the body of evidence offered herein that it is likely to resemble similar data drawn from the experience of members of most other societies.

Before leaving our general impact model, however, it is necessary to enter three caveats: (1) Beware of impacts that do not last. (2) Beware of things that only *appear* to evince an impact on someone. (3) Beware of attributing to the military those things that ought more appropriately to be attributed to the society that engendered it.

1. Military service or war may *temporarily* alter the attitude or behavior of, or opportunities available to, individuals, but in many instances the process completely reverses itself once the individual leaves the military or once the war ends. For example, an increasing percentage of women have found work in the twentieth century, but the most notable increase in any five-year span was that of the "Rosie the Riveter" era, 1940-45. Nevertheless, the period 1945-50 saw a *decline* in the percentage of women in the work force as men returning from the service forced women out of some positions and as other women reverted of their own volition to the roles of mother, wife, and homemaker.[8] The trend produced by the wartime circumstances simply did not persist. We shall examine several examples of this phenomenon—temporary changes that do not persist— in the discussion of the consequences of military service in this Introduction.

2. Some Vietnam veterans insist that military service or combat experience has made them more callous, has made them more willing to use force, or has given them a drug habit. For some this may very well be true, but for others who possess one or another of these traits it probably is not. One veteran spoke of how "different" he had become: "I never used dope before Nam, and I never picked no fights. Now I can't stay off the stuff and out of trouble. Once you've seen Nam, there's nothin' to it. I used to be a pretty easy-going guy. I gotta think the Army messed me up."[9] He may be correct in attributing his behavior to what he experienced, but then again he may not. What this veteran did not say during the interview, but what became known later, was that before entering the army he had been in trouble with the police several times, had been charged with more than one felony, and may well have been using drugs. Moreover, he had volunteered for and completed Airborne training. As William Cockerham has demonstrated, Airborne trainees are simply different from other army personnel. They are more physical, more adventure seeking, and more aggressive. And they self-select—that is, they are all volunteers.[10] The army does not transform them so much as it provides a vehicle for the reinforcing of already developed self-images. We shall offer several examples herein of this, for many traits seen in GIs and veterans are in fact properly attributable to values and attitudes acquired before entering the service.

3. Military organizations reflect the societies they serve.[11]. They have influence and powers of their own, to be sure, but only rarely do they have lives of their own. The military system in the United States often functions in ways that may be said to alter the lives of thousands of Americans, but we must remember that it is rarely the will and judgment of the uniformed leadership alone that produce these changes. Civilian elites, be they executive policy makers or congressional figures, are generally responsible for the key decisions that determine the ways in which the military services function and subsequently "affect" Americans, and these elites are themselves accountable and responsive to public opinion. Hence it is always appropriate to ask to what degree the military impact one is exploring is in fact more appropriately attributable to those forces that permeate society itself. The desegregation of the military affected many Americans, as we shall see (Sources 103 and 104), but it must be remembered that it was part of a broader impulse. The military-industrial-political complex affects society, to be sure, but the process is at least partly an open one. Those who stand to gain from the relationship vigorously defend it; those competing for national resources just as vigorously attack it. The complex's lobbyists may have more clout than the "peace lobby," but they must also compete at the public till with other lobbyists having clout and representing, for example, programs for highways, space research, education, health, and the like. And the public always reserves the right and power to elect a candidate who wants more (Goldwater) or less (McGovern) military spending. Hence there is impact, but it is not without sanction.

We may now begin to examine the specific historical context. What were the key steps, the "stages of development," in American history that explain the particular ways in which the evolving military and war-making institutions have altered the lives of "everyday Americans," and what were the impulses behind these developments?

To get a better sense of what has happened, we must say something of the beginnings, of the character of military and war-making institutions in the colonial era.[12] Briefly, the initial condition of all but the Pennsylvania colony is best characterized as that of the "garrison state." Military companies, composed of both local settlers and mercenaries from England, protected the survival and growth of Plymouth Plantation, the Massachusetts Bay Colony, the New Haven and New London settlements, the Virginia Company, Georgia, and the southern frontier. The nature of these unintegrated military systems eventually varied somewhat, with some relying more on small standing armies of mercenaries than on every-man-a-warrior militia forces. But when one compares the military systems and war-making ways of any one of these early colonies with their more modern, twentieth-century counterparts, it appears that they were more egalitarian and less centralized in the colonial era. Officers were often elected and could be voted out of "office." Discipline was lax, and training modest. Units from one colony rarely left their own environs, unless they were mercenaries, hired specifically with some elite's venture capital, to serve in a "foreign" expedition. Such institutions as these reflected the Englishman's fundamental distrust of standing armies and his localistic and independent values.

The American Revolution and the ensuing problems of the Confederation era led some to assume that a centralized standing army and a national navy, functioning alongside the various state militias in a federal system, were both necessary and reasonable for the new nation.[13] How else might one protect a growing overseas commerce? How else could one defend against possible threats to the Republic, or cope with British, Spanish, and Mexican bastions, with Native American tribes, with unsubmissive South Sea islanders, Central Americans, Koreans, Chinese, and Japanese? In order to accomplish any of these tasks in any rational, systematic way, one would need a body of career-minded professionals — individuals who would enter the military or naval service in their youth, become proficient mariners, gunners, and tacticians (or capable horsemen, riflemen, and leaders), and then remain in uniform until retiring. To this end warships and forts were built, professional schools for officers and enlisted personnel were created, drills and training exercises were organized, and bureaus overseeing supply, construction, repair, personnel, and deployment were provided. Progress was slow and somewhat uneven, with many innovations coming in fits and starts, but the process was steady. Service academies and specialized schools for gunnery, engineering, leadership, strategic planning, and the like, came into being throughout the nineteenth century, as did specialized professional journals and associations that provided for the dissemination of ideas and information within each of the various branches of each service. Promotion and retirement policies that rewarded exemplary qualities were adopted. General staffs and intelligence services emerged in order to provide for various "contingencies."[14]

Concurrently, cosmopolitans interested in centralized, rationalized control of military policy successfully dealt with more localistic leaders anxious to preserve the earlier militia and local volunteer organizations.[15] Only professionals, "regulars," could defend with any efficiency the increasingly important overseas interests of the United States. Throughout the twentieth century the National Guard was steadily subordinated to the Regular Army with its new arm, the Army Reserve.

With the outbreak of war in Europe, these same cosmopolitans insisted on a selective service system that would "Americanize" immigrants and channel persons who could easily be spared by those sectors of the economy deemed important by national leadership. They launched a prepar-

edness drive designed to convince Americans of the need for more powerful naval and military forces. They championed the improvement of
the military-industry liaison and the creation of a supreme coordinating
agency, the War Industries Board, to oversee production, finance, labor-
management relations, marketing, and transportation, and they turned to
censorship and propaganda, administered largely by the Committee on
Public Information.[16]

The end of World War I terminated Selective Service and wartime
regulations, but the military-industry liaison of World War I led to the
creation of the Army Industrial College in 1924. Logistics and planning in
the future would be more sophisticated and would be more systematically
administered.[17]

Wartime centralization of power in order to mobilize the nation's total
resources was first attempted by the Lincoln administration during the
Civil War. It was tried again by the Wilson administration during World
War I. But the Roosevelt administration's efforts of the early 1940s were
more successful than those of either of its predecessors. Every segment
of society was affected; every resource mobilized. Psychologists had been
utilized by the army in World War I, but on a smaller scale than they
would be during and after World War II. Indeed, by 1943 large numbers
of social and behavioral scientists of all descriptions were hard at work
on military assignments. Some studied combat behavior; others, soldier
attitudes; still others, training techniques. Psychologists designed and administered tests in order to improve the process of military personnel allocation. Sociologists and social psychologists studied troop morale,
motivation, and behavior under fire. Psychiatrists aided combatants unable to cope with the stress of combat. And the process continued after
the war had ended. Some social and behavioral scientists continued to
work on military-related projects, some of which dealt with the segregation of blacks in the military. Others, in the army's Human Resources Research Office, continued to study the motivation and behavior of military
personnel and to design training techniques and manuals. Still others examined military leadership and management and were involved in the
movement from coercion to persuasion in the military's managing of men
over the past thirty years.[18]

Other academics were not to be outdone. Economists and mathemati-
cians offered their skills to the war effort in the early 1940s. Cost account-
ing, systems analysis, and statistical probability became the standard bill
of fare among policy makers. Convoys burgeoned as a result of the analyses of these "whiz kids." Bombers were redeployed or sent airborne.
Missiles, aircraft, and other military hardware were either rejected or approved, in the optimal numbers.[19]

Physicists, chemists, and engineers offered their services as well. Military technology had made substantial advances in the century prior to World War II. The steam-driven steel warship, armed with rifled guns that were hydroelectrically keyed to a gyroscope to compensate for pitch and roll, threw enormous explosive shells some fifteen miles by 1940. Aircraft capable of delivering high explosives on factories or warships became available. Submarines, tanks, machine guns, repeating rifles, highly mobile artillery, and mechanized supply systems had all been created in the century prior to World War II, and each had contributed to what we might call the battlefield revolution. But the technological pace picked up during World War II and continued thereafter. Armor-piercing and VT-fuse shells, radar, electronic countermeasures, incendiary and "smart" bombs, jet aircraft, lightweight, high-velocity rifles, nuclear weapons, guided missiles, and the "electronic battlefield" continue to transform warfare.

One final phenomenon must not be forgotten: The American military system prior to World War II was small compared with what it would become in the years of the cold war. Tensions throughout the world in the 1940s—among them the Greek Civil War, the Soviet blockade of Berlin, the coups in Czechoslovakia and Bulgaria, the communist victory in China, the Soviet detonation of an atomic bomb, and the North Korean move into South Korea—appeared to many policy makers to confirm their image of the Soviet Union as an expansionistic military power in full command of an aggressive international movement ideologically committed to the destruction of the American system. Long-range aircraft and nuclear weapons posed the first truly credible threat to American security since the War of 1812. Consequently, the post-World War II American military was substantially larger than it had ever before been in peacetime (see Table 1).

The strain of maintaining such forces over several decades has been considerable and has affected both the availability of resources and the allocation of manpower. Dollars are spent for military aircraft, warships, and salaries rather than elsewhere in the public and private sectors.[20] During the quarter-century of peacetime Selective Service, young men were channeled into useful occupations; when they declined to flow with the current or were unable to qualify for one of the "useful" imprimaturs, they were generally drafted. Many physically or mentally unqualified young men have always been turned away by the military, but during the Vietnam War the military's manpower needs led to an experimental lowering of these standards, a phenomenon known as Project 100,000. The service and postservice experiences of these persons are being studied by social scientists today.[21]

So much for our survey "from the top down" of developments in America's military and war-making systems. We must now look at these devel-

TABLE 1
Military Personnel on Active Duty
as a Percent of the Total U.S. Labor Force, 1801-1967

YEAR	NUMBER IN THOUSANDS[a]	PERCENT OF LABOR FORCE[b]
1801	7	—
1810	12	—
1820	15	0.05
1830	12	0.03
1840	22	0.04
1850	21	0.03
1860	28	0.03
1865	1,063	—
1870	50	0.04
1880	38	0.02
1890	39	0.02
1898	236	—
1900	126	0.04
1910	139	0.04
1918	2,897	—
1920	343	0.08
1930	256	0.05
1939	334	0.06
1945	12,123	18.60
1950	1,460	2.30
1953	3,555	5.30
1960	2,476	3.50
1965	2,655	3.40
1967	3,377	4.20
1977 (est.)	2,000	3.00

[a]Office of the Secretary of Defense, Directorate of Statistical Services. Military personnel strengths as of June 30 of each year are cited.

[b]Labor force statistics refer to gainful workers, ten years and over, for 1820-1930, to total labor force, fourteen years and over, for 1939-63, and sixteen years and over, for 1965 and 1967. Data are from the U.S. Department of Commerce, *Statistical Abstract of the United States, 1960* (Washington, D.C.: Government Printing Office, 1961). See Tables 261 and 263, *Monthly Report on the Labor Force, April 1963* (Washington, D.C.: U.S. Department of Labor, 1963). See also *Employment and Earnings and Monthly Report on the Labor Force, July 1967* (Washington, D.C.: U.S. Department of Labor, 1967), Tables A-1 and A-27.

Labor force statistics are not available for those years marked with a dash.

Source: Harold Wool, *The Military Specialist* (Baltimore, 1968), p. 2.

opments and the resulting systems "from the bottom up." I have assembled a body of evidence (much of it the product of the work of other scholars) that may serve to illustrate the ways in which war and/or military service has affected Americans over the past several centuries, and I now wish to explain how that evidence has been organized in this book. I might have proceeded chronologically, offering materials from the colonial era first, to be followed by other materials in chronological sequence. But that organizational rationale seemed less sensible and useful than one that was primarily topical. In gathering these sources and in preparing this introduction, I was struck by the degree to which the experiences and attitudes of eighteenth-, nineteenth-, and twentieth-century American soldiers were more alike than they were different. As we shall see, there *were* differences, sometimes substantial ones, from one era to another in terms of: the level of sophistication of the training programs, the duration of the GI's exposure to combat dangers,[22] the availability of services and benefits for the GI's family or for the GI himself as a veteran, and the impact of war on the society and economy as a whole. But, on balance, the differences appear (to me, at least) to be less significant than the similarities. The same kind of men, for the same kinds of reasons, served in 1780 as those who served in 1861, 1917, 1942, or 1970. To the extent that their values, attitudes, or horizons were altered at all by such service, they were altered in one age in much the same fashion as they were in another. Some wars, such as the Civil War and World War II, are alleged to have been more popular than others, such as Vietnam. The attitudes, it is said, of World War II GIs were drawn in one direction by the "positive" atmosphere of American society in 1945, whereas the views of Vietnam veterans took a different turn as a result of the negative atmosphere *they* encountered at home. But this does not appear to have been the case,[23] probably because American society as a whole has never been either as positive or as negative about a war as historians who focus on editorials and congressional speeches presume. It is commonplace today to observe that the Vietnam War and the veterans of that war differ from wars and veterans of the past. But in preparing this book, I became convinced that many such differences may well be exaggerated.

In any event, I contend that one is more apt to develop a keener and clearer sense of the several, distinct ways in which war and military service have affected individuals and society throughout American history if one approaches the subject topically, not chronologically. (An appendix in which the sources are renumbered in a chronological fashion is provided for those who wish to use this volume to supplement a course that is organized in that fashion.)

Imagine a young man entering the military. He volunteers or is drafted; he is assigned to a unit and given training of some sort; his unit is assigned a mission, and he may be sent into combat; to one degree or another, he experiences and endures boredom, hardship, fear, anger, elation, and relief; discharged, he reenters the civilian community. He either has or has not been affected by such service or combat. Concurrently, his family, the rest of the society, and those in the community he is serving may, to one degree or another, also be affected. Let us first follow the American soldier from the day he entered the service to the day he left it, exploring the ways in which such service has affected different persons at different points of time. Then let us look at the ways in which these same phenomena—war and the military—have affected others. The evidence is arranged topically, but within each topic it is chronological, for we *will* consider those instances in which Americans living in one age were affected in ways significantly different from those that touched Americans of another era.

The business of assaying the record in order to provide truly illustrative materials has been time consuming and perplexing, for the "common folk" of yesteryear are not easily surveyed. Although they have left their marks on the past, deciphering those marks is not always an easy task, and it becomes more difficult the more pointed one's questions and the more systematic one attempts to be. The examination of any 100 veterans' autobiographies, diaries, or correspondence folders yields but a small handful of the kinds of passages that demonstrate how the individual (or his family) was affected (or unaffected) by his service experiences. And then one is hard-pressed to know what these passages are really worth. In the first place, how can one be sure that this individual *correctly* perceived what had happened to him? A number of scholars have discovered that what some veterans attribute to their military service is primarily a problem or characteristic that they possessed *prior* to such service.[24] In the second place, even if one can be satisfied that the individual correctly perceived and described the transformation wrought by war or military service, one must still ascertain as best one can how *representative* this phenomenon is of all those potentially so affected. Charles Bardeen, "a little fifer" in the Civil War, later edited and published his diary, noting that it constituted "a history of what the war did to poor little me," and claiming that it "indicates what it did to other little me's, thousands of them."[25] Should we take Bardeen's word for that? Sometimes aggregate data may be utilized to answer such questions, but in some instances it is either presently impossible to find such data or the question is such that aggregate data will not, in and of itself, provide an adequate answer.

One way of answering questions regarding the character or extent of a particular impact is to take the word of articulate elite observers (persons more likely than "common folk" to leave a record of their views) on the subject of what happened to these "common folk." We shall occasional-

ly consider the views of such "articulates," but only as setoffs for data
that reveal more objectively what actually *did* happen to "common folk."
To be sure, elites sometimes do perceive quite accurately what is happening to others, but these instances of insight are infrequent, for their
own backgrounds, values, and experiences are often so different from
those of the persons they are describing that they cannot sufficiently understand what is actually happening to these others. For example, many
military leaders, prominent philosophers, and civilian policy makers
alike throughout the nineteenth and twentieth century believed that the
average American recruit or draftee possessed an innate aggressiveness
and that he was sufficiently malleable to have that aggressiveness aroused
by various forms of combat indoctrination and strenuous activity. In a
pamphlet published in the 1920s Gen. William Haan put it thusly:

> Bayonet training is possible only because every red-blooded man
> naturally possesses the fighting instinct. This inherent desire to fight
> and kill must be carefully watched for and encouraged by the in-
> structors. . . . The recruit must long test his ability against an enemy's
> body, to prove that his bayonet is irresistable. He pictures an enemy
> at every practice thrust and drives home his bayonet with strength,
> precision, and satisfaction.[26]

Generals like Haan were utterly dismayed with the results of study
by social psychologists of some 400 randomly selected combat infantry
companies in the European and Pacific theaters during World War II.
Published in 1947 as *Men Against Fire,* this study revealed that only 1 in 5
trained infantrymen actually fired his weapon in combat. There appeared
to be several reasons for this—among them the sense of isolation from
comrades a soldier felt when he hit the deck, the ghostly character of the
unseen enemy, and the reluctance of the average GI to shoot to kill. It
was found that team-fired weapons, where responsibility was shared,
were fired at a much higher rate than were individually operated rifles.
Apparently, the Judeo-Christian ban on killing was much more difficult
to overcome than General Haan had imagined.[27] Bill — — — wrote home
from Vietnam in November 1965: ". . . every day I pray for only two things—
to be out of this hell and back home or be killed before I might have to
kill someone," and in this respect he was not unique.[28]

The evidence in this book is divided into two basic categories: (1) the
consequences of military service and (2) the effects that warfare and military institutions have on those not in the military itself. Each of these
basic categories is again further divided. The discussion of the consequences of military service includes sections on the recruitment process,
training, the tour of duty, combat, separation from the service, and veter-

ans. Included in the discussion of the effects that war and the military have on those not in the military itself are sections on the families of GIs, the economy, social and political values, and "the enemy within."

A. The Consequences of Military Service

1. THE RECRUITMENT PROCESS

Before one can properly discuss the impact of military service on those who have served, one must first know as much as possible about such persons before they entered the military. If we are to try to demonstrate the ways that military experience affected Americans, we must say something of what these Americans were like before they came into contact with the military institution if we are to establish any causal relationships.

There is another reason for examining the recruitment process. In and of itself this process may be said to affect Americans in substantial ways. Whether compulsion is involved or not, the very existence of the military service option has had a substantial effect on the lives of many young Americans, and this effect is clearly more pronounced in times when compulsion *is* present in one form or another.

When American society's legal mechanisms have not operated to compel young men to serve (and compulsory service has been the exception, not the rule, throughout most of the eighteenth, nineteenth, and twentieth centuries), men have volunteered for several reasons, among them, peer or family pressure, socioeconomic opportunities, a love of adventure, a desire to test one's mettle, or a sense of patriotism. Joseph Plumb Martin joined the Continental Army in 1776 in order to have some fun; William Scott, to "rise higher" (Source 1). Personal friendship and loyalty to king and country led Maurice Nowlan in two directions at once (Source 2). James Miller enlisted under "the influence of an unusual quantity of ardent spirits" (Source 3). Eugene Bandel, having "sold everything I owned that was value" in an unsuccessful search for a good job in the New World, enlisted in 1854 as "my only resort if I did not wish to steal or beg" (Source 4). John Faller and Henry Stanley marched off with the Union and Confederate armies (respectively) because they were "getting ashamed" of remaining in the rear while "the other boys are off" (Sources 5-8). Some blacks volunteered during the Civil War, World War I, and World War II first to secure and then to demonstrate their enduring claim to their rights (Sources 9-13). A survey in 1969 of high school male seniors indicated that a strong correlation existed between the attitudes of family and friends, on the one hand, and the decision to enlist, on the other (Source 14). As we shall see, some youth from the lower end of the socioeconomic spectrum enlist in order to "get ahead," but some from the other end of that spectrum do so in order to protect what they already have or what they feel the country offers. "Clerks and students" joined National Guard units in the late nineteenth century to defend "the rights of property." Professionals and skilled workers volunteered out of proportion to their numbers in the Civil War and in World Wars I and II (Sources 15-19), possibly because they were cosmopolitans, more conscious of "the best interests of the nation" (as those interests were perceived by those in power) than were more localistic rural men.[29]

Many have assumed that militarism and the pursuit of glory are the chief inspiration of young American volunteers. A. A. Livermore explained how the army managed to find recruits in 1850: It was

> by the wooden sword, and the tin drum of boyhood. It is by the training and the annual muster. It is by the red uniform and the white plume, and the prancing steed. It is by the cannon's thunder, and the gleam of the bayonet. It is by ballads of Robin Hood, and histories of Napoleon, and "Tales of the Crusaders." It is by the presentation of flags by the hands of the fair, and the huzzas for a victory. It is by the example of the father and the consent of the mother. It is by the fear of cowardice, and the laugh of the scorner. It is by the blood of youth, and the pride of manhood, and stories of revolutionary sires. It is by standing armies, and majestic men-of-war. It is by the maxims of self defense, and the cheapness of human life, and the love of excitement. It is by the bubble of glory, and the emulation of schools, and the graspings of money making. By one and all, the heart of the community is educated for war, from the cradle to the coffin.

The editor of *Youth's Companion* offered a similar verdict, albeit one with an economic and careerist dimension:

> [The parade] is the beginning of the war-spirit—this is the temptation which leads many, many to ruin. Then comes the Recruiting Officer with his delusive promises of "good pay, fine clothes, plenty of food, promotion and military glory"—and thus the foolish youth is caught in the snare. He soon finds that he has lost his liberty. If he lives through all this, and is one of the fortunate few who returns home, it will be with demoralized habits, a broken constitution, or the loss of a leg— and this is the glory the recruiting officer promised him.[30]

To be sure, the love of adventure and the pursuit of glory explain why some enlist. But two other reasons, which appear to be far more important, tell us much of the relationship between the recruitment process and the consequences of military service.

One might be styled the search for manhood or, more generously, the desire to test one's mettle. This ambition *may* explain why black applicants for the military, many of whom matured in an atmosphere constantly challenging their manhood and identity, appear to prefer the combat, action-oriented branches of the service (Source 20). It certainly explains the career patterns of most Airborne and Green Beret volunteers. William Cockerham asked Airborne trainees why they volunteered for such hazardous duty. Over half said they were primarily interested in meeting "a personal and physical challenge," and nearly all of the rest indicated that either their "self-identification with an elite military unit" or their love of excitement explained their decision. Only 3.8 percent cited the extra duty pay as the key motivation. When compared with a random sample of non-Airborne military personnel, Airborne trainees were found to be satisfied to a more substantial degree that what they were doing in the military was personally important (Source 21). David Mantell offers persuasive evidence that those who joined the Green Berets were disproportionately the children of harsh, narrow-minded, demanding parents who had displayed little affection and had offered few opportunities for independent thought or action (Sources 22 and 23). In effect, they were raised in a boot camp atmosphere and, consciously or unconsciously, were encouraged to seek the most demanding kind of military service.[31] Whatever the army may be said to have "done" to the Airborne and Green Beret volunteers was surely less important than what they brought with them into the service.

Conversely, those who acquired conscientious-objector status or who chose to resist the Selective Service system altogether were disproportionately from among well-educated, change-oriented youth (Sources 24 and 25), and Mantell's analysis of the family background of some twenty-five draft resisters suggests that they are the products of better-educated, warm and open-minded parents who sought to awaken independence and self-esteem in their children (Sources 26-28). A Survey Research Center study of high school seniors in 1969 predictably found a strong positive correlation between support for the war in Vietnam and an expressed intent to join the military (Source 29). In short, some are "opting in" for the same reason that others are "opting out" — because they sense that they will either flourish or wither in the military. To the extent that this self-selection phenomenon operates, the military recruitment process reduces the amount of impact that military service will have on the volunteer by narrowing the volunteer population to those already predisposed to thrive within the military environment.[32]

The other reason for volunteering is what we have called socioeconomic opportunities, what Henry Giles called "security and pride" in 1939 (Source 30). And this reason, unlike the one just discussed, is not as unlikely to reduce the potential impact of military service. Edward Papenfuse and

Gregory Stiverson have shown that the Continental Line recruits raised in
Maryland during the years 1776 and 1782 were disproportionately lower-
class souls who appear to have viewed military service as a means of ac-
quiring a nest egg or future stake in society.[33] More recent evidence regarding military recruitment points in the same direction. In the early
1960s a number of surveys of male high school seniors and of military recruits sought to discover the major advantages that teenagers saw in volunteering for one or another of the armed services. Respondents gave
similar responses (Source 31), indicating that the training for a trade and
the career opportunities that the military appeared to offer were more
important than any militaristic, impetuous, or solely patriotic impulses
the young men may have had. In 1964 a number of young men aged sixteen to nineteen years were asked by census takers to compare a career
in the military with one they were presently in or about to enter. When
their responses were organized according to their levels of education, it
became clear that those who had not completed high school were more
inclined to feel that military service offered more than their civilian futures
in terms of opportunity for advancement, long-term security, training and
skill acquisition, community respect, and variety, than were those who
had completed high school (Source 32). Another survey of teenagers revealed that only 17 percent of respondents from the industrial New England and Middle Atlantic regions displayed a positive attitude toward
military service, whereas 38 percent of those from the South gave positive
responses, and, once again, those who had not completed high school
were more likely to express a positive attitude toward military service (48
percent) than were those who had completed high school (33 percent) or
those who had gone on to college (18 percent).[34] Moreover, of those who
actually enlisted and were "true" volunteers, the undereducated and low
achievers (on the Armed Forces Qualification Test) predominated (Sources
33 and 33a). Army voluntary enlistment rates in the several regions of the
country in 1963 appear to be correlated inversely with long-term income
patterns (rather than short-term unemployment levels), suggesting that
young men from the South, where income levels are traditionally lower
than regions like the Great Lakes or Pacific Coast, enlist for economic
reasons (Source 34).

Blacks and other nonwhites have always been, on the whole, less well
off than whites in the United States. Prior to the desegregation of the
armed forces, the military was perceived as an avenue of social mobility
by some blacks, but, given the segregation and discrimination practiced
therein, not by all.[35] During World War I, some black recruits sang "Joinin'
the Army to get free clothes; what we're fightin' 'bout nobody knows."
Throughout World Wars I and II, they were less likely than whites to enlist and more likely to fail to report when drafted (Source 35). These wars

were the work and property of the white majority. If many black integra-
tionists (predominantly educated northerners) could optimistically support the war (Sources 36-38), many black separatists (predominately undereducated southerners) would not. On December 8, 1941, one black share-
cropper was reported to have remarked to his landlord: "Hey, Cap'n, I
hear the Japs done declared war on you white folks."[36] But with the desegregation of the armed services in 1951, conditions for blacks within
the military improved markedly (Source 39), resulting in an increased
nonwhite interest in military careers, a phenomenon reflected in the variations in reenlistment rates of servicemen of different races in the 1960s
(Source 40), in the comparison black GIs made in 1965 of conditions in
military and civilian life (Source 41), and in the remarks of Staff Sgt. John
T — —, who is black (Source 42). Clearly, many less fortunate youth regard
military service as a vehicle for upward mobility, and, as we shall see, for
many such youth the vehicle works. But since their prime objective in entering the service was socioeconomic mobility and *not* necessarily a craving for danger, challenge, or excitement, they may be affected by the experience in ways unlike those who joined for the latter reasons.

Thus far we have focused on volunteers. We must now consider the effect that the *compulsory* recruitment process has had on those it touched.

From time to time American policy makers have resorted to one or another form of conscription in order to ensure themselves adequate and
appropriate military forces. And, just as often, many of those faced with
conscription have protested mightily. John Simpson, a farmer who in
1917 was the head of the Oklahoma Farmers' Union (a group of lower-
income farmers), wrote to Senator Robert Owen of the anger that "nine
out of ten farmers" felt toward conscription (Source 43). The feeling was
not new in 1917. Colonists in Virginia had felt it as early as 1610, as had
citizens of several other colonies in the era of the American Revolution
and many from both the North and the South during the Civil War.[37]

Some refused to serve until compelled to do so by earnest Revolutionary
leaders (Source 44). Others sought nonhazardous alternative service in
one or another task deemed vital to the war effort by those in charge.
Several New Jersey farmers found jobs in Lord Stirling's ironworks in
1776 but proved to be indifferent employees. The superintendent of the
works complained that they were there "solely to be clear of the militia
and from no other motive. I find they are determined to shuffle the time
away [that] they are exempt and [to] do as little business as they possibly
can." He begged his employer, a leading rebel, to "send us some of the
[British] Regular and Hessian deserters" in order to pick up the slack.[38]
The Civil War draft of 1863 compelled into service those chosen who
could not pay the $300 commutation fee. When this fee was abolished in
1864, and the price of substitutes rose to three or four times that figure,

thousands of lower-middle-income persons were forced into uniform (Source 45). When Selective Service was introduced in September 1940, it precipitated thousands of "hasty marriages" (Source 46). Some were scrambling for dependents and the exemption it was hoped they would procure, and others were grasping for love and a semblance of romance before being shipped off to boot camp and North Africa. Some, notably those engaged in farming, were exempted.

More recently, between 1948 and 1971, millions of American young men were either conscripted or, as long as they were engaged in activities deemed vital to the national interest, were granted deferments. This process of channeling young men into science, engineering, tool or die making, teaching, or other scarce skills was described by the Selective Service System itself in a 1965 memo entitled "Channeling" (Source 47). The practice clearly altered the lives of many, causing some to leave the country, to fake illness, or to choose deferable jobs in order to avoid conscription, especially during the Vietnam War.[39] (Sources 48-54 may serve as examples.) Those unqualified for, or uninterested in, an "essential interest" deferment could still avoid conscription into the army, but only by agreeing to volunteer for a longer period of time in a noncombat Military Occupation Specialty (MOS) or in another of the armed services (the Navy, Air Force, Coast Guard, or the National Guard). Thus James W— — signed up for three years of naval service in 1966 to avoid being drafted for two years into a Vietnam-oriented army (Source 55). Others, while choosing the Army, were still able to avoid combat service by choosing a noncombat MOS, a privilege extended them as "volunteers" (Sources 56 and 57). It was a distressing situation, but one that was nevertheless accepted by most youth, even those on the campuses during the height of the Vietnam War. (A 1967 National Student Association pool found that 90 percent of college students felt the government had a basic right to conscript, and 68 percent felt that it had a right to do so even at times when no emergency conditions prevailed.) And the end results were both the channeling of many youth into roles that some of them did not prefer,[40] and the compelling of many others less gifted or affluent to enter the military in one capacity or another (Sources 58-60).

The draft has ended, and the numbers of persons sought by the armed services have declined, but 400,000 new enlistees per year will still be wanted through fiscal 1990, and this number represents no less than 37 percent of all those young men physically and mentally qualified who are not enrolled in college.[41] Little wonder that recruiting posters (Source 61) and TV "spots" are now being handled by seasoned Madison Avenue pros. If less awesome a machine than in the days of the draft, the recruitment process continues to have a substantial impact on the lives of some young Americans.

2. TRAINING

Upon entry into the military, recruits were provided with a measure of training to prepare them for service. This training may have been quite modest—a lecture by the regimental commander, a few days of close-order drill, and an hour of target practice—in the pre-twentieth-century fashion. Or it may have been quite elaborate—two to six months of basic and advanced schooling that provided rigorous regimentation, physical conditioning, and instruction in communications, tactical deployment, gunnery, and maintenance—the pattern increasingly prevalent in the century since the Civil War.

The more elaborate the training, the more likely it is that among its objectives was the implanting of the military ethos, by which was generally meant subordinating the recruit's self-image to the collective identity of the group, stimulating his aggressive impulses, and persuading him to accept and follow the leadership and orders given by his superiors. Many have assumed that such efforts by the military to "socialize" recruits produce substantial results. Some are pleased, others distressed, by this prospect, but only a few have explored the process sufficiently to say very precise or credible things about it.[42]

In fact, very little "rubs off" during the training cycle, and some of what does "rub off" is not what has been anticipated (Source 62). Trainees do appear to learn their military tasks, and they do appear to identify with the group (Sources 63 and 64), but this phenomenon is subject to rapid effervescense if the group is broken up and the trainees are allocated to entirely different groups or if the group is no longer subjected to the stress it endured in the training camp. One study finds the trainee coming to "love," or respect, his drill sergeant,[43] but another finds that respect for such authority figures declines in boot camp (Source 65), and other studies show trainees steadily becoming *less* dogmatic as basic training progresses[44] (Source 66). It would appear that trainees who initially scored high on the F-Scale learn that arbitrary and authoritarian leaders are most unpleasant chaps and that their faith in such an orderly way of life was mistaken. To be sure, brutal leaders can clearly create a brutal training environment; of that there is evidence;[45] but if the recruit is not predisposed to such an environment, he may merely learn to hate those in charge. "Fragging" (trying to kill one's superior) was clearly not uncommon in Vietnam, but just as clearly it did not originate there. It is a method of attacking unwanted disciplinarians in the American military that is at least as old as the war with Mexico (Sources 67, 67a, and 68).

Much of what *appears* to be the product of the training environment is, more accurately, a function of what the trainee himself brought into that environment. As we saw in our look at the recruitment process, the attitudes that teenagers hold on military-related subjects largely explain their personal decisions regarding military service, and the same may be said of the training experience: Soldiers who tend to thrive in boot camp or Officer Candidate School (OCS) are those who entered with values and personalities different from those who drop out or those who do poorly. The ones who do well in OCS, basic or advanced training, evidence the following : They score higher on the Armed Forces Qualification Test, have acquired more years of schooling, have fewer preservice delinquency traits (such as school truancy, running away from home, or civilian arrests), enter the service possessing more self-confidence, and appear more authoritative, aggressive, and orderly than do those who later fail or quit[47] (Sources 69-71). Given the uniformly subordinate nature of the trainee's status, some well-heeled recruits of the past were extremely distressed. The "leveling" experience angered them; they felt "put upon," their talents ignored (Sources 72 and 73). Conversely, some lower-class recruits had their first taste of success. Generally, poorly educated trainees were less affected by training films than were well-educated trainees (Source 74). Nonetheless, trainees having lower socioeconomic status (SES) did better in military training, with its emphasis on physical prowess and obedience, than they had done in high school.

All trainees were "socialized" in one way or another, but whereas for some the socialization process merely reinforced *positive* attitudes, for others it reinforced *negative* attitudes. Denying a recruit the particular military specialty training he hoped or expected to receive was one way of souring his attitude (Sources 75 and 76); separating him intentionally or unintentionally from his hometown friends, during or following basic training, was another (Sources 77 and 78); exposing northern black trainees (however unintentionally) to the more virulent racism of the rural South was still another (Sources 79 and 80).

In any event, the training experience was only intended as preparation for the more important tour of duty, which for some included combat. This post-training, on-the-job experience was longer and, in many ways, more likely to leave a lasting impact on the GI, and it is to this phase that we must now turn.

3. THE TOUR OF DUTY AND COMBAT

The training cycle lasts but a few months, but the rest of one's military service may amount to three or more years of regimented and sometimes hazardous living. In these years many individuals experience changes, be they lasting or temporary, as a result of the stress of discipline or of boredom, frustration, exhaustion, or fear.

Some of these changes are quite trivial—a greater ability to endure outdoor living and physical hardship, a heightened respect for creature comforts—a warm bed, dry socks, good food, lice-free clothing, soap and hot water (Sources 81-84). Other minor consequences of military service, ones as old as the military itself, include the familiar alterations in behavior that some may undergo who have learned to drink, gamble, or swear while in the armed services, away from home (Sources 85-90). Increased sexual promiscuity (Sources 91 and 92) is a commonly mentioned effect of service. Edmund Wilson's autobiographical character muses en route the front on a troop train in 1917:

> Now, he felt, he was really almost a man. He had discovered with excitement that the taboos of home need not be binding. You could curse like a baggage man if you wanted to, without its doing any harm, and the men who swore and drank most he found the most amusing of all; they seemed to have more fun in them, more imagination than others, and they had had more adventures. As long as he had been encamped near home, to be sure, he had left the whores alone, but when he should get to France—well, everybody knew what France was! And you didn't take much risk because the government would disinfect you afterward. In the States he hadn't been able to drink except furtively and it was with a thrill of adventure and freedom that he went into the English Y.M.C.A. and had beer among the absurd voices of the English soldiers.[48]

But John Cuber's study of GI promiscuity in 1941-42 indicated, once again, that preservice behavior explained most of what happened. "Not a great many men are initiated into prostitution when they are in the Army. . . . by and large the patrons in the army are the same patrons when at home, although the patronage seems to be more frequent and more open in the army situation."[49]

Obviously, military service has also had more important effects on Americans. It imparted greater self-confidence, self-control, and understanding to some; it broadened the horizons and opportunities of others; it cosmopolitanized certain localists. But the service affected others in ways *they* regarded as *undesirable* by making them more cynical, more tense, or by cutting away "the best years of our lives" (Sources 93-100). Some acquired more respect for the several new cultures and subcultures (American blacks) with which they came into contact (Sources 101-04); others developed a disdain for these unfamiliar peoples and societies and a heightened admiration of "the American way of life" (Sources 105-11).

Combat, of course, had a pronounced effect on many. Obviously, the effect was greatest of all on those killed or injured in action. Some 13 percent of Union and Confederate troops, and about 12.5 percent of all

who served during the American Revolution lost their lives, either to
enemy fire, poor treatment in hospitals or prisoner-of-war (POW) camps,
or disease. Because of improvements in the treatment of wounded personnel and the control of contagious diseases, fatalities suffered per
capita in twentieth-century wars have not been quite as severe, but battle
fatalities among those assigned to the combat arms have been just as
heavy as those of earlier wars.[50] Once again, background characteristics
have been critically important; enlisted men with lower SES have been
more likely to be killed or wounded than others, since they were more
likely to be channeled into the combat arms (Sources 112 and 113).

Crippling wounds and lifelong disabilities have been other consequences
of combat service, of course, as are the less visible, but no less real, physical disabilities sometimes produced by particularly grueling campaigns
or POW camp experiences (Sources 114 and 115).

Still another consequence of combat for some has been psychological
or physiological distress. Charles Genthe, upon examining the narratives
of scores of articulate American GIs published during World War I, con-
cluded that many had found the war a great and worthwhile challenge,
"a wonderful experience," as Pfc. Austin Abbey has put it.[51] But if this
had been the way that some literate, educated cosmopolitans described
combat, as a "moral renaissance" or "process of self-purification," it
would not appear to have been representative of those whose narratives
were not carefully prepared for publication in the Brahmin fashion or
were not approved for publication by boosterist censors in the Army or
the Committee on Public Information. Perhaps this is an example of the
mistake, alluded to earlier, that we make when we rely on the published
views of those strongly identified with elite decision makers. In any event,
the fact is that the stress of combat produced fear, hand tremors, sleep
difficulties, and physiological changes (detected through urinary analysis)
in vast numbers of American GIs and contributed to the psychiatric illnesses
others experienced. Troops waiting to storm enemy positions, air crews
about to take off, and personnel exposed to continual shelling often displayed a variety of fear symptoms (Sources 116-21), and the longer they
had served, the more comrades they had seen slain, the more missions
they had flown, the more likely they were to display signs of distress (Sources
122-28). Yosarrian, antihero of Joseph Heller's Catch 22, is a very believ-
able character.

For some this distress eventually precipitated psychiatric illness, but,
once again, background characteristics appear to have been as important
as military experiences. Soldiers with a history of family psychoses, childhood fears, unstable homes, poor health, and/or low intelligence were
especially prone to such illness whether they had served at length in heavy
combat or not[52] (Sources 129-31), though they were still more likely to

"crack" if they were subjected to considerable stress over an extended duration. And, to be sure, men with quite "normal" backgrounds, who were emotionally stable and self-confident, could also develop neuroses if they were frequently exposed to heavy enemy fire, if they saw their friends cut down, and if they lost confidence in their units or themselves. (Sources 132, 133, and 134 may serve as examples.)

In previous wars most neuropsychiatric casualties were removed permanently from the combat zone, but chemotherapy in Vietnam was sufficiently successful to allow the army to send many such casualties back into combat. Unfortunately, as Doctors Ron Glasser and Robert Jay Lifton have both observed, "there is no medical or psychiatric follow-up on [such] boys after they've returned to duty. No one knows if they are the ones who die in the next firefight, who miss the wire streched out across the track, or gun down unarmed civilians."[53]

Nor do we know much about "delayed" psychiatric casualties. In June 1920 there were 17,471 hospitalized vets; by 1940 there were 56,073, and 50 percent of these were neuropsychiatric patients, but we know very little about these patients. Jonathan Borus has found that Vietnam veterans were no more likely to experience emotional illness in the first seven months after leaving the combat zone than were noncombat veterans returning to the States from Korea and Germany.[54] But we cannot say how the mental health of these two groups will compare two, ten, or twenty years from now.

The fear of being killed was the more important of the two, in terms of the number of anxiety symptoms or psychiatric cases produced, but the fear of killing was a powerful fear too. To repeat the observation offered in this introduction, social scientists accompanying numerous American combat units in both theaters of World War II found that only about one in every five soldiers with individually operated weapons actually fired his weapon, and that this was so even during intense fire fights or when they were confronted with visible targets. Men who had to join together with others to fire weapons (machine gunners, artillery men), displayed no such reluctance to fire, in part, because they were drawn into the act by primary-group pressures. In like fashion, at Gettysburg over 18,000 muskets were found on the battlefield with unmistakable evidence that their owners had not fired them at anyone that day; 12,000 of them had two charges, neither of which had been discharged, rammed down the barrel; 6,000 more had from three to ten such charges, and another had no fewer than twenty-three charges![55] Some men had probably simply panicked and were loading their weapons purposelessly. But others were probably loading quite deliberately, in order to give the appearance that they were firing. Stonewall Jackson once complained that some of the more religiously inclined of his troops were reluctant to fire on the enemy, and when finally prevailed upon to shoot, were not likely to take correct aim. In short, many soldiers found it difficult to overcome the Judeo-Christian rule against the willful taking of human life (see Source 135).

The fears of killing and being killed are intermingled as men look for the first time upon dead bodies on the battlefield (Source 136). More trying is the moment when a soldier is expected to shoot to kill. Not all GIs found the act difficult, to be sure. Mantell's Green Beret subjects, for example, had few qualms (Source 137). But others were more reluctant (Sources 138 and 139).   What was the effect on the personality and value structure of the American soldier who killed and knew that he had killed? For many, of course, the act would not appear to have had substantial or lasting consequences. Writing from France in 1918, Harry Butters insisted that "a very few seconds after you are . . . turned sick by the sign of some uncleared remains of a late battlefield, you have forgotten about it." John Doyle, writing from Guadalcanal in 1942, asked himself what all the slaughter had "done to me" and answered: "I have not become cruel or callous. I am sure that I am hardened." (See Sources 140-43.) Others, however, believed that the killing had affected them in substantial ways (Sources 144-46). Two studies confirm these suspicions: Men drafted into the military in the 1940s and 1950s gave substantially more belligerent responses than did nonveterans to questions put to them in the early 1960s concerning U.S. military postures toward communist countries and the use of nuclear weapons (see Source 147). More recently, Vietnam veterans with heavy combat experience gave more violent responses to hypotheticals put to them concerning the appropriateness of violence than did any other group surveyed (Sources 148 and 149). Nonetheless, the question of the degree to which combat experience contributes to a future propensity toward violence is unresolved.

A related question, alluded to earlier, is that of the alleged criminal propensities of combat veterans. Commentators on American society have, at various times, claimed that battlefield mores tend to erode the servicemen's acquired values and render them unfit "for being comfortable and useful members of society in time of peace."[56] Reverend Brown Emerson, preaching at Salem in 1812, was not simply concerned with the "profaneness, blasphemy, debauchery," gambling, and drinking "which abound in any army," but also with the loss of "every spark of kindness and mercy" that ensued whenever soldiers became "accustomed to rapine and blood." They inevitably "became ferocious beasts, fitted for the work of cruelty and death."[57] Another minister, writing during the war with Mexico, maintained that "the brutal spirit" which the war "excites — the bad passions which it cherishes, tend to unhumanize all who are engaged in it. It tends to deaden the moral sense of those who . . . become familiar with its dreadful carnage." In *Review of the Mexican War* (1849) Charles Porter noted that:

This war has introduced crime and vice among us. A camp is the notorious home of unbridled passions. Soldiers in a foreign country feel that they are removed from all the restraints of civil law, and whenever the barrier of military discipline can be passed, unrestrained indulgence is sure to be sought. No one can know, until he has witnessed it, the hardening influence of war upon the characters of those who are engaged in it. He, who under the name of glory can coolly blow out the brains of his fellow man, or urge a bayonet into his bosom, has taken a lesson in blood, the effects of which he has rarely the ability or disposition to shake off. . . . Soldiers are commonly drawn from that class of society who most need the checks of civil law. Having been removed from its authority for a time, it is difficult for them to assume again the character of peaceable citizens. Martial law no longer holding them in restraint, they are too apt to feel a spirit of reckless defiance. And this inhumanity and lawlessness are scattered over the land. Its breath is infection, its touch is contagion. It breeds a moral miasma in every community which comes within its influence.[58]

It is not as obvious to me as it was to these writers that military service and combat experiences *erode* moral sensibilities, but they might *temporarily* weaken them. The "Last Words" of William Huggins, a veteran of the Revolutionary War executed for burglary in 1783, would tend to confirm the views of our authors, for Huggins claimed that he had learned his evil ways asoldiering.[59] But we know nothing of Huggins beyond what he tells us himself. He maintains that his military days had been his downfall, and he may have been correct. But that may have been what he *wanted* to believe, or what he thought his jailers *wanted* him to say; he may not have told us all there was to tell. What had he been like before becoming a soldier?

We are told that felonies increased sharply throughout the States at the close of the Civil War,[60] but we learn little from this kind of a statement. Of course, felonies increased sharply. Hundreds of thousands of young adult males (who are always disproportionately represented among felony convictions) were suddenly released from the firm control of the military services. More relevant would be comparisons, per capita, by age group, service experience, and socioeconomic status, of felonies one year *before* the war, one year *after* the war, and *five* years after the war. In 1866, according to a report in *The North American Review,* about 67 percent of all commitments to state prisons in the North were veterans; by 1867 the figure was below 50 percent, and it continued to fall thereafter. According to a study of Wisconsin prisons in 1922, most incarcerated veterans were guilty of property crimes or misdemeanors such as public drunkenness or disturbing the peace—*not* crimes of violence.[61]

In any event, a study of soldiers convicted of crimes while still in the service, between 1954 and 1963, revealed that the typical military prisoner had substantially lower test scores than the average recruit (Source 150). Once again, background characteristics may explain at least as much about a serviceman's propensity to commit unlawful acts as does his service experience. Ironically, felons paroled into the military during World War II had a substantially lower recidivism rate than did those paroled into the civilian community. Military service had actually helped to stabilize some of these young men; in that sense, it seems that it *did* affect their propensity to commit unlawful acts.[62]

Combat may or may not have eroded the moral sensibilities of GIs, but it was always a stressful experience, and it is time for us to ask how the typical GI managed to cope with the presence, day after day, of dying and killing. Our first answer is that he drew fugacious strength from those about him, from those with whose lot his was cast (Sources 151 and 152). This had the effect, especially after the integration of the armed forces in 1951, of drawing black and white GIs together in unfamiliar (albeit often impermanent) camaraderie (Sources 153-58). But extended periods of combat, during which buddies were killed and entire units decimated, weakened one's morale (Source 159), and ultimately the soldier simply hung on, hoping to "get it over with" and to survive (Source 160).

Once again, the more predisposed toward military service and combat one was, the more likely one was to succeed, and to remain, in the service.[63] Men who valued discipline and aggressiveness, who were in better physical condition, who were brighter, more self-confident, and sociable, and who had begun with a positive attitude toward the role of the military were more likely to be promoted and to reenlist (Sources 161-67).

Similarly, those who could not tolerate the service—those who turned to drugs in the service, who absented themselves without leave or deserted—did what they did because of their service experiences, because of what they had been before they had entered the service, or because of both preservice and in-service reasons. Union troops were much more inclined to desert in months when combat was intense and casualties high than during lulls in the fighting (Source 168). We do not know much about those who did and did not desert in the Civil War; we know a great deal about deserters and nondeserters in World War II. Arnold Rose's study of American desertions in the combat zone during World War II has demonstrated that those who deserted had experienced battle conditions (combat time, wounds, loss of comrades, strafing, etc.) quite comparable to those who did not desert. But they differed from their comrades in their attitudes: Unlike those who did not desert, they were far more likely to suffer from nervousness, fear, and a self-imposed isolation from other GIs, to claim that the officers were unfair or incompetent, and to feel that the war itself was "not worth fighting."[64] It would appear that these attitudes were not so much attributable to military experiences unique to these individuals as they were to values and behavior patterns acquired before the individuals entered the service.

The same may be said of peacetime desertion. Jack Foner has argued that the desertion rate of late nineteenth-century army personnel declined substantially as a result of the adoption by the officer corps of less heavy-handed treatment of enlisted men. He may well be right, but we would have to know more of those who enlisted in 1870 (when the desertion rate was high) and of those who enlisted in 1891 (when it was low) before we could say that their backgrounds were not relevant to an understanding of the variations he detected in the desertion rate.[65] We do know something of the preservice traits of modern peacetime army deserters, however, for there have been at least four studies of their characteristics in the past twenty years, and they all point in the same direction: Those who absent themselves without leave or desert from the peacetime military today tend to be younger, less educated, less intelligent, more rural, and less affluent than those who do not, and their flight "was found to be more highly related to [these] background and personal characteristics than to specific Army situations."[66]

During the war in Vietnam, some military personnel deserted or resigned in protest against U.S. policy, and such acts clearly affected their lives substantially (Source 169). Obviously, their decisions were informed both by the situation they found themselves in as a consequence of their being in the military and by the fact that the values they possessed defined that situation to be an untenable one. Many GIs were placed in the same military situation, and a number regarded that situation as constituting a moral dilemma, but few fixed on desertion, sabotage, or resignation as a course of action. Those who did must surely have had significantly different value structures than those who did not, and we may venture the guess that those value structures resembled those of Mantell's war resisters.

The evidence of drug use among Vietnam-era soldiers also indicates that both one's predisposition to use drugs and one's immediate military environment explain their use. The mere accessibility of the drugs themselves may have something to do with the differences, but the fact is that army personnel in Vietnam were more likely to use a number of drugs than were those in Europe, where drugs were also accessible (Source 170). And the stresses of the combat zone surely count heavily in explaining these differences (see Sources 171-73). But we have also learned that the user population was disproportionately composed of men who had used marijuana, narcotics, or amphetamines prior to entering the military, and of men with preservice records of arrests, truancy, unemployment, and low levels of education. A great many users in World War II and Vietnam were first-users, but this consequence of combat experience was not a lasting one. Some 93 percent of narcotics first-users and 86 percent of marijuana first-users stopped completely upon returning to the United States[67] (Sources 174 and 175).

Another consequence, for some, of military service has been politicization—that is, an increased political awareness, level of interest, and activity. Some combat personnel were politicized by a process of cognitive dissonance; in other words, they were distressed by the hazards that confronted them, but they recognized that they had no choice, and consequently they repressed all of their thoughts that were critical of the war and demanded that the civilian community, where such criticisms continued, suppress its critics and unite behind the war effort (Sources 176-78). They were also angered by workers who struck for wage increases during wartime. Source 179 demonstrates this phenomenon in the era of World War I. Ernie Pyle reported on the same phenomenon during World War II: "There was one thing concerning home life that soldiers were absolutely rabid on. That was strikes. Just mention a strike at home to either soldier or officer living on monotonous rations in the mud under frequent bombing, and you had a raving maniac on your hands." The most famous manifestation of this anger was the assault by two disabled veterans upon United Mine Workers President John L. Lewis during a coal strike in 1943.

Military service led other veterans to assume political reform positions, positions that were functions of the type of wartime experiences they had had. The most striking example of this may be that revealed by William Benton's study of Revolutionary War officer veterans from Pennsylvania.[68] Those who had served outside of the state, with either the Continental Line or the state militia, were far more likely to favor the creation of a strong federal government in 1787 than were those who had not seen such out-of-state duty. The two groups of officers were identical in every other respect—age, nativity, religion, social class, and county residence— but only one group had had a chance to grasp the "big picture," and only this group decided that the Confederation needed stronger bonding in its own defense. In like fashion, some World War II GIs indicated that they would not placidly "return to the 'old order of things'" (Source 180). Captain Lemuel Curtis, a black and a pilot in World War II, felt that members of his race in particular had been politicized by the war. "Negroes in far-flung corners of the earth are getting a new slant on things," he wrote in 1944. "When they come home they expect to get some of the things they've been learning about and fighting for. I believe they will be both aggressive and progressive about it all."[69]

Others, however, were completely alienated by their wartime experience. A. P. Hudson, a Southern folklorist, wrote that he had "never heard the cynical epithet 'rich man's war and poor man's fight' applied to the

Civil War in a public speech, nor have I seen it in a popular history, but I heard it many times from the lips of ex-Confederate soldiers."[70] A number of black (and white) veterans of World Wars I and II were thoroughly disgusted and "turned off" by what they had been subjected to (Source 181), and the same may be said of some Vietnam soldiers (Sources 182-84). John Helmer and David Cortwright maintain that Vietnam radicalized many GIs—that it caused them to embark on a sophisticated radical critique of the American polity.[71] But two other, more thorough studies of Vietnam veterans indicate that either a *conservative* reaction or a *lack* of political consciousness and commitment was the norm.[72] *Some* radicalization would appear to have occurred, but we know little of the preservice life of those radicalized,[73] and consequently cannot tell how much is due to Vietnam and how much is due to previous values and experiences.

Finally, some veterans, especially the regular army's "lifers," claim to have been, and probably were, unaffected altogether by their wartime experiences (Source 185).

4. HOMECOMING, ADJUSTMENT TO CIVILIAN LIFE, AND VETERAN STATUS

Upon being discharged, some GIs experience ambivalent feelings. From Revolutionary days to the present, discharged soldiers have longed to go home, but they have also sensed a loss upon parting with those by whose side they have fought and with whom they have shared hardships (Sources 186-89). Combat veterans acquired an incredulous outlook toward the spit-and-polish discipline and regimentation of boot camp, garrison life, and the peacetime army (Sources 190-91). More significantly, the attitudes GIs had come to hold toward a variety of issues—overseas allies, the enemy, "the cause," and even their sense of egalitarianism (sharing, racism-free camaraderie, cooperation) all tended to move back toward the preservice norm (Sources 192-97).

Upon reaching home, some experienced confusion. Those who were treated like heroes sometimes found the adjustment to civilian life easier and more pleasant, but they might also be led by this process to revise in their minds what it was that they had experienced. If their combat days had been particularly grim or terrifying, they might be transformed into more bearable, explicable, even amusing memories. If their military careers had been essentially boring, those careers might have undergone a metamorphosis and become more interesting and exciting (Sources 198 and 199).

Some were let down by the absence of a hero's welcome or by the realization, particularly common among low-income and nonwhite returnees,[74] that things at home were once again as they had been (Sources 200-06).

After World War II, one thing at home was not as it had been, though: A housing shortage forced many veterans to search for shelter for months (Source 205).

Search they did, for many veterans were not willing to be kept "down on the farm" after having seen "Paree" and other parts of the world. Many Union veterans moved their families south after the Civil War. About one in every four veterans of World Wars I and II moved away from his home county.[75] Military service had cosmopolitanized many GIs by bringing them into contact with different people, places, and life styles (Sources 206-08). Ironically, job opportunities during World Wars I and II had much the same impact on men of the GIs' same generation who had *not* served in the military. Although 28 percent of veterans were living by 1947 in counties different from those in which they had been raised, some 26 percent of their nonveteran peers were also living in new counties.[76]

Readjusting to civilian life was easier for some veterans than for others. On one level, certain army habits that conflicted with the ways of the civilian community sometimes had to be set aside (Source 209). On a more important level, the stark and grim memories of combat had to be dealt with, had to be lived with, now, in unfamiliar civilian surroundings, among people who had not "been there." A song popular with "doughboy" veterans of World War I went: "No one knows / No one cares, if I'm weary; / Oh, how soon they forgot Chateau-Thierry." It is a feeling that many veterans of American wars have felt at one moment or another in the first year or two after separation from the service (Sources 210-12). For quite a while upon returning home veterans of America's wars appear to prefer the company of other veterans (Source 213).

Getting back to the business of earning a living was a prime concern of most veterans, and many (especially before 1944) were angered, somewhat justifiably, by what they regarded as a lack of elite civilian concern for their plight (Sources 214 and 215). However, the 1944 GI Bill, the several Veteran's Administration business and home loan programs, and the New Deal's federal unemployment compensation altered the situation for post-World War II veterans. In the short term, nonveterans often seem to be doing better than veterans of the same age and level of education, but this is essentially due to the fact that veterans often use unemployment compensation (or GI Bill) funds for which young nonveterans are generally ineligible in order to readjust to civilian life and to find a job they like.[77] After World War II hundreds of thousands of veterans "joined" the "52-20 Club," by which they meant that they drew $20 per month for up to fifty-two weeks while settling back into things.[78].

Many veterans resumed their old jobs, while others sought different ones; the longer one served, the less likely one was to return to one's preservice job.[79] By 1945, veterans who had been union members were often able to retain their local seniority number and to move back into the job market with considerable security. Others, who had acquired a skill in the service, were able to find a job in that field, but since World War II some 80 percent of military jobs (those in infantry, artillery, ship mechanics, etc.) have been those in areas that account for only 10 percent of civilian jobs,[80] and the figures for the pre-World War II era are at least as skewed. Some 60 percent of World War II veterans surveyed in 1955 indicated that their military training had been of "no use" in their search. Among Korean War veterans some 15.8 percent of former officers had found their experience of "considerable use," whereas only 4 percent of combat arms veterans gave such a positive response.[81] In 1970, blacks and low SES whites were overrepresented in those military specialties that were not readily or effectively transferable to the civilian job sector (Source 216). Inner-city men who had been in the sevice in the 1960s were compared with those who had not; military training and U.S. Armed Forces Institute's educational courses taken by the former group were found to have been substantially less important in predicting their postservice employment and income success than were preservice traits such as father's occupation, race, or years of education.[82] Even career military personnel, retiring after twenty or more years of service from positions of some responsibility as lieutenant colonels or master sergeants or chief petty officers could be disappointed in their search for financially attractive civilian work.[83] The skills acquired in the service by the retiring person were less important to the future employer than was the retiree's level of formal education (Source 217). The Defense Department has long maintained that military training is of great value to the serviceman reentering the civilian community, but the evidence does not substantiate the claim. And there have been a steadily growing number of career military personnel retiring in the twentieth century (Table 2).

The GI Bill has been of considerable value to those who have taken advantage of its provisions, and about half of those eligible to use it have done so,[84] but it has not been as frequently used by those who presumably have the greatest need for it—that is, by those with the least preservice or in-service schooling—as it has by all others (Sources 218 and 219). In the words of James Alden Barber, "Folk wisdom has it that the veteran returns more mature and serious about getting an education; but the difficulty of [obtaining] adequate control [groups for comparative analysis] has prevented any clear findings by sociologists on the point."[85]

Other programs and benefits designed to aid veterans include loans for businesses and residences, health care services, and disability pensions. Some 170 Veteran's Administration hospitals, 87 nursing homes, and 218 outpatient clinics were in operation in 1975 at a cost of $3.4 billion. The veteran with financial need is entitled to such health care services free of

TABLE 2
Size of Retired Rolls by Five-Year Intervals
from 1900 to 1980

YEAR	NUMBER
1900	3,029
1905	4,102
1910	5,405
1915	6,739
1920	10,035
1925	19,369
1930	32,838
1935	37,437
1940	48,374
1945	64,456
1950	132,828
1955	180,817
1960	255,089
1965	462,463
1970	750,144
1975	1,076,000
1980 (est.)	1,320,000

Source: John McNeil, "Retirement from the Military Service," in Hamilton McCubbin, ed., *Families in the Military System* (Beverly Hills, Calif., 1976), p. 241.

charge, and if he was totally or partially disabled while in the service, he is entitled to vocational rehabilitation services and a disability pension. The average cost of a veteran's vocational rehabilitation services is over six times the average cost of a nonveteran in an HEW vocational rehabilitation program. The average monthly disability check for one with at least a 50 percent disability was about $363 in 1973, and this sum was neither taxable nor means-tested. Veterans' benefits today may not be all that they might be, but they are better than those available to nonveterans.[86]

One "bottom line" is the long-term economic consequence of military service. What differences between veteran and nonveteran income patterns are discernible several years after the completion of military service when one controls for age, ethnicity, level of education, geographic location, and occupation? Harley Browning, Sally Lopreato, and Dudley Poston analyzed the Census Bureau's 1971 Public Use Sample for males twenty-five to fifty years of age from California, Arizona, Colorado, New Mexico, and Texas who were working full time, and they controlled the income data for ethnicity, education, veteran status, and occupation.[87] Their findings (Source 220) are, I think, the most revealing yet produced by studies of this sort. They found that the incomes of Mexican-American and, to a lesser but still significant extent, black veterans were higher than Chicano and black nonveterans with comparable levels of education and occupations. It would appear that these veterans, and especially the Chicano veterans, had acquired a cosmopolitan outlook, some skills, and a sense of the Anglo's system. The military's regimen, its bureaucratic ways, its insistence on the use of the majority culture's language and symbols, and its egalitarianism ("all recruits are equal") appear to have provided youth from the *barrio,* for better or worse, with a greater degree of acculturation in "the Anglo's way," and thus increased the chance that he would move more effectively into the larger economy than did those of his peers who had not served.

Although the effects of military service on the lives of those who served are complex and often partially dependent on preservice values and experiences, it is still fair to say that the years in uniform were, for many, the most interesting years of their lives, and consequently it is not surprising that about one in every five veterans joins a veteran's organization (Source 221) and attends various veterans' outings, Memorial Day ceremonies, and reunions (Sources 222-30).

B. The Effects That War and the Military Have on Those Not in the Military Itself

1. THE GI'S FAMILY

The recruit who left behind a disabled and widowed mother or a pregnant wife with two children probably affected his family's fortunes in a substantial fashion. This was why deferments were eventually granted to many and why others, by 1942, were urged to send their dependents an allotment from their paycheck. Some wives took their husband's induction as a call to develop their own self-reliance (Sources 231 and 232); others used it as an opportunity to move away from their home communities temporarily in order to be with their husband at his stateside duty station, and some enjoyed the change of scenery immensely (Source 233). Many children also found the wartime atmosphere exciting and stimulating (Source 234). But other wives and children did not adjust as well to separation from the inducted soldiers (Sources 235-41), and some wives did what they could to obtain discharges for their husbands or to persuade them to desert (Sources 242 and 243). One Confederate soldier was entirely correct when he wrote home of how "depressing it is to get letters that breathe a spirit of discontent. I tell you sister Scottie that one half of the dissertions from the southern army is caused by the letters they receive from . . . home."[88]

If the family endured economic hardships as a result of induction or if the soldier's visits or letters home were few and far between, then the wife's adjustment to separation was a difficult one.[89] But, once again, this phenomenon was not entirely explicable by reference to the war or the military, in and of themselves. Unsuccessful adjustment to separation during World War II, for example, was also strongly associated with the family's socioeconomic status, the wife's psychological make-up and capabilities, and the family's previous record of marital stability.[90] European and Asian children and their families suffered (from bombs and fear-induced peptic ulcers or amenorrhea)[91] far more than the more secure American family during the several twentieth-century wars that the United States has participated in, but some American children suffered distress (see Source 244). American schools in the early stages of the cold war reported that about one-third of the children expected nuclear attack and feared fallout, poisoning, separation from their families, and injury.[92] Adults asked similar questions in 1952 indicated similar levels of alarm; for example, 21 percent "definitely" felt there was a real likelihood that their own city might be subjected to nuclear attack.[93] Later, in 1961, another sampling of public opinion revealed that those most fearful that such an attack would damage their own communities disproportionately believed such attacks to be "unlikely," an example of cognitive dissonance at work (Source 245).

Given the degree of family disruption inherent in the departure of one parent to the war (and often the other to a defense plant job), it is not surprising that some criminologists attributed the discernible rise in juvenile delinquency during the Civil War and World War II to the war itself. The children of such homes, in the words of one editor in 1866, constituted "a great army . . . marching by regiments to misery and crime." The U.S. Children's Bureau reported a per capita increase in juvenile delinquency of 16 percent between 1940 and 1942, and the increase was greatest in war production centers.[94]

Many veterans, wives, and children had considerable difficulties in getting accustomed to one another after the long separation. Wives had taken over the reins; some were uneasy about the return of a mate who had made all the decisions in the past (Sources 246 and 247). Sometimes tensions grew as husbands found themselves living with their wives' parents for weeks, until they could find work and an apartment. Frequently the veterans complained about the permissive attitude of wives toward children born during the war,[95] and in this regard the veteran was significantly different in his attitude toward his wife's child-rearing practices than was the nonveteran (Source 248).

Consequently, some married couples chose divorce or separation (Sources 249 and 250). Life with a brooding or bitter man, with one who drank, with one who had no interest in work or life, with one who preferred his buddies to his wife, with one who seemed to resent or detest the war-born child, or with one who aggressively reclaimed his prewar authority from a capable wife was too much for some women.[96] This pattern of separation and divorce appears to have been especially true of marriages formed at the outbreak of the war, or in the halycon days of victory parades and homecoming.[97]

What of the families whose menfolk never returned? Some wives and mothers experienced the same cognitive dissonance as had some GIs— that is, knowing that their husband or son was gone, they refused to consider that their "volunteer" might have been foolhardy or that their bellicose government might have been reckless. Instead, they lent their own support to "the cause." Their serviceman had not died in vain (Sources 251 and 252). Others, whose husbands may never have wanted to serve in the first place, were predisposed, often because of their disadvantaged place in American society, to be infuriated by the loss of their loved one (Source 253).

2. THE ECONOMY

War and the military have affected the American economy over the past three centuries in several ways. First, they facilitated the territorial expansion of the nation. Second, they defended a variety of economic relationships that were of benefit to the domestic economy. Third, they sometimes deprived the economy of important human, mineral, and energy resources. Fourth, they sometimes altered the wealth-holding and occupational patterns of Americans.

The constant strife with the Indian tribes and the defeat of French, British, and Mexican rivals for the control of portions of North America meant that millions of persons who might otherwise have been "pent up" in the original colonies, or even in Britain and Europe themselves, were free to occupy these newly acquired lands. Needless to say, the consequences for those who lost, and especially for the Indian tribes, were considerably less appealing. Euro-Americans benefited from the wars of conquest; Native Americans suffered terribly.

The military aided in the nation's economic development in a number of other ways, each of which significantly affected Americans of various walks of life. Colonists who had been abused by corrupt British customs officials were free to pursue their livelihoods in peace.[98] States and private firms that sought to construct bridges, dams, roads, canals, harbors, and railways often received direct assistance, in that many of those trained in civil engineering at West Point later resigned and took posts as civil engineers. Army topographical engineers mapped the American West and blazed trails, surveyed ranges, found water and mineral resources, and located passes. In effect, they totaled up the nation's resources and primed the resource-draining pump.[99] Infantry regiments built roads and provided local buying power. Other army and National Guard units sometimes acted to protect strike breakers, to curb industrial sabotage, or to protect property in the event of a riot or natural disaster.[100] Naval vessels went to the aid of merchants, whalers, and investors abroad[101] (Sources 254 and 255). This assistance to American business at home and abroad was sometimes regarded by certain Americans (especially nineteenth-century labor leaders) as being harmful to their economic condition, and at other times it appeared to be of value only to a handful of rich investors, but often it was at least indirectly useful to men engaged in pursuits that, as a result of naval or military assistance, found business easier and more profitable.

Military spending has, of course, always affected elements of the economy, from the days of frontier hamlets whose economy revolved around the local army post, to the cold war days of vast military bases and personnel payrolls and fat contracts to industries grinding out sophisticated new military hardware. The shipbuilding, firearms, and aerospace industries in particular have grown mightily as a result of defense spending, and those employed by those industries have benefited financially from the arrangement. But such expenditures tax other sectors of the public and private economies, for they channel human, monetary, technological, energy, and mineral resources away from those other sectors. One simple indicator of this effect might be revealed in Seymour Melman's comparison of U.S. and European Common Market GNP data for the year 1960:[102]

	UNITED STATES	COMMON MARKET
Military spending as a percent of GNP	9.2	4.2
Machinery and equipment as a percent of GNP	5.4	10.2

A more sophisticated picture of the effect of defense spending on the several sectors of the public and private economies has been compiled by Bruce Russett[103] (Sources 256 and 257). Inasmuch as the day-by-day particulars of defense spending are dependent upon decisions made in Washington, D.C., employment in a defense industry provides less job security than employment in some other sectors of the economy (Sources 258 and 259).

Peacetime defense expenses are steady and their impact modest, however, compared with those that ensue in wartime. Americans have long experienced substantial economic changes as a result of war. South Carolinians in 1707, before the Yamassee War, marketed some 120,000 deerskins. In 1716, after the war, the number produced had diminished to 5,000. During the American Revolution, the wealth-holding patterns of Americans continued to become more and more skewed—that is, compared with the poor, the rich were richer than they had been before the war.[104] Scholars disagree about the precise economic consequences of the Civil War, but some recent research indicates that the war may have had an accelerative effect on northern industry, finance, and GNP.[105] In any event, it is clear that many workers and their families were affected by the changes that flowed from the conflict.

The same may be said of World Wars I and II. Rural labor, black and white, moved to areas where war industries were located[106] (Sources 260-62). Many experienced prosperity for the first time in their lives, and many chose to remain in these new areas after the war (Sources 263 and 264). The cold war and Vietnam produced similar economic consequences.[107]

3. SOCIAL AND POLITICAL VALUES

War and the military have also at times affected the social and political values of Americans. If Confederate schoolchildren believed that "one Confederate soldier can whip 7 Yankees," it seems likely that the war, and militaristic textbooks, had something to do with it (Source 265). If many blacks experienced a resurgence of hope and the desire to secure their civil rights in the eras of the Civil War, World War I, and World War II, it may be that they regarded the courage and sacrifices of black soldiers, the look of determination on the faces of black veterans, as warranting such emotions (Source 266). "GI Joe" comic books were only nominally subject to censorship during World War II; their authors have never needed much direction from Washington. Nonetheless, they, like wartime textbooks and military-related toys and films, presented a positive image of the military to their young readers; at least some of these readers went on to enlist, and some continued to read these comics while in the real combat zone! (See Source 267.) The military itself, by its mere presence, and by its public relations efforts (Source 268), could also contribute to the shaping of a popular attitude in America that some style civilian militarism, but, once again, predispositions are important. Thus neither the United States government, the army or navy, nor any war was responsible for the mid-nineteenth-century growth of volunteer military companies. They grew because young men belonging to this raw, gun-toting nation weaned in war wanted to belong to a military organization.[108] Moreover, no one forces anyone to attend Armed Forces Day displays or "Blue Angels" demonstrations; the socialization that occurs at these gatherings is, at least partially, anticipated and desired.

Nevertheless, the omnipresent, modern defense establishment does appear to "socialize" some of those caught up in it who are not themselves in uniform. A recent study of defense plant workers in the era of the cold war indicated that the longer those workers remained on the job, the more likely they were to develop "hawkish" views (Source 269).

Although it is not necessarily a mark of militarism, Americans recently rated the military higher than any other of the nation's institutions when asked "how good a job" each was doing "for the country" (Source 270). Wartime admiration for "the men in khaki"[109] (Source 271) is not militarism either. Neither is the preference that political party leadership has traditionally displayed for veterans in nominating candidates for office, and in any event the voters do not confirm the hunches of these political leaders; voters do not prefer veterans to nonveterans per se[110] (Source 272). But if militarism implies a rejection of the notion of civilian control of the military, then it may be there does exist some evidence of civilian militarism in the United States[111] (Source 273). We cannot say precisely what has caused Americans to prefer to leave wartime decisions to the generals, but it seems reasonable to assume that the former's familiarity with war and the military has something to do with it.

4. THE "ENEMIES FROM WITHIN"

Needless to say, the American military has had a substantial impact on foreign peoples—on the populace of enemy and allied nations alike. We shall say nothing of this, as we are concerned here with the effects that war and military service have on *American* citizens. But the dividing line between "the enemy" and "the American" has not always existed. The Native American, the Confederate American, and the German-American, for example, were at times both "enemy" and "American." We shall restrict ourselves in the final pages of this Introduction to two such groups—the Tories of the American Revolution and the Japanese-Americans of World War II. Both were gravely affected by the outbreak of war; both were severely dealt with by military authorities (Sources 274-79).

But, once again, predispositions among those affected has as much to do with what happened to them as did the war itself. American Tories, for example, could always have changed their allegiance. If they feared confiscation, harassment, or death more than they cherished their loyalty to "King and Country," they might abjure in the fashion of Nathaniel Jones (Source 280). The fact that they did not cannot be blamed on the war. Japanese-Americans were less free to avoid their fate, inasmuch as it was their race, not their principles, that was the cause of their initial discomfort. But within six months of their internment they were put to another test—they were asked to swear that they were loyal. Many of those who declined to do so remained behind barbed wire, lost their citizenship, and in some cases were expatriated to Japan.

The Japanese-Americans who refused to swear allegiance had various motives for doing so. Some were recent immigrants whose loyalties were still with Japan; others were second generation (Nisei) who were infuriated with the discriminatory way that they had been treated; still others were members of families who did not want to be separated (Sources 281-84).

But not all recent immigrants refused to pledge loyalty to the United States. Not all children whose parents refused to declare their loyalty chose to follow those parents. Not all Nisei angered by discrimination chose to renounce their citizenship. Not all of those who had suffered economic loss chose to return to Japan. Some turned away from the United States; others were unable to do so.[112] Once again we learn, from the ways that Tories and Japanese-American behaved, that the effects a particular war appears to have had on some Americans are attributable in part to the values and personalities that these Americans possessed before the war began.

We do not want to overstate this, of course. Military service and war have substantially affected the lives of many Americans. But some of those affected by these systems (and we may properly call the waging of war a "system" or at least a systematic organizing of society) were decidedly more prone to the forces acting upon their lives than were others. Many Americans possessed values and personalities or were members of familial, social, or economic units that were so strong and enduring that military service or wartime measures left these persons essentially unchanged.

The institutions and systems created by the "leaders" have affected Americans, to be sure. But such artifacts of government (indeed, of business, the church, the school, and political parties) are not omnipotent. Some Americans do "go under" when one or another Leviathan washes over them. And it may well be that this is happening more frequently as these artifacts become larger, more complex, more imperious, more demanding, and more impersonal. But others bob back up to the surface and go on, swimming with (or against) the tide. Ernie Pyle did not exaggerate very much when he wrote, "the human spirit is just like a cork."

What you have just read should serve as an introduction to the sources that follow, and to the general question of the effects of military service and war on individuals and society in the United States. I hope that it has helped the reader to find some of the paths that one might follow in exploring this maze, and that the evidence offered provided the reader with some insights. But I make no claim that these paths are the only ones to follow, or that my evidence is in any sense complete. A single volume of sources could not possibly be definitive were I to have tried to be.

In any event, these materials are at least illustrative. I hope they will lead some readers to probe further, whenever my evidence on one or another dimension of the general question is insufficient.

Notes

1. See, for example, Jesse Clarkson and Thomas C. Cochran, eds., *War as a Social Institution* (New York, 1941); Alfred Kahler and Hans Speier, eds., *War in Our Time* (New York, 1939);

American Friends Service Committee, "The Psychological Effects of the Draft," in A.F.S.C., *The Draft?* (New York, 1968), pp. 10-23; Keith Nelson, ed., *The Impact of War on American Life: The 20th Century Experience* (New York, 1971).

2. See, for example, George Fredrickson, *The Inner Civil War: Northern Intellectuals and the Crisis of the Union* (New York, 1965); Stanley Cooperman, *World War I and the American Novel* (Baltimore, 1967); Edmund Wilson, *Patriotic Gore* (New York, 1962); Richard Resh, "Tutors to Society: Five American Intellectuals and War," unpublished Ph.D., University of Wisconsin, 1966; Daniel S. Greenberg, *The Politics of Pure Science* (New York, 1967); Ronald Tobey, *The American Ideology of National Science, 1919-1930* (Pittsburgh, 1971); Daniel Aaron, *The Unwritten War* (New York, 1973); Issac Kandel, *The Impact of the War upon American Education* (New York, 1948); I. L. Horowitz, *The Rise and Fall of Project Camelot* (New York, 1968).

3. Having offered this blanket critique of my professional predecessors, I hasten now to express my indebtedness to two historians, whose work I readily recommend to all: Bell Irwin Wiley, *The Life of Billy Yank* (New York, 1952); and *The Life of Johnny Reb* (New York, 1943); and Dixon Wecter, *When Johnny Comes Marching Home* (New York, 1944).

4. References to these studies appear in the essay or source materials where each study touches on the subject matter at hand. See also Kurt Lang's bibliographical essay and bibliography, *Military Institutions and the Sociology of War* (Beverly Hills, 1972).

5. Forrest McDonald, "The Relation of French Peasant Veterans of the American Revolution to the Fall of Feudalism in France, 1789-1972," *Agricultural History* 25 (January 1951): 151-61.

6. Gutteridge, *The Military in African Politics* (London, 1969), p. 4. Compare James Coleman, *Nigeria* (Berkeley, 1958), p. 254. But see K. W. Grundy and M. Shank, "African Ex-Servicemen and Independence Politics in British Africa," in Morris Janowitz and Jacques van Doorn, eds., *On Military Ideology* (Rotterdam, 1971), pp. 225-43, for a persuasive rebuttal of these arguments.

7. James Diehl, "Paramilitary Organizations and the Weimar Republic," unpublished Ph.D. dissertation, Berkeley, 1972.

8. William Chafe, *The American Woman . . . 1920-1970* (New York, 1972), pp. 135-95.

9. Resident of "Leadertown," a section of Pittsburgh, 1975, interviewed by Thomas Conley, to whom I am indebted for both the interview tape and the background information.

10. W. Cockerham, "Selective Socialization: Airforce Training as Status Passage," *Journal of Political and Military Sociology* 1 (Fall 1973): 215-29.

11. See Stanislav Andreski, *Military Organizations and Society*, rev. ed. (Berkeley, 1968), for one model of this interaction.

12. This paragraph is based essentially on John Shy, "A New Look at the Colonial Militia," *William and Mary Quarterly* 20 (1963): 175-85; Douglas Leach, *Arms for Empire* (New York, 1973); Howard Peckham, *The Colonial Wars, 1689-1763* (Chicago, 1964); Vernon Crane, *The Southern Frontier, 1670-1732* (Ann Arbor, Mich., 1956); and Howard Peckham, *The War for Independence* (Chicago, 1958).

13. The first half of this paragraph is based essentially on William Benton, "Pennsylvania Revolutionary Officers and the Federal Constitution," *Pennsylvania History* 31 (1964): 419-35; Russell Weigley, *History of the U.S. Army* (New York, 1973); Edward Billingsley, *In Defense of Neutral Rights* (Chapel Hill, N.C., 1967); Peter Karsten, *The Naval Aristocracy* (New York, 1972); and Richard Kohn, *Sword of the Republic* (New York, 1974).

14. Peter Karsten, "Armed Progressives: The Military Reorganizes for the 'American Century,'" in Jerry Israel, ed., *Building the Organizational Society* (New York, 1972), pp. 197-232.

15. *Ibid.*

16. John Chambers, "Conscripting for Colossus: The Adoption of the Military Draft in the U.S. in World War I," paper presented at OAH meeting, 1972; Paul Koistinen, "The Indus-

trial-Military Complex: World War I," *Business History Review* 41 (1967): 378-403; Robert Cuff, "The Cooperative Impulse and War," in Israel, *op. cit.,* pp. 233-46; John G. Clifford, *The Citizen Soldiers: The Plattsburg Training Camp Movement, 1913-1920* (Lexington, Mass., 1972); John P. Finnegan, "Military Preparedness in the Progressive Era," Ph.D. dissertation, University of Wisconsin, 1969.

17. Walter Millis, *Arms and Men* (New York, 1958), pp. 237-71; Paul Koistinen, "The Military-Industrial Complex . . . The Inter-War Years," *Journal of American History* 47 (1970): 819 ff.

18. See Leo Bogart et al., eds., *Social Research and the Desegregation of the Armed Services* (Chicago, 1969); Morris Janowitz, "Changing Patterns of Organizational Authority: The Military Establishment," *Administrative Science Quarterly* 3 (March 1959): 473-93; Walter Millis, "The War," in his *Arms and the State* (New York, 1958), pp. 61-90; Morris Janowitz and Roger Little, *Sociology and the Military Establishment,* rev. ed. (New York, 1965); David G. Mandlebaum, *Soldier Groups and Negro Soldiers* (Berkeley, 1952); Samuel Stouffer et al., *Studies in Social Psychology in World War II,* 4 vols. (Princeton, N.J., 1948-52); HumRRO, *Bibliography* (Washington, D.C., 1969). One consequence of the shift "from coercion to persuasion" was a revolt of "old-timers" who feared that the leaders were "getting soft." See especially Robert Heinl, "Special Trust and Confidence," *U.S. Naval Institute Proceedings* 82 (1956): 463 ff.

19. Louis Morton and Gene Lyons, *Schools for Strategy* (New York, 1965); Paul Dickson, *Think Tanks* (New York, 1971); Bruce L. Smith, *The Rand Corporation* (Cambridge, Mass., 1966).

20. Bruce Russett, *What Price Vigilance?* (New Haven, Conn., 1970).

21. Much of the work is available as publications of the Human Resources Research Office and the U.S. Army's Behavioral Research Office, and as discussion papers at various meetings of the Inter-University Seminar on Armed Forces and Society.

22. See especially Source 159 and notes 44, 47, and 64.

23. See, for example, Opinion Research Corporation, *The Image of the Army* (Princeton, N.J., 1969); and Norma Wikler, "Vietnam and the Veteran's Consciousness . . . ," unpublished Ph.D. dissertation, University of California, Berkeley, 1973.

24. Examples of this are cited in notes 52, 54, 64, 73, 74, and throughout the source materials.

25. Charles Bardeen, *A Little Fifer's War Diary* (Syracuse, N.Y., 1910), p. 9.

26. Haan, cited in Edward Sherman, "A Bureaucracy Adrift," *Nation* (March 1, 1971). Compare William James, *The Moral Equivalent of War* (New York, 1910).

27. S. L. A. Marshall, *Men Against Fire* (New York, 1947).

28. Glenn Munson, ed., *Letters from Vietnam* (New York, 1966), p. 120.

29. Captain H. R. Brinkerhoff, "The Regular Army and the National Guard," *United Service,* n.s., 13 (1895): 505; Norman Pollack, *The Populist Response to Industrial America* (Cambridge, Mass., 1962), pp. 59-60; Martha Derthick, *The National Guard in Politics* (Cambridge, Mass., 1965), p. 12.

30. Marcus Cunliffe, *Soldiers and Civilians* (Boston, 1969), p. 81.

31. Cockerham, *op. cit.;* David M. Mantell, *True Americanism* (New York, 1974).

32. Mantell, *op. cit.;* William Lucas, "The American Lieutenant," unpublished Ph.D. dissertation, University of North Carolina, 1971. Compare Cornelius Lammers, "Midshipmen and Candidate Reserve Officers at the Royal Netherlands Naval College," *Sociologica Neerlandica* 2 (1965): 98-123.

33. Edward Papenfuse and Gregory Stiverson, "General Smallwood's Recruits," *William and Mary Quarterly* 30 (January 1973): 117-32.

34. Harold Wool, *The Military Specialist* (Baltimore, 1968), p. 108. Compare Milton Holmen and Robert Katter, *Attitude and Information Patterns of OCS Eligibles* (HumRRO, October 1953).

35. Jack Foner, *The U.S. Soldier Between Two Wars* (New York, 1970), p. 137.

36. Arthur Barbeau, "The Black American Soldier in World War I," Ph.D. dissertation, University of Pittsburgh, 1970, p. 198; Richard Dalfiume, *Desegregation of the U.S. Armed Forces* (Columbia, Mo., 1969), p. 11.

37. See, for example, Eugene Murdock, *Patriotism Limited, 1862-1865* (Kent, Ohio, 1967); Edward Wright, *Conscientious Objectors in the Civil War* (Philadelphia, 1931); and Peter Brock, *Pacifism in the U.S. from the Colonial Era to World War II* (Princeton, N.J., 1968).

38. Andrew Mellick, Jr., *Lesser Crossroads* (Rutgers, 1948 [originally published 1889]), 168.

39. However, when the lottery draft was reintroduced in 1971, students were asked their opinion of the Vietnam War both *before* they had learned of their draft number and *after* they had learned of it. A low number (high draft eligibility) did not appear to cause a student to change his views regarding the war. Thus it is probably not correct to say that previous students who had opposed the war while in a deferred status did so essentially because their deferred status allowed them a freedom others lacked. They opposed the war out of conviction. See Charles Longino, "Draft Lottery Numbers and Student Opposition to War," *Sociology of Education* 46 (Fall 1973): 499-506.

40. Irwin Sperber, "The Sociological Dimensions of Military Co-optation in the U.S.," *Sociological Inquiry* 40 (1970): 61-71.

41. Department of Defense, *Commander's Digest*, 17 (April 10, 1975), p. 6.

42. For an inadequate job see the American Friends Service Committee, *The Draft?* (New York, 1968), pp. 10-23. For a better one see John Farris, "The Impact of Basic Combat Training," *Armed Forces and Society* 2 (November 1975): 115 ff.

43. Farris, *loc. cit.*

44. Paul Hood et al., *Evaluation of Three Experimental Systems for Noncommissioned Officer Training* (HumRRO, September 1967); Peter Petersen, *Against the Grain* (1972), 152; Janowitz and Little, *op. cit.*, p. 63; Donald Campbell and Thelma McCormack, "Military Experience and Attitudes Towards Authority," *American Journal of Sociology* 62 (March 1957): 480; Badgett et al., "Authoritarianism and Military Ideology of Military and Civilian Students," *Psychology* 7 (1970): 13-16. Compare Klaus Roghmann and Wolfgang Sodeur, "The Impact of Military Service upon Authoritarian Attitudes: Evidence from West Germany," *American Journal of Sociology* (September 1972): 418-33, who demonstrate that the decline in dogmatism during training has no lasting effect.

45. Alan Horton, "Marine Recruit Training Under Fire," *Pittsburgh Press* (March 26, 1976); U.P.I., "Marines Hint D.I. Screening," *ibid.* (April 28, 1976).

46. Bell Irwin Wiley, *The Life of Johnny Reb* (New York, 1943), p. 338; D. Cortwright, *Soldiers in Revolt* (New York, 1974), p. 44. Compare William Willcox, *Portrait of a General* (New York, 1962), p. 80, on fragging in the British army, around 1776. (I thank Van Beck Hall for bringing this to my attention.)

47. S. James Goffard et al., *A Study of Category IV Personnel in Basic Training* (HumRRO, April 1966); George D. Greer, Jr., "Predictors, Descriptions and Correlates of Basic Training Delinquents," paper read at annual meeting of Western Psychological Association, Spring 1966; Raymond Fink and George Gray, *Effects of Four Orientation Procedures on Airborne Trainees* (HumRRO, October 1953); Faris, *op. cit.*, p. 126.

48. *New Yorker* (May 13, 1967), p. 67.

49. Cuber, "Changing Courtship and Marriage Customs," in *The American Family in World War II*, Annals of American Academy of Political & Social Science, September 1943.

50. Howard Peckham, ed., *The Toll of Independence* (Chicago, 1974), pp. 130-33; *Armed Forces and Society* (Spring 1976), pp. 356, 358.

51. Abbey, *An American Soldier* (Boston, 1918), p. 92, cited in Genthe, *American War Narratives, 1917-1918* (New York, 1969), p. 67.

52. See, for example, G. A. Braatz, G. K. Lumry, and M. S. Wright, "The Young Veteran as

a Psychiatric Patient in Three Eras of Conflict," *Military Medicine* 136 (1971): 455-57; R. Grinker and J. Spiegel, *Men Under Stress* (Philadelphia, 1945), p. 350; Robert Egbert, "A Study of the Characteristics of Successful and Unsuccessful Men Working in Situations of Extreme Stress," a paper read at the American Psychology Association meeting, 1954; Gary Tischler, in Peter Bourne, ed., *The Psychology and Physiology of Stress* (New York, 1969), pp. 21-22; Jonathan Borus, "The Reentry Transition of the Vietnam Veteran," *Armed Forces and Society* 2 (Fall 1975): p. 106.

53. Glasser, *365 Days* (New York, 1971), p. 178; Lifton, *Home from the War* (Boston, 1973), p. 420.

54. Borus, *op. cit.*, pp. 97 ff; Borus, "The Incidence of Maladjustment in Vietnam Returnees," *Archives of General Psychiatry* 30 (1974): 554-57. Compare R. E. Strange and D. E. Brown, "Home from the War," *American Journal of Psychiatry* 128 (1970): 488-92; W. B. Gault, "Some Remarks on Slaughter," *American Journal of Psychiatry* 128 (1971): 450-54.

55. Marshall, *op. cit.*; F. A. Shannon, *Organization and Administration of the Union Army* (Cleveland, 1928), I, p. 137.

56. Noah Worcester, *Abraham and Lot . . .* (Concord, Mass., 1812), p. 12. I am indebted to Professor William Gribbin for this reference.

57. Emerson, *The Causes and Effects of War . . .* (Salem, Mass., 1812), p. 12. I am indebted to Professor Gribbin for this reference as well.

58. Reverend Eli E. Hall, *Ahab and Naboth; or the United States and Mexico . . .* (New Haven, Conn., 1847), pp. 13-15; Porter, *Review . . .* (Auburn, N.Y., 1849), pp. 162-63. Both selections appear in George W. Smith and Charles Judah, eds., *Chronicles of the Gringos* (Albuquerque, N.M., 1968), pp. 446-47.

59. Wecter, *op. cit.*, p. 70.

60. *Ibid.*, p. 233.

61. Betty Rosenbaum, "The Relationship Between War and Crime in the U.S.," *Journal of Criminal Law and Criminology* 31 (1940): 722-40, esp. 725; W. F. Lorenz, "Delinquency and the Ex-Soldier," *Mental Hygiene* 7 (1923): 472-84.

62. Hans Mattick, *Parole in the Army* (1957), cited in Janowitz and Little, *op. cit.*, p. 54.

63. Compare Yehuda Amir, "Effectiveness of Kibbutz-Born Soldiers in Israeli Defense Forces," *Human Relations* 22 (1969): 333-44.

64. A. Rose, "The Social Psychology of Desertion," *American Sociological Review* 26 (1951):618-24.

65. Foner, *op. cit.*, p. 222. As this book was going to press I discovered some confirmation of my preferred alternative to Foner's explanation of the decline in the desertion rate. Frederick Harrod's *Manning the New Navy* (Westport, 1978, p. 117) demonstrates that it was the successful recruitment of a better caliber of sailor in the early twentieth century that essentially explains the steady decline in the desertion rate in the U.S. Navy between 1905 and 1935.

66. Hobart G. Osburn et al., *A Preliminary Investigation of Delinquency in the Army* (HumRRO Technical Report no. 5, April 1954); David Cortwright, *Soldiers in Revolt* (New York, 1974), p. p. 14; Kurt Boyd and Harry Jones, "An Analysis of Factors Relating to Desertion Among FY 68 and FY 69 Army Accessions," *Catalog of Selected Documents in Psychology* 4 (Spring 1974): 59; John Kifner, *New York Times* (October 5, 1969), p. 58.

67. *Armed Forces and Society* (Spring 1976): 374, 450, 452.

68. W. Benton, "Pennsylvania Revolutionary Officers and the Federal Constitution," *Pennsylvania History* 31 (1964): 419 ff.

69. Wecter, *op. cit.*, p. 552.

70. Arthur Palmer Hudson, *Specimens of Mississippi Folklore* (Ann Arbor, Mich., 1928), v.

71. J. Helmer, *Bringing the War Home* (New York, 1974); Cortwright, *op. cit.*

72. Norma J. Wikler, "Vietnam and the Veteran's Consciousness: Pre-Political Thinking Among American Soldiers," unpublished Ph.D. dissertation, University of California, Berkeley, 1973, pp. 315-34; M. K. Jennings and G. B. Markus, "Political Participation and Vietnam-Era War Veterans: A Longitudinal Study," in Nancy Goldman and David Segal, eds., *The Social Psychology of Military Service* (Beverly Hills, Calif., 1976), pp. 180-81; both studies cited by Jack Ladinsky in *Armed Forces and Society* 3 (Spring 1976): 448. Compare Stephen Ward, ed., *The War Generation: Veterans of the First World War* (New York, 1975).

73. The Jennings-Markus study does indicate that those Vietnam veterans who participated in antiwar and other political rallies after returning to the States were disproportionately made up of men who had attended such meetings before entering the service *(loc. cit.).*

74. James Fendrich and Michael Pearson, "Black Veterans Return," in Martin Oppenheimer, ed., *The American Military* (1971), pp. 163-78.

75. S. Stouffer et al., *Studies in Social Psychology* . . . , II, p. 641. In this regard, then, Dixon Wecter was misled by earlier opinion figures (gathered from GIs at separation centers in 1944) that indicated that over 40 percent of veterans did not intend to return to their home communities. The 1947 census returns showed that 72 percent had, in fact, returned.

76. Stouffer, *op. cit.,* p. 64; Robert Havighurst, *The American Veteran Back Home* (New York, 1951), p. 236.

77. Michael Taussig, *Those Who Served* (20th Century Fund, New York, 1974), p. 99.

78. Havighurst, *op. cit.*

79. Wecter, *op. cit.,* p. 197, citing Carl Fish, "Back to Peace in 1865," *American Historical Review* 19 (1919): 437-40. Compare Stouffer, *op. cit.,* IV, p. 630; Wilbur Brookover, "Adjustment of Veterans to Civilian Life," *American Sociological Review* 10 (October 1945): 581.

80. Cortwright, *Soldiers in Revolt,* p. 194, citing Harold Wool, *The Military Specialist* (Baltimore, 1968). Compare Herbert Kelley, "Effects of Military Experience on Socialization of Vietnam Era Veterans in Work Roles," unpublished Ph.D. dissertation, University of South Carolina, 1972.

81. Charles Moskos, *The American Enlisted Man,* p. 205.

82. Research report to 1972 meeting of the Inter-University Seminar on Armed Forces and Society in Chicago by Jack Ladinsky, Department of Sociology, University of Wisconsin.

83. Albert Biderman and Laura Sharp, "The Convergence of Military and Civilian Occupational Structures," *American Journal of Sociology* 73 (January 1968): 381-99.

84. Neil Fligstein, "Military Service, the Draft, and the GI Bill: Their Effects on the Lives of American Males 1940-1973," M.A. thesis, University of Wisconsin, 1976; M. Taussig, *Those Who Served,* p. 102.

85. J. Barber and S. Ambrose, *The Military in American Society* (New York, 1973), p. 156. Compare Fligstein, *loc. cit.*

86. Taussig, *op. cit.,* pp. 66, 71, 79, 116.

87. Browning et al., "Income and Veteran Status," *American Sociological Review* 38 (1973): 74-85.

88. Robert Hill of Texas to his wife, April 29, 1864, cited in Bell Irwin Wiley, *The Life of Johnny Reb,* p. 210. Compare Ella Lonn, *Desertions During the Civil War* (New York, 1928).

89. Reuben Hill et al., *Families Under Stress* (New York, 1949), pp. 150-51.

90. *Ibid.,* pp. 109, 113, 131, passim.

91. Irving Janis, *Air War and Emotional Stress* (New York, 1951), pp. 90-92. Compare Fred C. Ikle, *The Social Impact of Bomb Destruction* (Norman, Okla., 1958).

92. Seymour Melman, *Our Depleted Society* (New York, 1965), p. 170.

93. *The Public and Civil Defense: A Report Based on Two Sample Surveys in Eleven Major American Cities,* University of Michigan, March 1952, p. 32.

94. Wecter, *op. cit.,* 169; John Gillin, *Criminology and Penology* (New York, 1945), p. 211.

Compare W. A. Lunden, "Juvenile Delinquency in Japan, Pre-War, War and Post-War," *Journal of Criminal Law, Criminology and Political Science* (November-December 1953): 428-32; F. E. Louage, "Delinquency in Europe After World War II," *Journal of Criminal Law, Criminology and Political Science* 44 (May-June 1951): 53-56; Demetre Karanikas, "Le Service Militaire et son Influence sur la Criminalité," *Annales Internationales de Criminologie* (1966): 363-70.

Conversely, there were no substantial differences between prewar and wartime civilian suicide, insanity, or serious crime rates in the United States during the same period of time (1940-42). See H. W. Dunham, "War and Personality Disorganization," *American Journal of Sociology* 48 (November 1942): 387 ff; W. Reckless, "The Impact of War on Crime, Delinquency and Prostitution," *American Journal of Sociology* 48 (1942): 378-86; and Walter Bromberg, "The Effects of the War on Crime," *American Sociological Review* 8 (1943): 686.

95. Wecter, *When Johnny Comes Marching Home*, p. 169 (for post-Civil War evidence of this phenomenon); Lois and Herbert Stolz, *Father Relations of War-Born Children* (New York, 1950), pp. 31, 66 (for World War II evidence).

96. Cathrine Breslin, "Vietnam Veterans," *Redbook* (May 1973): 95 ff; Corrine Browne, "The War in the Bedroom," *New Times* (December 12, 1975), pp. 32 ff., esp. p. 40.

97. Calvin Hall, "The Instability of Post-War Marriages," *Journal of Social Psychology* 5 (1934):523 ff.

98. Jesse Lemisch, "The American Revolution Seen from the Bottom Up," in Barton Bernstein, ed., *Towards a New Past* (New York, 1968), pp. 21-28.

99. Forest Hill, *Roads, Rails and Waterways: The Army Engineers and Early Transportation* (Norman, Okla., 1957), p. 150; William Goetsmann, *Army Exploration in the American West, 1803-1863* (New Haven, Conn., 1959), passim.

100. William Ganoe, *History of the United States Army* (New York, 1924), pp. 501-05; Jerry M. Cooper, "The Wisconsin National Guard in the Milwaukee Riots of 1886," *Wisconsin Magazine of History* (Autumn 1971), 31-48; Robin Higham, ed., *Bayonets in the Streets: The Use of Troops in Civil Disorders* (Manhattan, Kan., 1969); Francis P. Prucha, *Broadax and Bayonet: The Role of the U.S. Army in the Development of the Northwest, 1815-1860* (Madison, Wis., 1953); Barton C. Hacker, "The U.S. Army as a National Police Force, 1877-98," *Military Affairs* (1969): 255 ff.

101. Peter Karsten, *The Naval Aristocracy* (New York, 1972), pp. 140-85.

102. Seymour Melman, *Our Depleted Society* (New York, 1965), pp. 69, 78. The same inverse relationship exists between the percentage of GNP devoted to military spending in the United States, Europe, and Japan, and the annual GNP growth rates of these nations. Compare Albert Szymanski, "Military Spending and Economic Stagnation," *American Journal of Sociology* 78 (July 1973): 1-14.

103. Bruce Russett, *What Price Vigilance?* passim.

104. Douglas Leach, *Arms for Empire* (New York, 1973), p. 268; J. Lemon and G. Nash, "The Distribution of Wealth in 18th Century . . . Chester County, Pa. . . .," *Journal of Social History* (Fall 1968): 11.

105. Harry Scheiber, "Economic Change in the Civil War Era: An Analysis of Recent Studies," *Civil War History* 11 (1965): 396-411.

106. E. D. Tetreau, "The Impact of War on Some Communities in the Southwest," *American Sociological Review* 8 (1943): 240-55; Louis Ducoff et al., "Effects of the War on the Agricultural Working Force and on the Rural-Farm Population," *Social Forces* 21 (1943), 406-12; Rudolph Heberle, *The Impact of the War on Population Redistribution in the South* (no. 7 in Papers of the Institute of Research and Training in the Social Sciences, Nashville, Tenn., 1945).

107. James Clayton, ed., *The Economic Impact of the Cold War* (New York, 1970); Robert Stevens, *Vain Hopes, Grim Realities* (New York, 1975).

108. Marcus Cunliffe, *Soldiers and Civilians* (Boston, 1969), pp. 213-54.

109. That this was so indicates that the military's fear that the public blames it for Vietnam is unwarranted. See, for example, Ambrose and Barber, *op. cit.,* p. 309. Compare James Clotfelter, *The Military in American Politics* (New York, 1973), p. 125.

110. Albert Somit and Joseph Tanenhaus, "The Veteran in the Electoral Process: The House of Representatives," *The Journal of Politics* 19 (May 1957): 184-201.

111. Clotfelter, *op. cit.,* pp. 124 ff.

112. Dorothy Swaine Thomas and Richard S. Niskimoto, *Japanese-American Evacuation and Resettlement: Vol. 1: The Spoilage* (Berkeley, Calif., 1946); D. S. Thomas, *ibid.: Vol. II: The Salvage* (Berkeley, Calif., 1952). Compare Anthony F. C. Wallace, *The Death and Rebirth of the Seneca Nation* (New York, 1970); Leonard Broom and Ruth Riemer, *Removal and Return* (Berkeley, Calif., 1973).

PART I

The consequences of military service

1

The Recruitment Process

SOURCE 1

> *Young Joseph Plumb Martin of Milford, Connecticut, decided to enlist during the American Revolution:*

The winter of this year passed off without any very frightening alarms, and the spring of 1775 arrived. Expectation of some fatal event seemed to fill the minds of most of the considerate people throughout the country. I was ploughing in the field about half a mile from home, about the twenty-first day of April, when all of a sudden the bells fell to ringing and three guns were repeatedly fired in succession down in the village; what the cause was we could not conjecture. I had some fearful forebodings that something more than the sound of a carriage wheel was in the wind. The regulars are coming in good earnest, thought I. My grandsire sighed, he "smelt the rat." He immediately turned out the team and repaired homeward. I set off to see what the cause of the commotion was. I found most of the male kind of the people together; soldiers for Boston were in requisition. A dollar deposited upon the drumhead was taken up by someone as soon as placed there, and the holder's name taken, and he enrolled with orders to equip himself as quick as possible. My spirits began to revive at the sight of the money offered; the seeds of courage began to sprout; for, contrary to my knowledge, there was a scattering of them sowed, but they had not as yet germinated; I felt a strong inclination, when I found I had them, to cultivate them. O, thought I, if I were but old enough to put myself forward, I would be the possessor of one dollar, the dangers of war to the contrary notwithstanding; but I durst not put my-

Source: George Scheer, ed., *Private Yankee Doodle: Being a Narrative of Some of the Dangers and Sufferings of a Revolutionary Soldier* (Boston: Little, Brown and Co., 1962), pp. 6-17.

self up for a soldier for fear of being refused, and that would have quite upset all the courage I had drawn forth.

The men that had engaged "to go to war" went as far as the next town, where they received orders to return, as there was a sufficiency of men already engaged, so that I should have had but a short campaign had I have gone.

This year there were troops raised both for Boston and New York. Some from the back towns were billeted at my grandsire's; their company and conversation began to warm my courage to such a degree that I resolved at all events to "go a sogering." Accordingly I used to pump my grandsire, in a roundabout manner, to know how he stood affected respecting it. For a long time he appeared to take but little notice of it. At length, one day, I pushed the matter so hard upon him, he was compelled to give me a direct answer, which was, that he should never give his consent for me to go into the army unless I had the previous consent of my parents. And now I was completely graveled; my parents were too far off to obtain their consent before it would be too late for the present campaign. What was I to do? Why, I must give up the idea, and that was hard; for I was as earnest now to call myself and be called a soldier as I had been a year before *not* to be called one. I thought over many things and formed many plans, but they all fell through, and poor disconsolate I was forced to set down and gnaw my fingernails in silence.

I said but little more about "soldiering" until the troops raised in and near the town in which I resided came to march off for New York; then I felt bitterly again. I accompanied them as far as the town line, and it was hard parting with them then. Many of my young associates were with them, my heart and soul went with them, but my mortal part must stay behind. By and by, they will come swaggering back, thought I, and tell me of all their exploits, all their "hairbreadth 'scapes," and poor Huff will not have a single sentence to advance. O, that was too much to be borne with by me.

The thoughts of the service still haunted me after the troops were gone, and the town clear of them; but what plan to form to get the consent of all, parents and grandparents, that I might procure thereby to myself the (to me then) bewitching name of a soldier, I could not devise. Sometimes I thought I would enlist at all hazards, let the consequences be what they would; then again, I would think how kind my grandparents were to me, and ever had been, my grandsire in particular: I could not bear to hurt their feelings so much. I did sincerely love my grandsire; my grandma'am I did not love so well, and I feared her less. At length a thought struck my mind: should they affront me grossly, I would make that a plea with my conscience to settle the controversy with. Accordingly, I wished nothing more than to have them, or either of them, give "His Honor" a high affront, that I might thereby form an excuse to engage in the service *without* their consent, leave, or approbation.

It happened that in the early part of the autumn of this year, I was gratified in my wishes; for I thought I had received provocation enough to justify me in engaging in the army during life, little thinking that I was inflicting the punishment on myself that I fancied I was laying on my grandparents for their (as I thought) willful obstinacy.

. . . enlisting orders were out. I used frequently to go to the rendezvous, where I saw many of my young associates enlist, had repeated banterings to engage with them, but still when it came "case in hand," I had my misgivings. If I once undertake, thought I, I must stick to it; there will be no receding. Thoughts like these would, at times, almost overset my resolutions.

But mauger all these "doleful ideas," I one evening went off with a full determination to enlist at all hazards. When I arrived at the place of rendezvous I found a number of young men of my acquaintance there. The old bantering began—come, if you will enlist I will, says one; you have long been talking about it, says another—come, now is the time. "Thinks I to myself" I will not be laughed into it or out of it, at any rate; I will act my own pleasure after all. But what did I come here for tonight? Why, to enlist. Then enlist I will. So seating myself at the table, enlisting orders were immediately presented to me; I took up the pen, loaded it with the fatal charge, made several mimic imitations of writing my name, but took especial care not to touch the paper with the pen until an unlucky wight who was leaning over my shoulder gave my hand a stroke, which caused the pen to make a woeful scratch on the paper. "O, he has enlisted," said he. "He had made his mark; he is fast enough now." Well, thought I, I may as well go through with the business now as not. So I wrote my name fairly upon the indentures.[1] And now I was a *soldier,* in name at least, if not in practice. . . .

[1] Martin enlisted on July 6, 1776.

Peter Oliver, a prominent Tory active in the service of "King and Country," asked a Revolutionary lieutenant captured at Bunker Hill how he had decided to serve. The lieutenant, William Scott, replied:

Source: *Peter Oliver's Origin and Progress of the American Revolution,* ed. Douglass Adair and John A. Shutz (San Marino, Calif., 1961), p. 130. For a discussion of Scott see John Shy, *A People Numerous and Armed* (New York, 1976), pp. 165-79.

The case was this Sir! I lived in a Country Town; I was a Shoemaker, & got my Living by my Labor. When this Rebellion came on, I saw some of my Neighbors get into Commission, who were no better than myself. I was very ambitious, & did not like to see those Men above me. I was asked to enlist, as a private Soldier. My Ambition was too great for so low a Rank; I offered to enlist upon having a Lieutenants Commission; which was granted. I imagined my self now in a way of Promotion: if I was killed in Battle, there would be an end of me, but if my Captain was killed, I should rise in Rank, & should still have a Chance to rise higher. These Sir! were the only Motives of my entering into the Service; for as to the Dispute between great Britain & the Colonies, I know nothing of it; neither am I capable of judging whether it is right or wrong.

SOURCE 2

Maurice Nowland, a Tory veteran, told a royal commission that he had served briefly as a Revolutionary soldier "by Compulsion" and/or "from attachment to a friend":

Memorial of Maurice Nowland
26th of May 1785.

Maurice Nowlan — the Claimant — sworn.

Is a Native of Ireland & went to America in 1770 to New York. He was settled in 1774 at Cross Creek & followed a Mercantile Line & carried out 200 Gas. He took part with Gov^t at first & rais'd a Company in 1776 & join'd Col^l Macdonald at Cross Creek. Produces a Warrant for the rank of Captn with the Pay as such. He was four Years & ten Months in Captivity. He broke Gaol at Reading in Octr 1780 & got to New York from whence he went in 1781 to Charlestown. He got a Warrant from Col^l Stuart to raise a Company in North Carolina but being obliged to evacuate Wilmington suddenly he was not able to raise the Company. Warrant produced dated 30th of Octr 1781. At the Evacuation of Charlestown he came to Eng^d. He never sign'd any Association or took any Oath. When he was in confinement he was offer'd his whole property if he would join them. He rec^d the pay of Captn up to this time & now receives half pay. He has an Allowance of £50 a Y^r from the Treasury which he has had from the Ist of Jany 1783 & he now continues to receive it.

Neil McArthur — sworn.

Knew Mr Nowland in 1774. He was a very loyal Subject. He was a Storekeeper. He raised a Company in 1776. He was a long time confined. He married a Dau^r of one Wm White he married in Ireland. Wm White was an

Source: H. E. Egerton, ed., *Royal Commission on the Losses and Services of American Loyalists* (London 1915), pp. 368-69.

Irishman. He is not acquainted with any of [Maurice Nowlan's] Lands. He knows he had an House at Cross Creek can't tell what he gave for it. Does not know what it was worth but believes £500 S. Would have given £500 for it.

Further Testimony to the Memorial of Maurice Nowlan

2^d of June 1785.

Maurice Nowlan—sworn.

Admits that he was one of the Party who went by the desire of the Rebel Committee to intercept a letter written by Govr Martin which they effected. Says however that he did not go by choice. Says he went by Compulsion & that he was taken out of his Bed. Says however that he should have been in no personal Danger if he had avoided going. Says there were two Companies in Arms in America at that time for the purpose of learning their Exercise. One Co was attach'd to America & the other to G. B. He was in that which was attached to America. He was an Assist^t Lieut^t. Being asked why he did not tell this Story when he spoke of his own Case he says he was confused & that he was not asked. Thinks notwithstanding this that a Man may be said to have been uniformly loyal. He chose his Co. from attachment to his friend. He join'd the British because he always meant to do it. Admits that he always thought that the British would succeed.

Alexander McKay—sworn.

Did not know that Mr Nowlan was one of the Party to take Captⁿ Cunningham till this Day. Says in the Case of Vardy [another claimant] this affected his Opinion because he knew his Sentiments but it does not alter his opinion of Nowlan's Loyalty.

SOURCE 3

> *James Miller claimed to Lt. Col. Thomas Randolph, commander of the Virginia Volunteer Regiment in 1847, that he had been "shanghaied":*

The reputed justice and honor of character for which I have heard you [are] distinguished has emboldened me to ask exoneration from the constrained and unjust oppression imposed upon me by Captain John P. Young, of your Regiment, who tore me from my lawful employment,

---

Source: George W. Smith and Charles Judah, eds., *Chronicles of the Gringos* (Albany, N.Y., 1968), pp. 16-19.

forced me to embark for this distant Country, and now, per might, holds me an involuntary soldier in his company.

In order to enlighten you as to the outrage perpetrated upon my liberty and rights, let me bespeak your patience while I detail a plain and unvarnished tho' tedious narrative of the facts of my hard case as they occurred: I, James Miller was born in Renfordshire, Scotland. When only thirteen years of age I emigrated to Nova Scotia, and in the town of New Glasgow of that province I served an apprenticeship to the trade of ship carpenter. On the last of Aug. 1846, I left Nova Scotia for Philadelphia, U.S. where I remained only about the space of six weeks, when I sailed in the capacity of second Mate and Carpenter aboard the Barque Ann Hood, bound to New Orleans, which vessel having been forced by distress to enter the Harbor of Norfolk, Virg. to repair damages sustained at sea, I left her by consent of the Captain and engaged myself in employment in the U.S. Navy-Yard at Gosport.

While so employed I first met, on or about the 1st day of Decr. '46, Captain Young, then engaged in raising a Volunteer Company to serve the Government of the U.States in the existing war with the Republic of Mexico. Stimulated by the influence of an unusual quantity of ardent spirits and incited by persuasion I signed a paper purporting to be an enrollment of the names of men about to organize themselves for said service. At the time of signing my name I was under the impression that the term of service was limited to a twelve months [*sic*]. Not more than ten days thereafter, having maturely reflected on the nature and consequences of the engagement into which I had in part entered and having ascertained the indefinite term for which, upon being mustered into the service, I was expected to enlist, I informed said Capt. Young that circumstances and after consideration had determined me, while yet in my power, to recede from my first intention; therefore I wished him no longer to consider me as a member of the Company certain to consummate the enlistment.

Subsequently, in the Collection of the individuals into Rendezvous, their organization as a Company, election of Officers &c I took no part nor concern. I neither ate, drank, slept nor appeared with them under the guise or semblence of membership. Far from it. I went several times to their quarters, continuing only there long enough at each visit to undeceive the Company as to my ultimate intentions, by declaring unequivocally my disinclination to adhere to my yet incomplete compact with them. When the Company was organized by the election of Officers, in this all important matter, involving as it does the reputation, order, peace and comfort of the soldier, I participated in no manner. Captain Young, having been duly elected and commissioned the head, moved the Company to Richmond, Va. without insisting upon my attendance or the attendance of several other men who recanted after signing. Thinking myself free from further trouble on this score, I continued to labor daily for about eight days following in the Navy Yard.

When, that time elapsed, Capt. Young returned and endeavoured to persuade me to accompany him back to Richmond for the purpose of suffering myself to be mustered into the service of the U. States; but upon my steady refusal to take this last decisive and deciding step, he threatened me with force and violence with so much earnestness of manner as constrained me to accompany him to Richmond, not with any intention on my part of submitting to the proposed order &c., but by the intervention of a writ of habeas corpus to free myself from the entanglement. . . .

I returned to my employment in the Navy Yard pursuing it without molestation for the period of a week more. On the first day of the succeeding week Lieut. John Cook appeared in Portsmouth and descrying [illeg. word] me standing, with some others, my fellow-laborers at the door of my boarding house, he made diagonally across the street for the place where I stood, accosted me as he came up with "well, Miller, you ran away from Richmond and must surrender and go with me." I replied that I had not run away, but had acted in my departure thence according to the advice of a legal friend; that I recognized no authority subsisting in him to control my actions or impel my movements, and that I should not yield obedience to any of his dictates. He swore a mighty oath that he would compel me, following the threat by the act of clutching me by the collar of my coat. By an effort I parried his hold upon my collar, whereupon he instantly drew a revolver-pistol, vociferating oaths that he would take me dead or alive. Yielding to the persuasions of my friends present, and to the force of my necessity, I submitted myself a prisoner first to be led by said Lieut. Cook's order to the jail, wherein the jailer refusing to confine me, I was taken to a tavern and committed to the custody of two men of the Company for the night.

Next morning, I was dragged aboard of a boat landed at Fort Monroe, and closely immuned in the guard house for sixteen days, at the expiration of which time, I was again transported to Richmond reiterating at every suitable opportunity my determination not to consent to be mustered into service. There I was taken before a Capt. Smith who asking me my name and if I was a sound man, received for reply from me that I was "a pressed man" and that I should answer no questions the drift and bearings of which I did not clearly comprehend. Capt. Smith then accosting Lieut. Cook said, "I want to have nothing more to do with this man." Immediately after this, Lieut. Cook[sic] took me away and delivered me to the custody of the City Guard.

On the day following, a writ of habeas corpus brought me before a Judge of the City who at the close of the trial consigned me and my blighted hopes to military domination remarking that if it were not for some order emanating from the Adjutant General's Office then before him, the tenor and purport of which I was before then, and am now, profoundly ignorant, he would feel himself bound to discharge me. My lawyer promised to make one more effort to rescue me, but was frustrated in his humane design by my being hurried next morning, at 5 o'clock, on board of a boat bound to Fort Monroe, and remaining there only one short night, I was chucked aboard a barque, and have been dragged into this lawless land [Mexico], devoid of any hope of release, but that which I repose in your magnanimity and love of equal justice.

SOURCE 4

Young Eugene Bandel, a Silesian-born migrant to the United States, tried to find a good job for several months in New York, Washington, Wheeling, Cincinnati, Louisville, and St. Louis. In the process, he consumed his tiny supply of capital, and, finding himself broke and without work in St. Louis, he enlisted:

I reached Cincinnati and was there told that I could find work in Louisville, and I thereupon left Cincinnati by steamboat for that place. That took the last of my money. In Louisville I found work. I did piecework— that is, I was paid so much per lock. Not being accustomed to work of that sort, I earned only five dollars the first week. . . . I traveled on, although the season was advancing, and perhaps no one would give employment to a stranger shortly before the approach of winter.

I went to St. Louis. There too, after looking around in vain for several weeks, I found work in a machine shop. Of course I knew nothing of this kind of work, and the foreman at first would give me only four dollars a week. On this I could not live—at least, could not live as I was accustomed to live. So I gave that up and commenced anew. I went sixty miles west of St. Louis, where I had heard work could be had in the lead mines; but there was no work for me there—probably because I looked as though I had not been accustomed to hard work. I was forced to go back. It was toward the end of October. I had no money. My trunk was in a boarding house in St. Louis. I had with me only a few shirts tied up in a handkerchief. These I sold but did not receive enough to pay my fare back by train; therefore I had to walk back to St. Louis. I spent one night in the woods without a roof over my head, without a fire, and without blankets. The wolves howled round about me. I could not sleep but froze all the more; and it was too dark to go farther without danger of losing my way.

Source: Eugene Bandel, *Frontier Life in the Army, 1854-1861,* ed. Ralph Bieber (Glendale, Calif., 1932), pp. 70-72.

After three days I finally reached St. Louis. I had sold everything I owned that was of value. I owed six dollars at my boarding house. I did not know what to do. By chance I saw a flag hanging from a house and under it a sign. It was a notice that the United States wanted recruits for the army. This was my only resort if I did not wish to steal or beg. I went in. I was accepted soon enough and sworn in. I was bound to remain a soldier for five years, for clothes, lodging, and food, and eleven dollars a month, with extra pay for any extra work done for the government.

SOURCE 5

In 1861 young John Faller told his family that he was enlisting:

They say we will be mustard in on Friday. Five of our men went with Col. Geary's regiment last week. I received the music. Remeber Mother you said that if the company would go I could go. Several folks that meet us say, "well aint you off to the war yet" and I am getting ashamed running around playing soldier when the other boys are off.

Give my love to all at home and Uncel John and
the rest
of the folks.
I will let you know before
we go if we go at all.
Tell Lou & Gust that I will
go down south & burn some of
the Rebels

No more at present
your affectionate
Brother
JOHN

Source: Milton E. Flower, ed., *Dear Folks at Home* (Carlisle, Pa., 1963), p. 52.

SOURCE 6

Henry Stanley, who had been a young English resident of Arkansas, in 1861, later recalled the impulse that had led him to enlist in an Arkansas regiment:

Source: Dorothy Stanley, ed., *The Autobiography of Sir Henry M. Stanley* (Boston and London, 1909), pp. 165-66.

The young men joined hands and shouted, "Is there a man with soul so dead, Who never to himself hath said—This is my own, my native land?' 'An honourable death is better than a base life,' etc., etc. In the strident tones of passion, they said they would welcome a bloody grave rather than survive to see the proud foe violating their altars and their hearths, and desecrating the sacred soil of the South with their unholy feet. But, inflamed as the men and youths were, the warlike fire that burned within their breasts was as nothing to the intense heat that glowed within the bosoms of the women. No suggestion of compromise was possible in their presence. If every man did not hasten to the battle, they vowed they would themselves rush out and meet the Yankee vandals. In a land where women are worshipped by the men, such language made them war-mad.

Then one day I heard that enlistment was going on. Men were actually enrolling themselves as soldiers! A Captain Smith, owner of a plantation a few miles above Auburn, was raising a Company to be called the 'Dixie Greys.' A Mr. Penny Mason, living on a plantation below us, was to be the First-lieutenant, and Mr. Lee, nephew of the great General Lee, was to be Second-lieutenant. The youth of the neighbourhood were flocking to them and registering their names. Our Doctor,—Weston Jones,—Mr. Newton Story, and the brothers Varner, had enlisted. Then the boy Dan Goree prevailed upon his father to permit him to join the gallant braves. Little Rich, of Richmond Store, gave in his name. Henry Parker, the boy nephew of one of the richest planters in the vicinity, volunteered, until it seemed as if Arkansas County was to be emptied of all the youth and men I had known.

About this time, I received a parcel which I half-suspected, as the address was written in a feminine hand, to be a token of some lady's regard; but, on opening it, I discovered it to be a chemise and petticoat, such as a negro lady's-maid might wear. I hastily hid it from view, and retired to the back room, that my burning cheeks might not betray me to some onlooker. In the afternoon, Dr. Goree called, and was excessively cordial and kind. He asked me if I did not intend to join the valiant children of Arkansas to fight? and I answered 'Yes.'

At my present age [60] the whole thing appears to be a very laughable affair altogether; but, at that time, it was far from being a laughing matter. He praised my courage, and my *patriotism,* and said I should win undying glory, and then he added, in a lower voice, 'We shall see what we can do for you when you come back.'

What *did* he mean? Did he suspect my secret love for that sweet child who sometimes came shopping with her mother? From that confidential promise I believed he did, and was, accordingly, ready to go anywhere for her sake. . . .

About the beginning of July we embarked on the steamer 'Frederick

Notrebe.' At various landings, as we ascended the river, the volunteers crowded aboard; and the jubilation of so many youths was intoxicating. Near Pine Bluff, while we were making merry, singing, 'I wish I was in Dixie,' the steamer struck a snag which pierced her hull, and we sank down until the water was up to the furnace-doors. We remained fixed for several hours, but, fortunately, the 'Rose Douglas' came up, and took us and our baggage safely up to Little Rock.

We were marched to the Arsenal, and, in a short time, the Dixie Greys were sworn by Adjutant-General Burgevine into the service of the Confederate States of America for twelve months. We were served with heavy flint-lock muskets, knapsacks, and accoutrements, and were attached to the 6th Arkansas Regiment of Volunteers, Colonel Lyons commanding, and A. T. Hawthorn, Lieutenant-colonel.

SOURCE 7

> Will Judy, a Chicago attorney in 1917, experienced a similar sensation that led to his enlistment:

I fell asleep with the dread gone that in my old age the children might point to me and laugh among themselves that in the great war I stayed at home.

Source: Will Judy, A Soldier's Diary (Chicago, 1931), p. 13.

SOURCE 8

> Richard Marks described the "support" that he and his fellow marine recruits had offered to a comrade in boot camp:

We did have one boy break down and ask to quite [sic] today—he is quite a problemed boy—His parents were separated, father died, mother more interested in herself. . . . He joined the Marine Corp. to prove himself, to himself, but the discipline, and demands have taken their toll—There is no way out for him except through a medical, or bad conduct discharge— none would serve his purpose. A few of us took him under the wing, and we hope he makes it—we keep his mind off all things, but the bright side— he's a good kid, and if he makes it he'll be a good dedicated Marine.

Source: Gloria Marks Kramer, ed., The Letters of Richard Marks, PFC, USMC (Philadelphia, 1967), p. 23.

SOURCE 9

> Sayles Bowen argued that blacks should respond to the call for
> black volunteers, at a meeting of blacks in Asbury Church, Wash-
> ington, D.C., June 1863:

When we show that we are men, we can then demand our liberty, as did
the revolutionary fathers—peacably if we can, forcibly if we must. If we
do not fight, we are traitors to our God, traitors to our country, traitors to
our race, and traitors to ourselves. (Applause.) Richmond is the place for
us, and we mean to go there. (Applause.) Our friend, Jeff. Davis, says we
shall go there (laughter), and we will go; but they won't be glad to see us.

[One hundred and forty men volunteered at the end of the meeting.]

Source: James MacPherson, The Negro's Civil War (New York, 1967), p. 179. Compare Fred-
rick Douglass's appeal in his Monthly Magazine, March 1863, cited in MacPherson, The Negro's Civil War, p. 176.

SOURCE 10

> Jerry Sullivan spoke at a meeting of blacks in Nashville, Ten-
> nessee, November 1863:

God is in this war. He will lead us on to victory. Folks talk about the fighting being nearly over, but I believe there is a heap yet to come. Let the
colored men accept the offer of the President and Cabinet, take arms,
join the army, and then we will whip the rebels, even if Longstreet and all
the Streets of the South, concentrate at Chattanooga. (Laughter and applause.) Why, don't you remember how afraid they used to be that we
would rise? And you know we would, too, if we could. (Cries of 'that's so.")
I ran away two years ago. . . . I got to Cincinnati, and from there I went
straight to General Rosecrans' headquarters. And now I am going to be
Corporal. (Shouts of laughter.)
  Come, boys, let's get some guns from Uncle Sam, and go coon hunting;
shooting those gray back coons [Confederates] that go poking about the
country now a days. (Laughter.) Tomorrow morning, don't eat too much
breakfast, but as soon as you get back from market, start the first thing

---

Source: James MacPherson, The Negro's Civil War (New York, 1967), p. 206.

for our camp. Don't ask your wife, for if she is a wife worth having she will call you a coward for asking her. (Applause, and waving of handkerchiefs by the ladies.) I've got a wife and she says to me, the other day, "Jerry, if you don't go to the war mighty soon, I'll go off and leave you, as some of the Northern gentlemen want me to go home to cook for them." (Laughter.) . . . The ladies are now busy making us a flag, and let us prove ourselves men worthy to bear it.

SOURCE 11

> W. E. B. DuBois echoed the arguments of Bowen, Sullivan, and of Fredrick Douglass fifty-five years later on the editorial page of the NAACP's magazine, The Crisis:

Close Ranks

This is the crisis of the world. For all the long years to come men will point to the year 1918 as the great Day of Decision, the day when the world decided whether it would submit to military despotism and an endless armed peace—if peace it could be called—or whether they would put down the menace of German militarism and inaugurate the United States of the World.

We of the colored race have no ordinary interest in the outcome. That which the German power represents today spells death to the aspirations of Negroes and all darker races for equality, freedom and democracy. Let us not hesitate. Let us, while this war lasts, forget our special grievances and close our ranks shoulder to shoulder with our own white fellow citizens and the allied nations that are fighting for democracy. We make no ordinary sacrifice, but we make it gladly and willingly with our eyes lifted to the hills.

Source: The Crisis 16 (July 1918): 1. I am indebted to Arthur Barbeau for bringing this to my attention.

SOURCE 12

> Cpl. Thomas Long of the 54th Massachusetts regiment, a black regiment, spoke to his comrades while serving as chaplain during Sunday services, March 1864:

Source: James MacPherson, The Negro's Civil War (New York, 1967), p. 213.

If we hadn't become sojers, all might have gone back as it was before; our freedom might have slipped through de two houses of Congress & President Linkum's four years might have passed by & notin been done for we. But now tings can never go back, because we have showed our energy & our courage & our naturally manhood.

Anoder ting is, suppose you had kept your freedom widout enlisting in dis army; your chilen might have grown up free, & been *well cultivated* so as to be equal to any business; but it would have been always flung in dere faces—"Your fader never fought for he own freedom"—and what could dey answer? *Neber can say that to dis African race any more,* (bringing down his hand with the greatest emphasis on the table). Tanks to dis regiment, never can say dat any more, because we first showed dem we could fight by dere side.

SOURCE 13

> *A black sergeant spoke to his comrades in a Louisiana regiment, July 1863:*

I has been a-thinkin' I was old man; for, on de plantation, I was put down wid de old hands, and I quinsicontly feeled myself dat I was a old man. But since I has come here to de Yankees, and been made a soldier for de United States, an' got dese beautiful clothes on, I feels like one young man; and I doesn't call myself a old man nebber no more. An' I feels dis ebenin' dat, if de rebs came down here to dis old Fort Hudson, dat I could jus fight um as brave as any man what is in the Sebenth Regiment. Sometimes I has mighty feelins in dis ole heart of mine, when I considers how dese ere ossifers come all de way from de North to fight in de cause what we is fighten fur. How many ossifers has died, and how many white soldiers has died, in dis great and glorious war what we is in! And now I feels dat, fore I would turn coward away from dese ossifers, I feels dat I could drink my own blood, and be pierced through wid five thousand bullets. I feels sometimes as doe I ought to tank Massa Linkern for dis blessin what we has; but again I comes to de solemn conclusion dat I ought to tank de Lord, Massa Linkern, and all dese ossifers. Fore I would be a slave 'gain, I would fight till de last drop of blood was gone. I has 'cluded to fight for my liberty, and for dis eddication what we is now to receive in dis beautiful new house what we has. Aldo I hasn't got any eddication nor no book-learnin', I has rose up dis blessed ebenin' to do my best afore dis congregation. Dat's all what I has to say now.

Source: James MacPherson, *The Negro's Civil War* (New York, 1967), pp. 187-88.

SOURCE 14

Two sociologists asked high school male seniors in 1969 to speculate on how their parents, siblings, and peers "would feel if you enlisted in the military in the next twelve months." They then correlated these responses with the actual behavior of these young men in the next twelve months:

CATEGORY	PERCENT OF SAMPLE (N = 1691)[a]	PERCENT OF CATEGORY THAT TRIED TO ENLIST
Parents		
1. Happy	15%	29.7%
2. Wouldn't care	13	14.6
3. Unhappy	72	7.3
	100	
Grand Mean = 11.6	Eta = .250	Eta-square = .063
Brothers and Sisters		
1. Happy	13%	27.3%
2. Wouldn't care	24	12.9
3. Unhappy	63	7.2
	100	
Grand Mean = 11.1	Eta = .212	Eta-square = .045
Best Friends		
1. Happy	9%	24.2%
2. Wouldn't care	47	13.0
3. Unhappy	44	7.9
	100	
Grand Mean = 11.8	Eta = .143	Eta-square = .020

[a]For "Brothers and Sisters," N = 1589. The remaining 102 cases were the only child in their family.

Source: Jerome Johnston and Jerald G. Bachman, *Youth in Transition: Vol. V: Young Men & Military Service* (Ann Arbor, Mich., 1972), p. 118.

SOURCE 15

Ratios of Union Volunteers to Draftees by Profession, 1861-64[a]

Professional men	1.863
Farmers	1.420
Printers	1.016
Commercial men	0.947
Mechanics	0.926
Laborers	0.479

[a]The U.S. Sanitary Commission estimated that these figures greatly underrepresented the voluntary services of "the professional classes," inasmuch as many from these classes served voluntarily as officers (*loc. cit.,* p. 209). The same *might* be said of commercial men as well, but of that we have no hard evidence.

Source: Compiled from figures in U.S. Sanitary Commission Memoirs, *Statistical Investigations in the Military and Anthropological Status of American Soldiers,* by B. A. Gould (New York, 1869), pp. 210-11. I am indebted to David Montgomery for bringing this volume of curious tables to my attention.

SOURCE 16

In World War I the Old South contributed only 15 percent of the nation's volunteers and 25 percent of its draftees. The following list shows the percentage of recruits (volunteer and draftee) from each of several northern and southern states who had volunteered for service:

Oregon	53%
Massachusetts	51%
California	49%
Virginia	25.7%
Georgia	23.2%
North Carolina	21.8%
Louisiana	21.1%
South Carolina	18.8%

Source: Fred Baldwin, "The American Enlisted Man in World War I," unpublished Ph.D. dissertation, Princeton University, 1964, pp. 61-62.

SOURCE 17

Major Civilian Occupational Groups of Males Inducted and Voluntarily Enlisted in the Army and Navy, November 1940 Through June 1945 and Employed in 1940

MAJOR OCCUPATION GROUP	INDUCTIONS (1940-45)	ENLISTMENTS (1940-45)	EMPLOYED MALES, 18-44 (1940)
Operatives and kindred occupations and laborers	41.7%	30.4%	29.4%
Craftsmen, foremen, and kindred occupations	12.9	18.9	12.9
Farmers and farm laborers	12.6	5.0	18.6
Clerical, sales, and kindred occupations	12.0	12.7	13.5
Service occupations	4.9	4.0	6.4
Students[a]	4.9	3.8	5.4
Professional and semiprofessional	3.3	4.6	5.5
Managerial and official[a]	2.8	1.3	7.5
Nonclassifiable	4.9	19.3	0.7
Total	100.0	100.0	100.0

[a]Students, professionals, managers, and officials were more likely to enter as officers than to be drafted or to enlist as privates. Consequently, they are underrepresented in this table.

Source: Mapheus Smith, "The Differential Impact of Selective Service Inductions on Occupations in the U.S.," American Sociological Review 11 (1946): 568-72.

SOURCE 18

Social psychologists interviewing GIs in World War II discovered that soldiers who had entered from rural areas and with little education had greater anxieties about combat than others:

Source: Samuel Stouffer et al., Studies in Social Psychology in World War II: Volume I: The American Soldier (Princeton, N.J.: Princeton University Press, 1949), p. 334.

**Worry about Battle Injury as Related to Preference for Infantry or
Overseas Service — Attitudes of Rural Non High School Graduates
Compared with All Others**

(Infantrymen in the United States, 3 Months to 3 Years of Service, April 1944)

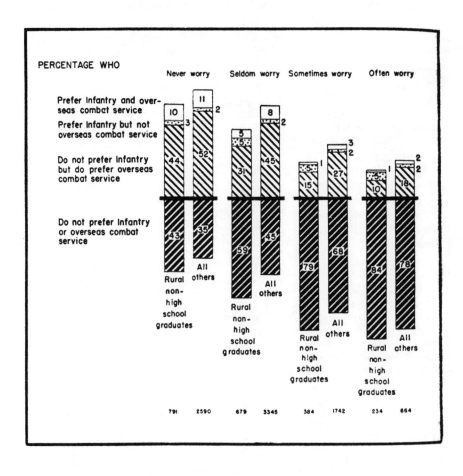

SOURCE 19

Percent of Enlistments of All Those Entering the Military from South Carolina, 1940–46, by County's Index of Industrial Development[a]

LOW LEVEL OF INDUSTRIAL DEVELOPMENT		SECOND QUARTER (INDEX OF 21–40)		THIRD QUARTER (INDEX OF 41–100)		HIGH LEVEL OF INDUSTRIAL DEVELOPMENT	
LOWEST QUARTER (INDEX OF 0–20)						HIGHEST QUARTER (INDEX OF OVER 100)	
COUNTY	ENLISTED (%)	COUNTY	ENLISTED (%)	COUNTY	ENLISTED (%)	COUNTY	ENLISTED (%)
Allendale	6.2	Bamberg	7.8	Barnwell	6.6	Anderson	14.4
Calhoun	7.0	Berkeley	5.9	Charleston	15.2	Cherokee	11.4
Clarendon	4.7	Chesterfield	9.8	Jasper	8.5	Chester	13.1
Colleton	8.8	Dillon	10.9	Lexington	12.0	Darlington	11.4
Edgefield	8.4	Dorchester	8.5	Marion	10.0	Greenville	15.6
Horry	8.9	Florence	11.4	Ocone	12.8	Greenwood	14.8
Lee	5.8	Hampton	8.1	Pickens	13.8	Lancaster	11.6
Saluda	6.8	Kershaw	12.6	Richland	16.5	Laurens	11.9
Williamsburg	5.6	Marlboro	9.1	Sumter	9.1	Newberry	12.8
		Orangeburg	8.6	Union	15.8	Spartanburg	14.5
						York	14.8
Average	7.3	Average	9.3	Average	12.0	Average	14.6

[a]Index of Industrial Development = Value added by manufacture per capita in county, compiled from the 16th Census of U.S., 1940, Manufactures, 1939, Vol. III, pp. 942-43, and Holmes Springs, Selective Service in South Carolina, 1940-1947 (Columbia, S.C., 1948), 70-71.

SOURCE 19 — continued

It is, of course, possible that these percentages are not as meaningful as they might at first appear. Thus if industrial workers
were to have been especially favored with exemptions by the
Selective Service system, then our figures of enlistments as a
percentage of all inductees might be extremely misleading. In
fact, however, agricultural occupations were favored with
exemptions from Selective Service (Springs, p. 85). Hence these
percentages would understate the greater propensity of persons
from industrial regions to enlist. And that is exactly what they
do. If we divide the numbers enlisting from each county into
the total population of each county, we find that the least industrial counties (Lowest Quarter) saw only 1 enlistment for
every 66 persons, whereas in the most industrial counties (Highest
Quarter) 1 in every 24 persons enlisted, a ratio of 2.75, which
figure is greater than the ratio (2.0) of our averages shown in the
preceding table.

However, it might still be the case that persons from industrial
areas are enlisting precisely in order to avoid being drafted into
less desirable, combat roles. Surely this would explain some of
these enlistments. However, when we compare enlistments by
county in an obviously high-risk combat service (the Marine
Corps) with those in an obviously low-risk combat service (the
Coast Guard), we find that the ratio of Marine Corps to Coast
Guard recruitment in highly industrial areas (Highest Quarter)
is 9.0, whereas it is only 2.5 in the least industrial areas (Lowest
Quarter). It would seem that industrial areas in World War II
yielded more persons per capita "willing to fight" than did agricultural areas, a phenomenon that Source 16 would appear to
confirm for World War I.

What accounts for this propensity? I suspect that it is largely
due to the fact that persons in industrial areas tend to be more
cosmopolitan than their localistic agrarian counterparts. Persons whose informational diet is purely localistic, who are rarely
told of the link between distant events and their own lives, rights,
values, jobs, standard of living, and so on, are simply less likely
to see the need for military action than those who are. For more
on the significance of the local-cosmopolitan rift see Samuel P.
Hays, "Political Parties and the Community-Society Continuum,"
in W. N. Chambers and W. D. Burnham, eds., The American
Party Systems (New York, 1967), 152-81.

We do know that blacks were disproportionately located in nonindustrial areas and that until recently (Source 20), they were much less willing to enlist than whites (Source 35). For several reasons (page 19) blacks were very "localistic" when it came to World War II. This explains part of the industrial-nonindustrial differential. But it does not explain all of it. If we manipulate county census materials and selective service records in order to isolate the white population, we find that eligible whites in heavily industrial areas enlisted at a rate 33 percent greater than that of eligible whites in the least industrial areas.

SOURCE 20

Nonwhites were more inclined to volunteer for the army or Marine Corps than were whites in fiscal years (FY) 1972 and 1973:

Male Applicants for Enlistment: Distribution on Initial Examination, by Race and Military Service Applied (Fiscal Years 1972 and 1973)

MILITARY SERVICE	TOTAL		CAUCASIAN		NEGRO		"OTHER RACES"	
	NUMBER	PERCENT	NUMBER	PERCENT	NUMBER	PERCENT	NUMBER	PERCENT
FY 1972								
Total	439,187	100.0	348,362	100.0	85,571	100.0	5,254	100.0
Army	191,319	43.6	149,679	43.0	39,161	45.8	2,479	47.2
Navy	97,353	22.2	81,603	23.4	14,709	17.2	1,041	19.8
Marine Corps	47,188	10.7	34,578	9.9	11,919	13.9	691	13.2
Air Force	103,327	23.5	82,502	23.7	19,782	23.1	1,043	19.8
FY 1973								
Total	414,263	100.0	320,493	100.0	88,445	100.0	5,325	100.0
Army	184,257	44.5	135,162	42.2	46,451	52.5	2,644	49.7
Navy	92,374	22.3	79,981	24.9	11,494	13.0	899	16.9
Marine Corps	47,884	11.5	33,316	10.4	13,768	15.6	800	15.0
Air Force	89,748	21.7	72,034	22.5	16,732	18.9	982	13.4

DISTRIBUTION BY RACE

Source: Human Resources Research Organization, *Applicants for Enlistment . . .* by Bernard Karpinos (July 1975), p. 12.

SOURCE 21

A social scientist asked Airborne trainees and nonairborne military personnel identical questions in 1970:

Percentage of Responses to Question: "How Important Is It to You Personally to Make Good as a Soldier?"

RESPONSE	AIRBORNE SUBJECTS (N = 52)	NON-AIRBORNE SUBJECTS (N = 48)
It is very important	77.0	6.4
It is pretty important	17.3	20.8
It is not so important	3.8	52.0
It is not important at all	1.9	20.8
Total	100.0	100.0

Source: William Cockerham, "Selective Socialization . . . ," *Journal of Political and Military Sociology* 1 (1973): 227.

SOURCE 22

A psychologist interviewed "Green Beret" soldiers stationed in Europe in 1969:

Case 202

Yeah, my school was pretty bad. Cops in there all the time. Three people got killed. You know, Bedford-Stuyvesant. . . . One day, I was supposed to be the baddest thing there, and these guys were ribbing me, you know, saying I was a quitter and then followed me into a candy store and just kept ribbing me, ribbing me. So I ordered another Coke and told him not to open it, and so while they was ribbing me I was shaking the Coke up and pretty soon I just turned around and hit him with it. . . . He was playing with his knife. . . . Shaked it up to get pressure inside. When it bursts, then it blows glass all over. . . . Hit him on the head. . . . He got cuts, on the top of his head, and a pretty good one right here. . . . I think he was unconscious. Maybe he wasn't. I don't know. I just hit him and left. . . . No, I wasn't nervous. I was elated. . . .

Source: Selections from D. M. Mantell, *True Americanism: Green Berets and War Resisters* (New York: Teachers College Press, 1975), pp. 18, 19, 34, 39, 74, 76, 80, 93, 166.

Case 204

When either mother or father would tell us to do something we went
ahead and did it. Like with mother, you know, I mean, if we were bad,
she'd spank us with a hairbrush. She usually took care of most of the
whippin'. And we'd go ahead and behave. Her beatin's weren't as bad as
our father's, 'cause he'd usually get out the belt, you know. He'd wear
us out. . . . -

Case 205

[Mom was] a little hot tempered, you know. There was always the thing
that, you know, you don't want to say the wrong thing and get her started.
. . . She did most of the punishing. For about just about anything. She had
heart trouble and didn't like any noise so I didn't play much. So I didn't
run around the house and this jazz. She was, uh, the type of person who
said something once and she was stern. When she said, move, you moved
then and there or you got killed. She'd take us and beat us half to death
. . . with anything . . . yeah, with a chair too [laughs]. If she was standing
there, you're going to do what she says or she'd beat you to death. . . . Hell,
no. You din't run. You stood there and took it until she decided to quit.
You'd get it for anything. . . . She used to get on my ass. . . . I realized, shit,
she was just the type of woman, you know, just got furious all of a sudden
and that was it. . . . No, my mother wasn't affectionate with anybody
except my younger brother.

Did your mother ever hit you with a belt?
Hell, yes.

On your bare bottom?
Shit, yes.

Did you ever have welts?
Bled.

You actually bled?
Hell, yes. My mother didn't play.

Did she hit you on the head too?
Shit, yes. Anywhere, wherever she connected, that's where you got it. . . .
Hell, it would hurt like hell, you know. You'd cry and then she would continue beating you until you stopped crying and shit, you know. And she
had a thing, that you didn't look at her while she was beating you, you
know. You wouldn't dare look up at her. I never understood it. She called
it, rollin' your eyes. I mean, if you looked up at her she would beat the
hell out of you. The last time I told her I wasn't goin' to cry, I told her, shit,

I wasn't going to cry anymore, you know, and if she beat me to death I wasn't going to cry. She continued beating me and, hell, I wouldn't cry.

What was she beating you with?
A stick.

And you just stood there and took it?
Yes, till I got so weak. She was beating me till I just couldn't hold up anymore, you know. So when I slumped down to my knees, you know, and then she had one of these heart flutters or something and her heart wouldn't hold it out any more. So when I went down, hell, she almost went down too. But I didn't cry for her anymore. I figured, well, the hell, I wasn't going to do that shit anymore. . . .

Case 207

I've always wanted to do something adventurous like jumping out of planes which I do. I'm going to start skydiving tonight. I'm in a skydiving class that starts tonight. And, uh, I raced stock cars for a year. Nothing big-time like, you know, like you read in the papers. Just a little dirt track. But I think a lot of that had to do with the kid that lived downstairs. He was, like I say, he was two years older than I was and we always grew up together. And ever since I can remember, we've always done something exciting, you know. We've always done dangerous things for some reason. We jumped off bridges and in the water, you know. I guess all kids do it. Today I look at the bridge where I used to jump off and it scares the hell out of me, 'cause it seems so, it was about a hundred foot drop into the water and, you know, you wonder why you did something like that. At the time I never gave it a thought of getting hurt. And if my folks knew about it, I would have got whipped. And, uh, I think, he, he and I together more or less built adventures, you know, an adventuresome attitude in us because he's, he's now a professional stock car racer. You know, I think if I had gotten out of the Army last year, instead of reenlisting, I probably would be, you know, racing this year. . . . The best thing that ever happened to me, was, well, I won a race one day and I thought that was about the greatest thing. . . .

Case 209

Well, they'd just bring out the strap and whip us a few times. That would usually straighten us up. That was the usual way or send us to bed early sometimes, when we were younger. . . . Well, for fighting, calling somebody names, destroying something around the house. Just did something you weren't supposed to do, you know. . . . My mother usually dished it out 'cause she was around more when things happened and took care of it on the spot. My father used a board a couple of times. That's, uh, maybe why I feared my father more [chuckles]. . . . My mother whipped me, you know, it's hard to recall, but I'd say, about twenty or thirty times. Something like that. Maybe a couple of times a week. . . . My father would hit me maybe five or six times [with the board], that'd be enough. Most of the time you knew you deserved it. . . . No, they weren't too hard in that respect. . . . Yeah, it was hard to know 'cause it was up to them, you know, how they felt at the time. They were nervous people and you'd get on their nerves after a while. . . . There were certain things you did every day. You didn't think about them. You just did 'em. And you never talked back. . . .

Case 210

I got close enough to some [V.C.] to kiss 'em. . . . What was it like? I can't describe it. It's an accomplishment, more or less stalking a person, stalking something alive, just like going hunting for deer. You're stalking deer, you get in your position, you wait, you wait and finally the deer will come and you get him, and if you snag the deer, you feel—you feel good. It's the same way. If I had made one move I would have been shot. It was the same way. He [my father] would have been proud, if he heard a twig snap. . . .

Case 215

Between my freshman and sophomore year in college I worked for the sheriff's department. I took the job. See, the rifle team I used to shoot for was under the sheriff's department, the sheriff's department rifle team for the parish. I knew all the people there very well 'cause I shot with them 'til I was eighteen years old.

How old were you when your father first introduced you to guns?
Six or seven. . . . I've been shooting ever since.

Have you ever been in trouble with the police?
Well, I had quite an advantage because when I did get into any kind of trouble I had them [sheriff] to help me out.

Case 217

I remember all the way through clear up to when I got into high school. I had to get into a fight with every kid in the class, 'cause I could beat everybody. The first thing was to beat everybody at school. Didn't fight so much in high school. Started growing up, started getting a bit older. No use for fighting.

Did you have fights in high school?
Yeah. The biggest fight I got into was with a guy, he was the middle age between my brother and myself. My brother was a senior and I was a sophomore and this guy was a junior and on the football team. He got into a fight with my brother. It was my brother's fault. He's a loud-mouth and wise guy. He was about 240 pounds and my brother was only 150. And the next day I got a hold of him and did him in a number. Broke his nose, couple of ribs. Put him in the hospital. Actually didn't even know him. We got to be good friends. . . . No, I didn't even get scratched. At that time I had been studying karate for a couple of years. Also had been weight lifting since I was thirteen. . . . No, I didn't get into trouble. Where I come from out in California is quite a rough place. Gang fights, hoodlums and everything else. Bloody motorcycle gangs and car clubs. A lot of gang fights going on all the time. A few broken ribs and stuff is nothing. Nobody even looks at it. It's a waste of time for the cops.

Were you ever involved in any gang fights?
No.

Why?
More or less, the—the people that I ran around with, the gang that I ran with weren't thugs or anything but the football team. And I weighed 230 pounds and I was the smallest one, and we always went around together. We had two guys that weighed 310, and we always stayed together, and nobody'd mess with us. We always had eight or nine of us together. And nobody wanted to fight us. Never had to get into any fights, gang wars. Didn't cause anybody any trouble. . . .

What was your favorite sport in high school?
Football. . . .

Why?
Body contact. Plow over everybody else. That you would beat the other person. And when they'd come in to tackle, you'd be able to hit them back harder and move them out of the way. I couldn't do any of this zig-zag fancy stuff. Just a straight line. . . . As long as you're going after the ball it's legal. Stepping on legs and breaking ribs and stuff, going for the ball. It's all legal.

Case 218

Which sport did you like the best?
Football.

Why?
Well, it was just, uh, more I guess, more—well, physical, I suppose. More

hard and you'd hit people and everything. Show your cruelty in there. . . .
. . . My father was pretty stubborn, and hard headed really. He was a
perfectionist, a real perfectionist. He used to make my mother so damn
mad. He always expected everything in the house to be, and he's still that
way, pretty much, he expects everything in the house to be exactly in its
certain place. And, uh, I don't know if this is just a personal characteristic
or if he became this way while he was in the army, uh, demanding exact
precision as far as the cleaning of the house, the placement of things and
the alignment of things. But he was real exact with us and he had a very
good eye. He has very good vision and I remember one example my mother
told me about. This one particular vase on the table, a vase. Uh, every
day when he came home he'd always—he just made a routine inspection,
like it was a barracks. When he came home, you know, he'd walk around
and he'd move this ashtray or that ashtray or check this or that. Every day
he always moved this one vase just a fraction of an inch, you know, to
put it right in the middle. And so my mother, this made her so mad. So
one day she took a ruler and she measured it right down to the exact center
of the table and placed the vase right exactly in the center. And my father
came home and he looked at the vase and he started to move it and he
looked at it again and he said it was exactly right [laughs]. That made it
worse because my mother expected him to move it a little fraction and
then she was going to say, ha, I caught you this time, you know. But no,
it's exactly right.

And, uh, I remember on two occasions I didn't make my own bed. As
long as I can remember this was one of my tasks that he made me learn
how to do as soon as I was able to and that was to maintain my own room
and to make my own bed. This one time I overslept and I didn't get up. In
fact, if I'm not mistaken, I was an altar boy then and I was late getting up
and going to church and so I didn't make my bed. And so for the next two
weeks to make sure I had plenty of time to get my bed made I had to get
up an hour early [laughs]. And so it was pretty decent punishment. It made
me think about getting up and doing what I was required to do and then
the second time that I did it, I was a little older but he made sure that I
didn't go anywhere for a week or two. I forget, a week or two, something
like that. After school I had to come immediately home and, uh, work
around the house. And he believed in, uh, if I wanted something I should
work for it and get it myself, to have ambition, you know. For some reason, he always stressed the military. He always wanted me to go into the
Army. And, uh, I remember this, very many times he talked about the army
and that it's good life and that it's good for a man to be in the Army. . . .
But I think more or less in his mind he pictured a fairly secure way of
making a living and something that would be more or less interesting for
a young man. You know, one that is possibly aggressive or interested in a

little bit of adventure. I think maybe he pictured himself actually. I think he always mentioned that he regretted that he got out of the Army. He always wanted to stay in the Army. And I think since he wanted this so much for himself, he wanted me to do it.

Did you ever get the feeling when you were growing up, while on the one hand your father was encouraging you to join the service that he was also pretty much of an army man in the way he lived?
He was very much because, like I mentioned, the way he'd more or less conduct inspections. Every day he'd come home and he'd insist on preciseness. And not only that. He was real systematic about other things that he did, such as, oh, just little minor examples, such as the way he would, uh, he was real fanatic about the way he would, like before he'd go to work he'd pack his lunch. Everything had to be just so so and always he was prepared hours before it was time to go to work. He always insisted on everything being—he had a certain place and he'd put his cigarettes and his thermos jug and his lunch and his jacket and a certain pair of shoes and socks. And he wore a uniform. In his later years, on his present job, he wears a uniform and he always keeps a spotless uniform.

Tell me something. Is it possible that your father emphasized military virtue, you know, in terms of responsibility, discipline, neatness, orderliness, stuff like that, but never in connection with any particular set of values? You have to be disciplined and orderly and neat because you have to protect this, that, and the other thing. For example, a person would say, uh, you might have had the training that you have to be patriotic and fight for your country, you know.
He never indicated patriotism.

Right. I get the feeling your father was more interested in just the general military value.
I believe so.

As opposed to the general military value in defense of a particular set of values, as for example the U.S. and what it stands for. Is that true would you say?
That's true. I never thought about it before but this is basically true because every time he mentioned military, the way he mentioned it it had to do with certain, uh, things, self-discipline or neatness and precision or being a man as far as building, he never actually mentioned character so much, anything that would lead toward, for instance, punctuality and neatness had something to do with a person's character. He never indicated this but I think he pictured the military life as being a well-disciplined man that was neat and orderly. But he never mentioned patriotism or defending any such thing as the U. S. anything like this, never. No.

Do you think it would be fair to say in the case of your father that he was more interested in the form of the military life and what the military life represented than in any particular virtue like, I mean, these were the virtues, but he wasn't interested in the concepts of good and bad. You know, this is evil, this is good?
That's true. I would say he was more interested in the military life. . . . He never really expressed too many feelings or thoughts about, I think, he more or less thought that it was understood that you should do good. If it's in your mind to do good and not to do bad. Uh, I mean, he was a good marr in that way but he never really did much to try and form my character. He never really did much, only to the extent that he wanted me to be punctual and well disciplined and neat and this form of the military life. . . .

Case 221

[My dad] was furious. He would have just—she was trying to cook and I don't remember, this was just told to me, I mean I was real too small. Anyway, yeah, he was just—it was at my grandparents' house there in Arizona. And she was fixing something to eat and he come up and goosed her or messing around with her or something. And it must have just caught her 'cause she had a knife in her hand and he turned around and she took it and threw it. I know one good fight they had because she was at fault. It was in—we was living in Portland, Oregon and I don't know what started it, 'cause I guess he was drinking and she kept hitting on him and slapping him and he threw her under ice cold water in the shower. That's all he did was keep her under the shower till she cooled down.

That time that she threw the knife at him, you say that he smashed her. Where?
He slapped her.

Did she kind of cool off after that?
Yes.

Did your parents ever have any arguments besides those two times?
Oh yeah. Constantly. She almost run him down once with a car. She caught him out with a barmaid one time on New Year's Eve. I was in the eighth grade too, that's right. It happened in Phoenix. And my brother—my brother —well, my father's—well, I guess you could—my uncle, him and my father are just like—they're both big men, 250 pounds. And they're always kicking around, you know. Running around together. And my mother and my aunt caught them in a bar making some advance to some barmaids and they really had a fight that night. But Dad didn't do anything to her. She did it all. She was pulling his hair, pinching him and all this bit.

You said she tried to run him down with a car?
Yeah, she stopped right before, 'cause he said, you know. She cursed him out to start with and we was going home and he took out walking and she went to chase him, you know, with the car. . . .

Well, I mean, she [his mother] didn't want me to, you know, go out and don't want me to fight, don't want me to, you know, anything that was dangerous. She didn't want me to do this and that, you know. And thank God! My old man. He—he cut her off short, you know, 'cause my old— well, anyway, my old man also was very interested and used to take me and show me how to knife fight. . . .

Do you remember why your father wanted to show you how to knife fight?
Yeah, because I asked him to. I mean, he used to do all kinds of things when I was small. Teach me how to march and stuff like this. You know, all basic movements that you do in the Army. I got interested in knives because he gave me an old Navy Burnett, a Burnett he had. And I asked him to show me how to, you know, to use it. How to work with it. 'Cause he used to box when he was in the Army. And he used to show me how to box and wrestle. . . .

SOURCE 23

> These same "Green Berets" (V) were asked questions that were also put to a number of army draftees (D) and war resisters (R):

Question	Nos.		
1. In general how do you feel about being in the Army?	V	D	
(a) it's a complete waste of time	0	9	
(b) I could be doing better things	2	16	
(c) it's all right	5	4	
(d) I like it	13	3	
(e) Army life is great	5	2	
2. When you were in High School, did you get into fights?	V	D	R
(a) all the time	0	0	0
(b) often	2	1	0
(c) sometimes	10	8	0
(d) seldom	11	17	10
(e) never	2	9	10

Source: Appendix to D. M. Mantell, *True Americanism: Green Berets and War Resisters* (New York: Teachers College Press, 1975), pp. 267-69, 274-81.

3. In High school, did you have

		V	D	R
(a)	many close friends?	7	11	1
(b)	several close friends?	11	10	7
(c)	a couple of close friends?	6	12	9
(d)	one close friend?	0	1	0
(e)	no really close friends?	1	1	3

4. Do you remember arguing with teachers?

		V	D	R
(a)	many times (more than 10 times)	1	6	5
(b)	several times (8-10 times)	1	6	3
(c)	a few times (3 to 7 times)	5	6	5
(d)	once or twice	11	14	3
(e)	never	7	3	4

5. How do you think you would feel about killing a Vietcong?

		V	D
(a)	I would really like to kill a Vietcong soldier	3	1
(b)	I would feel it is part of my job without liking or disliking it	18	5
(c)	I would feel it is part of my job, but I wouldn't like it		
(d)	I would probably be able to do it, but would feel very badly	0	10
(e)	I don't feel I would kill a Vietcong soldier	0	0

6. If you were to volunteer for Vietnam or have already done so, which of the following would best describe your reason for doing so?

		V	D
(a)	advance one's military career	3	1
(b)	earn extra money	3	14
(c)	get some different and new military experience	7	4
(d)	serve our country	11	9
(e)	chance to see another part of the world	1	6

7. If you were in a battle zone in Vietnam and a 14- to 15-year-old Vietcong tried to shoot you, how would you feel about shooting him?

		V	D
(a)	I would want to shoot him.	15	5
(b)	I would feel it is part of my job to shoot him.	10	9
(c)	I would feel it is part of my job, but would feel very badly.	0	8
(d)	I would only shoot him if it is unavoidable and would feel very badly about it.	0	13
(e)	I couldn't shoot a 14- to 15-year-old boy.	0	0

SOURCE 24

A Selective Service survey of those classified as conscientious objectors awaiting work assignment, in September 1971, included a tabulation of these conscientious objectors by level of education:

LEVEL	DISTRIBUTION (%)
Trade school	4
High school graduate	18
Some college	35
College graduate	42

Source: Michael Useem, Conscription, Protest and Social Conflict (New York: John Wiley & Sons, Inc. 1973), p. 144.

SOURCE 25

College and noncollege youth responded to questions about the draft in 1968 and 1969:

Attitudes of American Youth on Draft Resistance, 1968–1969

			COLLEGE YOUTH (%)		
QUESTION	DATE	NON-COLLEGE YOUTH (%)	ALL	"PRACTICAL" STUDENTS	"CHANGE-ORIENTED" STUDENTS[a]
Do you feel that draft resistance is justified under any circumstances? . . . Yes	October 1968	17		36	67
Resisting the draft is basically wrong — a citizen is obligated to serve his country regardless of his personal views about the justness of a war.	March–April 1969	72	44		
Using the draft as a political weapon is always or sometimes justified.	March–April 1969	29	49		

Source: 1968 data from Fortune Magazine (1969, 35); 1969 data from Columbia Broadcasting System (1969, 22, 31) [reproduced in M. Useem, *Conscription, Protest and Social Conflict* (New York: John Wiley and Sons, Inc., 1973) p. 121].

[a]The distinction between "practical" and "change-oriented" college students is based on which of the following two statements respondents identified as most representative of their views on college and career: "For me, college is mainly a practical matter. With a college education I can earn more money, have a more interesting career, and enjoy a better position in society." "I'm not really concerned with the practical benefits of college. I suppose I take them for granted. College for me means something more intangible, perhaps the opportunity to change things rather than make out well within the existing system."

SOURCE 26

> *War resisters, interviewed by the same psychologist who had interviewed "Green Berets," described their relations with their parents:*

Case 128

They encouraged both my brother and myself to think for ourselves whenever it was feasible. . . . Well, first of all we had certain responsibilities at home. They were, you know, that either my brother or I had to take care of like the garbage or cleaning our rooms. Helping to keep the house straight or helping to keep the yard clean and things like that. And they very, very rarely interfered with my reading. Quite often if there was something that puzzled me in a book or something, I would come and ask for an explanation. And they usually solved it. . . . Once I had gotten into high school there was never any big trouble about hours. Like if I was going to stay at a friend's house late Friday evening or Saturday evening, I would call up and say, you know, this is where I am and I'll be here until such and such a time and then I'll be home. And unless there was a particular reason to be home he [father] would say, fine, see you later, see you in the morning. . . . They never put any limitations on where I was going. Where I went, what I did, the friends I had, there never seemed to be any interference with it. The only things that they would say to me in some situations, when they felt that I wasn't considering all the factors that were involved and they would say, "Look, we think there are other things involved in this that you don't realize. We think it would be wiser if you

---

Source: D. M. Mantell, *True Americanism: Green Berets and War Resisters* (New York, Teachers College Press, 1975), pp. 59, 105.

did this." And, you know, of course there wasn't total freedom. . . . Yeah, they felt that the most sane approach was to introduce me to thinking for myself as early as they could and to teach me to be responsible.

Case 128

I remember talking more with my father, really getting some idea of what he thought and felt. And this is when we talked about the war. We talked about politics. We're able to talk to each other quite frankly now. You know, it doesn't really matter what the subject is because he knows where I stand politically. In fact he's in agreement with me in a lot of things. . . . Whenever I would voice an opinion that my father would disagree with, he would say, "Well, I don't agree with that," and he would say, "Now this is why I don't agree with it." But he never, you know, he wouldn't force it upon me and say, well, look, you know, this is the thing you ought to believe.

SOURCE 27

Characteristics of Parent-Child Relationships
as Reported by Volunteers and Resisters

	BOTH PARENTS		NEITHER PARENT	
	VOLUNTEER	RESISTER	VOLUNTEER	RESISTER
Strictness	18	3	0	16
Mechanical-formal-cold	12	1	3	20
Parental dominance	9	0	3	20
Freedom of movement (permissiveness)	0	13	14	6
Respect for child's rights, individuality	1	15	21	1

Source: D. M. Mantell, *True Americanism: Green Berets and War Resisters* (New York: Teachers College Press, 1975), pp. 261, 263.

Explicit Child-Rearing Values Held Most and Least Frequently by Parents

| | VOLUNTEERS | | | | RESISTERS | | | |
| | FATHERS | | MOTHERS | | FATHERS | | MOTHERS | |
	N	%	N	%	N	%	N	%
Respect for property	24	96	24	96	12	48	14	56
Respectability	23	92	25	100	12	48	17	68
Orderliness and cleanliness	21	84	21	84	8	32	10	40
Discipline	21	84	23	92	3	12	8	32
Conformity within the community	21	84	24	96	10	40	12	48
Obedience and submission to authority	20	80	22	88	2	8	7	28
Physical strength	20	80	5	20	2	8	0	0
Individual achievement	16	64	10	40	22	88	21	84
Respect for adults	16	64	21	84	0	0	0	0
Intellectual achievement	6	24	9	36	20	80	23	92
Rationality and reasoning	6	24	3	12	20	80	17	68
Individual privacy	5	20	4	16	19	76	15	60
Kindliness	5	20	11	44	17	68	24	96
Love of life	5	20	12	48	21	84	22	88
Community responsibility (sociopolitical engagement)	4	16	2	8	14	56	15	60
Philanthropy	3	12	8	32	8	32	17	68
Social justice	1	4	1	4	17	68	19	76
Love of art, music, literature	1	4	4	16	11	44	17	68
Humanitarianism	0	0	3	12	17	68	24	96

SOURCE 28

Do the views of this "Green Beret" and this war resister regarding religion correlate with their varying need for structure in their lives?

Case 219 [a Green Beret]

When I was little my parents were Methodists. But they never went to church. My brother and I went to church every Sunday. When I was ten or twelve I got a little tired of going to that church mainly because my very best friend that I went to school with, he was an Episcopalian, and so I started going to church with him and became an altar boy. It's the most similar religion to Catholicism. I got real close with the minister and took an active part in it. Then I had a real close girlfriend in my eleventh year of high school and she was Catholic and so I started going to church with her. . . . My father was threatening me to move out of the house if I changed over and that made things worse. . . . And I was trying to go along with the beliefs of the Catholic church. . . . I took private instruction two or three nights a week for about a year. And then I convinced them [his parents] that I wanted to change before I got out of school because I was planning to go into the Army and wouldn't have time. . . . Well, when I went there I knew very little about the religion. It seemed to me the people were more dedicated to their religion. The priests impressed me because they dedicated their entire lives to being priests. The actual ceremony itself, the Mass, impressed me with its tradition.

Do you think it was the particular theological principles that attracted you to Catholicism?
No, I don't think I had this too much in mind.

Was it the fact that it was much more disciplined and much more dedicated?
Yeah.

There was more ceremony?
This is what drew me.

The ceremony was colorful, well prepared, and well executed.
This is what drew me more than the actual meaning behind the theo— how do you pronounce that word? . . .

Case 101 [a War Resister]

My main objection to the concept of organized religion, uh, is this whole thing of—you sign up, you join, you take your thing and then you sort of —I wouldn't say you sold out, but you relinquish, uh, to your bishops, to

---

Source: D. M. Mantell, *True Americanism: Green Berets and War Resisters* (New York: Teachers College Press, 1975), pp. 88, 106.

your Mother Superior, to your abbess, to your Pope or whatever, and you accept the framework they give you. Obedience and that sort of thing to their dogma, their particular whim. Well, I object to that. . . .

SOURCE 29

Anticipation of entering the military and support for the Vietnam War were positively correlated among young men in 1969:

Vietnam War Dissent Index
by Probability of Entering Service

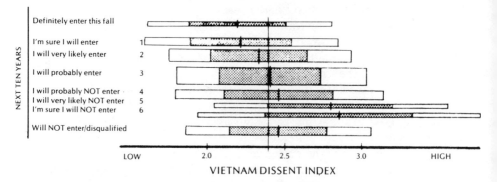

Note: The height of the bar is proportional to the number of cases in that category. The length of the bar represents the range of scores of those respondents between the 10th and 90th centiles; the length of the shaded portion represents the range of those between the 25th and 75th centiles.

Source: J. Johnston and J. Bachman, *Youth in Transition:* Vol. V: *Young Men and Military Service* (Ann Arbor, Mich., 1972), 34. Compare Ronald Inglehart, "Changing Values and Attitudes to Military Service Among the American Public," in Nancy Goldman and David Segal, eds., *The Social Psychology of Military Service* (Beverly Hills, Calif., 1976), pp. 276-77.

SOURCE 30

Sgt. Henry Giles recalled his reasons for enlisting in 1939:

"When I enlisted [in the old army] I didn't even think about a war. . . . The depression hadn't ended in 1939 down our way and I was sick and tired of the scrabbling and the shame of the commodity [lines] and no jobs but the WPA. . . . the army meant security and pride and something fine and good. [When I put on the uniform for the first time] not only had I clothes now that I wasn't ashamed of, but for the first time in my life I was *somebody.*"

Source: Janice H. Giles, ed., *The GI Journal of Sergeant [Henry] Giles* (Boston, 1965), p. 23.

SOURCE 31

Young men ranked relative advantages of the military as an occupation, 1960:

**Numbers of Times That Certain Factors Were Mentioned
as Among the Three Most Important Factors
in Choosing a Military Program**

	FIRST ANSWER	SECOND ANSWER	THIRD ANSWER	TOTAL
Opportunities for training	156	115	83	354
Choice of career field	152	94	55	301
Opportunities for advancement	78	113	103	294
Length of enlistment	51	38	38	127
Branch of service	48	37	24	109
Good living conditions (personal and family)	7	29	35	71
Opportunities for travel and adventure	14	20	22	56
Opportunity to become an officer	7	9	10	26
Other responses	45	60	69	174

Source: Robert Dear and Ledyard Ducher, *The Measurement of the Relative Appeal of Military Service Programs* (Princeton, N.J.: Educational Testing Service, 1961), p. 43.

SOURCE 32

U.S. Army Recruiting Poster, ca. 1930:

SOURCE 33

Comparison by Male Teenagers in 1964 of Military Service and Civilian Jobs in Terms of Selected Job Characteristics[a]

SELECTED JOB CHARACTERISTICS	PERCENT DISTRIBUTION "CIVILIAN BETTER"
Pay	
Total	65.0
Less than high school graduate	50.6
High school graduate	80.4
Some college	85.5
Chances for Advancement	
Total	38.2
Less than high school graduate	29.0
High school graduate	46.2
Some college	55.1
Interesting Work	
Total	37.6
Less than high school graduate	31.8
High school graduate	41.4
Some college	54.6
Retirement Plan, Medical Plan, and Fringe Benefits	
Total	21.6
Less than high school graduate	17.4
High school graduate	24.8
Some college	32.3
Chances for Further Training and Learning Job Skills	
Total	19.7
Less than high school graduate	14.7
High school graduate	25.1
Some college	26.9
Highly Respected Job	
Total	26.1
Less than high school graduate	18.7
High school graduate	32.7
Some college	41.3

Source: U.S. Bureau of the Census Survey of Civilian Men, 16 to 34 years old, October 1964.
[a]Based on responses of nonveterans, aged 16 to 19 years, and not enrolled in school, to

the following question: "Based on the military service you have seen, how does military work compare with your present, full-time civilian job? (If you do not have a full-time, civilian job now, answer in terms of the next one you plan to get.)" Cited in H. Wool, *The Military Specialist* (Baltimore, Md.: Johns Hopkins University Press, 1967), p. 114.

SOURCE 33a

Extent of Draft-Motivated Enlistments Among Regular Enlisted Personnel on Their First Tour of Active Duty, October 1964 (by Selected Characteristics)

CHARACTERISTIC	DRAFT MOTIVATED (%)
Service	
Army	43.2
Navy	32.6
Air Force	42.9
Marine Corps	30.4
Age at Enlistment	
17-19 years	31.4
20-25 years	57.9
Education	
Less than high school graduate	23.0
High school graduate	40.2
Some college or more	58.2
Mental Category	
Groups I and II	44.0
Group III	33.2
Group IV	29.2

Source: Reference Materials from the Department of Defense Study of the Draft, OASD (Manpower) (July 1966), p. 18.6; cited in K. H. Kim et al., *The All-Volunteer Army* (New York, 1971), p. 81.

SOURCE 34

Army Voluntary Enlistment Rates and Civilian Earnings and Employment, Males Ages 16 to 21, by Region, 1963

REGIONS	ARMY ENLISTMENTS WITHOUT A DRAFT[a]		MEDIAN CIVILIAN INCOME, MALES 16 to 21[b]		UNEMPLOYMENT, MALES 16 TO 21[b]	
	RATE (PERCENT)	INDEX	AMOUNT	INDEX	RATE (PERCENT)	INDEX
New England	3.36	96.3	$3,567	98.5	11.3	99.1
Middle Atlantic	2.97	85.1	3,748	103.5	14.2	124.6
South Atlantic	4.65	133.2	2,849	78.7	9.4	82.5
South	4.93	141.3	2,441	67.4	13.9	121.9
Western South	4.25	121.8	3,148	86.9	9.2	80.7
Great Lakes	3.10	88.8	4,184	115.5	11.1	97.4
Great Plains	2.05	58.7	3,725	102.9	6.0	52.6
Mountain	3.25	93.1	3,640	100.5	9.8	86.0
Pacific	3.35	96.0	4,257	117.5	16.2	142.1
U.S. average	3.49	100.0	3,621	100.0	11.4	100.0

[a]Army enlistments in mental groups I-III, excluding those motivated by the draft, per 100 civilian out-of-school males, ages 16 to 21, who meet minimum enlistment standards.
[b]Derived from Department of Defense survey of civilian men, 16 to 34 years old. October 1964.

Source: Joint Economic Committee, *Economic Effects of Vietnam Spending* (90th U.S. Congress, 1st sess., 1967), I, 317; cited in H. Wool, *The Military Specialist* (Baltimore, Md., Johns Hopkins University Press, 1967), p. 219.

SOURCE 35

South Carolina Induction and Enlistment Statistics, 1940-46

	WHITE	BLACK
Men called	137,360	117,533
Failed to report	2,465	4,602
Percent who failed to report	1.8%	3.9%
Men enlisting	58,345	3,687

Source: Holmes Springs, *Selective Service in South Carolina, 1940-1947* (Columbia, S.C., 1948), pp. 63, 65.

SOURCE 36

Relationship of Background and Army Experience to Choice of Overseas Outfits and Fighting Jobs Among Black and White Enlisted Men, March 1943

| | PERCENTAGE CHOOSING | |
| | BOTH AN OVERSEAS OUTFIT AND A FIGHTING JOB | |
	BLACK	WHITE
Type of enlistment		
Volunteers	26	49
Selectees	10	30
Length of time in army		
Over 2 years	24	53
1 to 2 years	15	45
6 months to 1 year	12	33
Under 6 months	11	31
Age		
30 and over	9	28
25-29	13	34
20-24	15	41
Under 20 years	23	43
Education		
College	24	40
High school graduate	22	43
Some high school	17	37
Grade school	8	25
Marital condition		
Married	12	29
Single	14	39
Regional origin		
North	20	37
South	9	33

Source: S. Stouffer et al., *Studies in Social Psychology in World War II,* 4 vols. (Princeton, N.J.: Princeton University Press, 1949-50), II, p. 524.

SOURCE 37

Differences in Attitudes Toward Combat Between Blacks Who Reject Racial Separation in the Army and Those Who Do Not, by Region of Origin and Educational Level (March 1943) (Numbers Following Bars = Number of Cases on Which Percentages Are Based)

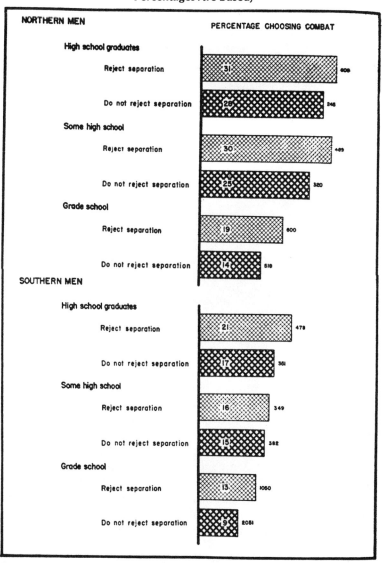

Source: S. Stouffer et al., *Studies in Social Psychology in World War II*, 4 vols. (Princeton, N.J.; Princeton University Press, 1949-50), II, p. 525.

SOURCE 38

Data on Black Infantry Replacement Volunteers
During "Battle of the Bulge," 1944:

	PERCENTAGE WHO WERE HIGH SCHOOL GRADUATES	PERCENTAGE WITH HIGH TEST SCORES
Black riflemen in white companies	22	29
All blacks in European theater	18	17

Source: S. Stouffer et al., Studies in Social Psychology in World War II, 4 vols. (Princeton, N.J.: Princeton University Press, 1949-50), II, p. 588.

SOURCE 39

The integration of army posts originally had no effect on nearby segregated communities, as the remarks of this southern politician in 1951 suggest:

(White civic leader): All of the facilities are separate. A separate place is given them in theaters. They have separate entrances in the bars. They are not allowed to eat in down-town places. . . . I can't see any change in this town since I have been here. None due to the presence of the Fort. When the colored come to town, they conform to the way we do things.

[But the army slowly intervened, first by attacking certain discriminatory practices:]

(Colonel, division staff officer): At present we have no post school for children of the families of Army men. We have in the unit a colored sergeant whose child was of school age. He was forced to send his child to the segregated grade school for Negro children. He came to me with the story that the school was in a deplorable state, so I decided to investigate myself. Well, when I got to this school, I was completely flabbergasted.

Source: Leo Bogart, Social Research and the Desegregation of the U.S. Army (Chicago, 1969 [orig. written 1951], pp. 302, 306; Edward Glick, Soldiers, Scholars and Society (Pacific Pal., Calif., 1971), pp. 22-25.

The physical plant was not bad in itself, but the facilities had never been completed. For water the whole school relied upon an open spring across the road. It was located at the base of a large ravine. Up on the slopes were several Negro shacks with their outhouses so located that the drainage could only flow towards the spring. Now there was a good size well dug and cemented in near the school, yet for some time now this new well had not been put into operation, because the pipes had never been connected! A cafeteria was operating without water except for what could be carried from the spring . . . temporary latrines had been set up . . . indescribably filthy and crude. I was shocked by it all. . . . But when I went to the superintendent of schools he gave me to understand that the Army was not running his school system! I had the post surgeon induce the county health officer to inspect the school. The health officer offered every conceivable excuse. Finally when he ran out, he accompanied the post surgeon on an inspection tour. . . . I heard that corrective measures were being taken, and I more or less forgot the matter till Christmas time. The school superintendent invited me out to dinner given on the last day before Christmas vacation. I was surprised at how much improvement had been made. The spring was closed, toilets in good order, well and well house operating, and there seemed to be a general sprucing up of the whole place.

[The Army eventually attacked segregation itself. A 1967 Defense Department study revealed that a third of all potential rental properties in the vicinity of military bases were segregated. A black GI was quoted on the problem:]

August 1965 — I attempted to find housing close to base in Maryland. The housing I checked had advertised vacancies. Phone conversations with the resident managers confirmed vacancies. But when I checked in person, I was greeted with the same problem so many Negroes have when they try to get off-base quarters close to the base. "I'm sorry [,] sir, but we do not rent to colored." So I found suitable housing in S. E. Washington. Rent was higher and I had to drive further, but I had no racial problem. Fourteen months later I was lucky to get on-base housing (October 1966). I'm very pleased with my present quarters.

[In 1968, consequently, the Defense Department made segregated housing off limits to military personnel, and within six months over half of the segregated properties were desegregated.]

SOURCE 40

First-Term Reenlistment Rates, by Race, 1964-66

SERVICE	CALENDAR YEAR	TOTAL	WHITE	BLACK	OTHER
All Services	1964	22.4	20.1	45.8	76.1
	1965	19.3	17.1	45.7	19.3
	1966	20.1	18.0	45.8	19.3
Army	1964	21.1	18.5	49.1	—
	1965	16.3	13.7	49.1	18.3
	1966	23.2	20.0	66.5	11.2
Navy	1964	21.0	20.9	19.9	81.9
	1965	26.1	24.2	44.8	81.2
	1966	18.7	17.6	24.7	68.6
Marine Corps	1964	14.0	12.9	25.1	22.6
	1965	20.4	18.9	38.9	42.3
	1966	11.2	10.5	19.8	12.4
Air Force	1964	28.3	26.1	48.8	—
	1965	20.7	19.1	39.2	27.6
	1966	17.3	16.0	30.1	16.6

Source: U.S. Department of Defense, Office of Assistant Secretary of Defense (Manpower), cited in H. Wool, *The Military Specialist* (Baltimore, Md., Johns Hopkins University Press, 1967), p. 144.

SOURCE 41

Attitudes of Negro Soldiers in 1965 Comparing Racial Equality in Military and Civilian Life, Total and by Home Region

WHERE MORE RACIAL EQUALITY	PERCENT		
	TOTAL	HOME REGION	
		NORTH	SOUTH
Military life	84	75	93
Civilian life	3	6	0
No difference	13	19	7
Total	100	100	100
(No. of cases)	(67)	(36)	(31)

Source: Charles Moskos, "Racial Integration in the Armed Forces," *American Journal of Sociology* 72 (1966): 140.

SOURCE 42

> Staff Sgt. John T— —, a black artilleryman, explained in 1975
> why he had chosen the military as a career:

"I enlisted in '72 and three months ago [reenlisted]. I'm from Louisville,
and I *know* I'm better off in the Army. There ain't no jobs out there for
what I do, and them that are ain't goin' to my people; y' understand? — I
got a family and they're a whole lot better off with me where I am. I'll
worry about [the civilian job market] later [when I retire seventeen years
from now]."

Source: Personal interview with author, August 1975.

SOURCE 43

> John Simpson, head of the small-farm oriented Farmer's Union
> of Oklahoma, wrote to his senator on March 31, 1917, offering a
> farmer's opinions on proposals to draft men to fight in France:

My work puts me in touch with farmer audiences in country schoolhouses
nearly every night. We always discuss the war question and universal
military service. I know nine out of ten farmers are absolutely opposed to
both. We farmers are unalterably opposed to war unless an enemy lands
on our shores.

Source: George Tindall, *The Emergence of the New South* (Baton Rouge, La., 1967), p. 47. I
am indebted to John Chambers for bringing this to my attention.

SOURCE 44

> Joseph Seeley, Jr., a prisoner in Hartford (Connecticut) jail, prom-
> ised to enlist in the Continental Line if he were released, May
> 1777:

Upon the memorial of Joseph Seeley jun', a prisoner in the goal at Hartford, representing to this Assembly that he had for inimical practices been
sentenced to suffer two years imprisonment and pay a fine of £20 0 0; that
he had served the United States in the present war with faithfulness, and

Source: Charles Hoadly, ed., *Public Records of the State of Connecticut* 1 (Hartford, Conn.,
1894), p. 303.

professing repentance for his evil conduct, promising reformation in future; praying this Assembly to liberate him from his imprisonment upon his inlisting into the continental service, as per memorial on file: Therefore resolved by this Assembly, that the said Joseph Seeley jun^r be and hereby is liberated from his imprisonment upon his paying or securing to be paid the cost of prosecution arising against him and he inlisting into some one of the battalions raising in the United States of America for continental service; and the goaler in such case is ordered to discharge the said Joseph from his imprisonment.

SOURCE 45

**Draftees from Four Ohio Counties in Late 1864, When
$300 Commutation Fee Was No Longer Allowed, by Profession and Disposition**

	NO. DRAFTED	PERCENT HIRING SUBSTITUTES	PERCENT EXEMPTED	PERCENT FAILING TO REPORT	PERCENT HELD FOR SERVICE	RATIO OF COLUMNS (2) and (5)
	(1)	(2)	(3)	(4)	(5)	(6)
Merchant	373	24.4	46.4	23.8	5.4	4.518
Clerk, public servant	283	16.2	48.4	31.5	3.9	4.154
Manufacturer	38	9.0	55.3	34.2	3.0	3.000
Doctor, lawyer, banker, broker	42	19.0	57.1	12.0	11.9	1.597
Teacher, minister, artist	85	20.0	43.5	21.2	15.3	1.307
Laborer, mechanic	1,510	15.4	41.1	31.9	11.6	1.319
Farmer	2,584	20.3	34.3	18.8	26.6	0.763

Source: Computed by author from tables compiled and provided from draft records by Hugh Earnhart in *Civil War History* 12 (1966), pp. 139-42.

Note: "Failing to Report" *could* have been a religious, an ideological, or a political gesture, especially among Quakers and Peace Democrats. "Exemption" was a measure designed by Union leadership to achieve military ends. Hence these two categories ought not to be considered in measuring the economic hardship that the elimination of commutation imposed on those drafted who were not eligible for exemption and who possessed no deep-seated objection to military service. The "Ratio of Columns (2) and (5)," then, would appear to be a measure of the ability of different occupational groups to buy substitutes.

SOURCE 46

A sociologist noted the correlation of marriages, births, and the passage of the Selective Service Act of 1940:

The Crude Birth Rate for the United States and the Crude Marriage Rate for Sixteen Selected States, by Months: 1939 to 1941

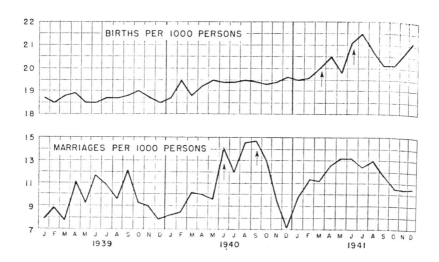

Note: *Arrows on chart showing birth rate indicate dates nine months after introduction into and passage by Congress of the Selective Service Act. Arrows on chart showing marriage rate indicate dates of introduction into and passage by Congress of the Selective Service Act.*

Source: Philip Hauser, "Population and Vital Phenomena," in *American Journal of Sociology* (November 1942): 312. Compare Ernest Burgess, "Effect of the War on the American Family," *American Journal of Sociology* 48 (November 1942): 343 ff.

SOURCE 47

> The Selective Service System's leadership in Washington de-
> scribed "channeling" in an "Orientation Kit" for new draft board
> members, July 1965:

One of the major products of the Selective Service classification process
is the channeling of manpower into many endeavors and occupations;
activities that are in the national interest. This function is a counterpart
and amplification of the System's responsibility to deliver manpower to
the armed forces in such a manner as to reduce to a minimum any adverse
effect upon the national health, safety, interest, and progress. By identifying and applying this process intelligently, the System is able not only
to minimize any adverse effect, but to exert an effect beneficial to the
national health, safety and interest.

The line dividing the primary function of armed forces manpower procurement from the process of channeling manpower into civilian support
is often finely drawn. The process of channeling by not taking men from
certain activities who are otherwise liable for service, or by giving deferments to qualified men in certain occupations, is actual procurement by
inducement of manpower of civilian activities which are manifestly in
the national interest.

While the best known purpose of Selective Service is to procure manpower for the armed forces, a variety of related processes takes place
outside delivery of manpower to the active armed forces. Many of these
may be put under the heading of "channeling manpower." Many young
men would have not pursued a higher education if there had not been a
program of student deferments. Many young scientists, engineers, tool
and die makers, and other possessors of scarce skills would not remain in
their jobs in the defense effort if it were not for a program of occupational
deferment. Even though the salary of a teacher has historically been
meager, many young men remain in that job seeking the reward of deferment. The process of channeling manpower by deferment is entitled to
much credit for the large amount of graduate students in technical fields
and for the fact that there is not a greater shortage of teachers, engineers,
and other scientists working in activities which are essential to the national
interest.

. . .

The opportunity to enhance the national well-being by inducing more
registrants to participate in fields which relate directly to the national
interest came about as a consequence, soon after the close of the Korean

---

Source: The Selective Service: Its Concepts, History and Operation (Washington, D.C.: U.S.
Government Printing Office, September 1967).

episode, of the knowledge within the System that there was enough registrant personnel to allow stringent deferment practices employed during
war time to be relaxed or tightened as the situation might require. Circumstances had become favorable to induce registrants, by the attraction
of deferment, to matriculate in schools and pursue subjects in which there
was beginning to be a national shortage of personnel. These were particularly in the engineering, scientific, and teaching professions.

...

In the Selective Service System, the term "deferment" has been used
millions of times to describe the method and means used to attract to the
kind of service considered to be the most important, the individuals who
were not compelled to do it. The club of induction has been used to drive
out of areas considered to be less important to the areas of greater importance in which deferments were given, the individuals who did not or
could not participate in activities which were considered essential to the
Nation. The Selective Service System anticipates evolution in this area.
It is promoting the process by the granting of deferments in liberal numbers where the national need clearly would benefit.

Soon after Sputnik I was launched it became popular to reappraise critically our educational, scientific, and technological inventory. Many de-
plored our shortage of scientific and technical personnel, inadequacies
of our schools, and shortage of teachers. Since any analysis having any
connection with manpower and its relation to the Nation's survival vitally involves the Selective Service System, it is well to point out that for quite some
time the System had been following a policy of deferring instructors who
were engaged in the teaching of mathematics and physical and biological
sciences. It is appropriate also to recall the System's previously invoked
practice of deferring students to prepare themselves for work in some
essential activity and the established program of deferring engineers,
scientists, and other critically skilled persons who were working in essential
fields.

The Congress, in enacting the Universal Military Training and Service
legislation declared that adequate provisions for national security required
maximum effort in the fields of scientific research and development, and
the fullest possible utilization of the Nation's technological, scientific,
and other critical manpower resources. To give effect to this philosophy,
the classifying boards of the Selective Service System defer registrants
determined by them to be necessary in the national health, safety, or interest. This is accomplished on the basis of evidence of record in each
individual case. No group deferments are permitted. Deferments are
granted, however, in a realistic atmosphere so that the fullest effect of
channeling will be felt, rather than be terminated by military service at
too early a time.

Registrants and their employers are encouraged and required to make available to the classifying authorities detailed evidence as to the occupations and activities in which registrants are engaged. It is not necessary for any registrant to specifically request deferment, but his selective service file must contain sufficient current evidence on which can be based a proper determination as to whether he should remain where he is or be made available for service. Since occupational deferments are granted for no more than a year at a time, a process of periodically receiving current information and repeated review assures that every deferred registrant continues to contribute to the overall national good. This reminds him of the basis of his deferment. The skills as well as the activities are periodically reevaluated. A critical skill that is not employed in an essential activity does not qualify for deferment.

...

It is in this atmosphere that the young man registers at age 18 and pressure begins to force his choice. He does not have the inhibitions that a philosophy of universal service in uniform would engender. The door is open for him as a student to qualify if capable in a skill needed by his nation. He has many choices and he is prodded to make a decision.

The psychological effect of this circumstantial climate depends upon the individual, his sense of good citizenship, his love of country and its way of life. He can obtain a sense of well being and satisfaction that he is doing as a civilian what will help his country most. This process encourages him to put forth his best effort and removes to some degree the stigma that has been attached to being out of uniform.

In the less patriotic and more selfish individual it engenders a sense of fear, uncertainty, and dissatisfaction which motivates him, nevertheless, in the same direction. He complains of the uncertainty which he must endure; he would like to be able to do as he pleases; he would appreciate a certain future with no prospect of military service or civilian contribution, but he complies with the needs of the national health, safety, or interest—or he is denied deferment.

Throughout his career as a student, the pressure—the threat of loss of deferment—continues. It continues with equal intensity after graduation. His local board requires periodic reports to find out what he is up to. He is impelled to pursue his skill rather than embark upon some less important enterprise and is encouraged to apply high skill in an essential activity in the national interest. The loss of deferred status is the consequence for the individual who has acquired the skill and either does not use it, or uses it in a nonessential activity.

The psychology of granting wide choice under pressure to take action is the American or indirect way of achieving what is done by direction in foreign countries where choice is not allowed. Here, choice is limited but not denied, and it is fundamental that an individual generally applies himself better to something he has decided to do rather than something he has been told to do.

The effects of channeling are manifested among student physicians. They are deferred to complete their education through school and internship. This permits them to serve in the armed forces in their skills rather than as unskilled enlisted men.

The device of pressurized guidance, or channeling, is employed on Standby Reservists of which more than 2½ million have been referred by all services for availability determinations. The appeal to the Reservist who knows he is subject to recall to active duty unless he is determined to be unavailable is virtually identical to that extended to other registrants.

The psychological impact of being rejected for service in uniform is severe. The earlier this occurs in a young man's life, the sooner the beneficial effects of pressured motivation by the Selective Service System are lost. He is labeled unwanted. His patriotism is not desired. Once the label of "rejectee" is upon him all efforts at guidance by persuasion are futile. If he attempts to enlist at 17 or 18 and is rejected, then he receives virtually none of the impulsion the System is capable of giving him. If he makes no effort to enlist and as a result is not rejected until delivered for examination by the Selective Service System at about age 23, he has felt some of the pressure but thereafter is a free agent.

This contributed to establishment of a new classification of I-Y (registrant qualified for military service only in time of war or national emergency). The classification reminds the registrant of his ultimate qualification to serve and preserves some of the benefit of what we call channeling. Without it or any other similar method of categorizing men in degrees of acceptability, men rejected for military service would be left with the understanding that they are unfit to defend their country, even in war time.

. . .

From the individual's viewpoint, he is standing in a room which has been made uncomfortably warm. Several doors are open, but they all lead to various forms of recognized, patriotic service to the Nation. Some accept the alternatives gladly—some with reluctance. The consequence is approximately the same.

The so-called Doctor Draft was set up during the Korean episode to insure sufficient physicians, dentists, and veterinarians in the armed forces as officers. The objective of that law was to exert sufficient pressure to furnish an incentive for application for commission. However, the indirect effect was to induce many physicians, dentists, and veterinarians to specialize in areas of medical personnel shortage and to seek outlets for their skills in areas of greatest demand and national need rather than of greatest financial return.

Selective Service processes do not compel people by edict as in foreign systems to enter pursuits having to do with essentiality and progress. They go because they know that by going they will be deferred.

...

Delivery of manpower for induction, the process of providing a few thousand men with transportation to a reception center, is not much of an administrative or financial challenge. It is in dealing with the other millions of registrants that the system is heavily occupied, developing more effective human beings in the national interest....

SOURCE 48

Male high school seniors indicated what things "could interfere" with their "future career plans," 1969:

	PERCENTAGE FREQUENCIES	
	FIRST MENTION	SECOND MENTION
What thing(s) could interfere with your future career plans?		
1. Grades not good enough; won't finish school; won't get enough education	14.8	3.0
2. Not enough money	8.2	2.6
3. Might change my mind; might not like it; something I like better may come along	8.1	2.8
4. The draft; the war; military service	29.1	5.1
5. If something (illness, accident, death) happens to me or my family	10.4	2.7
6. No jobs available; no openings; no need for that type of worker	1.2	0.1
7. Other	5.7	4.6
8. Marriage	3.4	1.5
Missing data	19.1	77.7

Source: J. Johnston and J. Bachman, *Youth in Transition:* Vol. II. *Young Men and Military Service* (Ann Arbor, Mich., 1972), p. 108.

SOURCE 49

*In 1969 "Craig T." told Franklin Stevens of the ways that the
Selective Service System had affected his life:*

"I've managed to stay out of the Army," says twenty-five-year-old Craig T.,
"but for the last six years, my life has been so shaped and directed by the
draft—so 'channeled' I guess you could say—that in some ways I might
as well have gone in.

"Of course, it wasn't only the pressures of the draft. My parents, my
home, and my whole background came into it, too."

. . .

"I certainly wasn't going to work in anything remotely connected with
a defense industry, because as far as I was concerned that was no better
than going into the military. It would have been doing the same things,
but just not having to be directly confronted with the consequences of
my actions. [A friend] suggested teaching, in a high . . . or grammar school.
At that time there was a severe shortage of teachers in several of the East-
ern states, and you could take a two- or three-month crash program to
qualify, rather than several years of education courses. But the trouble
was that most of the assignments were to slum areas, and as far as I can
see it takes a lot more to teach in a slum area than it does in a middle-class
white suburb. I mean, actually getting deprived kids to learn, to orient
toward literacy and toward thinking in an abstract way, is a tremendously
difficult thing. At that time I was occasionally going out with a girl who
was a student teacher in Boston, and she said she spent most of her time,
and so did the other teachers, just getting the kids in this slum school to
stay in their seats and not rip the classroom apart.

"Well, I don't think it's fair to those kids to send a teacher into their
classroom who doesn't know what he's doing, doesn't have any ideas on
how to make those kids start to learn, and what's worse, doesn't have any
real feeling along those lines. And I didn't have any of those things. Teaching in a college is a lot different from teaching in a grammar or high school
in a slum. I wasn't a dedicated teacher, and if there's anyplace you need
a dedicated teacher it's in a situation like that. So I just couldn't see myself cheating those kids, taking away whatever slim chance they might
have to learn something, in order to stay out of the draft.

"But I did remember from what a couple of my friends around home
had told me that the local draft board, which was dealing with mostly
ghetto black guys, and working-class poor, had been fairly generous in
giving deferments for things like VISTA, and the poverty programs. This
was probably because the guys who applied for these deferments were

Source: Franklin Stevens, *If This Be Treason* (New York: David McKay Co., Inc., 1970), pp.
84, 95-97, 104-08. Reprinted by permission of David McKay Co., Inc.

from that small section of the area that was white, upper-middle-class, and the board was just prejudiced in favor of nice, literate, middle-class kids. It was unfair, but at that point I didn't see any other alternative, so about a week after I graduated from college I went to see the minister of our church, and asked him about working on this poverty program they had going in the Baltimore slums. I didn't know very much about it, but I did know it was concerned primarily with community action regarding housing, and neighborhood improvement, so I wouldn't be put in the phony position of pretending to be a teacher.

"At that time, what I was most worried about was that I thought I'd have to lie, if he asked me why I wanted to work on the program, pretend to be a dedicated social worker or something to that effect. This minister is no radical. He's a fairly good friend of my mother's, because she does a lot of church charity work, of the society-lady type, unfortunately, and I've more or less been acquainted with him most of my life.

"But he didn't ask me why. He just said something like, 'Are you doing this to stay out of the military?' and without thinking I simply told him the truth, yes, and then I thought, well, that's done it.

"But he just shuffled the papers on his desk around a bit, and then said something to the effect of, 'Well, you'll do a lot more good here than in Vietnam.' Which almost knocked me over flat, but made me feel much better. Like having an ally you didn't know about, showing up in a totally unexpected quarter."

[So Craig began to work with the poverty program. His father was angry. Craig recalled the conversation:]

"This is simply a way of staying out of uniform, isn't it?

I tried to explain to you, I can't go into the military.

I think you know what your brother would have thought of you, and I'm sure you know what I think of you. Apparently you don't feel you have any obligations toward your country, but you might have given some slight thought to your obligations to your family."

If I hadn't thought about my family, I'd be a C.O. now.

I don't think I have anything more to say to you, Craig. I didn't think it would ever be possible, but I'm actually ashamed of my own son.

"And I thought, well, it's a question of having him ashamed of me, or being ashamed of myself.

[Soon he decided that the poverty program was ineffective and a waste of time and energy. He spoke to the minister again:]

"I told him what my situation was: that I couldn't destroy my family by becoming a C.O., but I couldn't destroy myself, and others, by going into the military. And I couldn't face any more nonwork on nonprojects. Then, before I could say it myself, he said: 'Have you thought about divinity school?'

[Craig entered divinity school:]

". . . the executives of the seminary knew they were getting a substantial number of students who were interested in divinity school primarily because it was a deferment, and because of the militancy of their antidraft sentiment they had no objection to this.* One of my roommates was there for exactly the same reason I was. The other, who did want to become a minister, burned his draft card during the demonstration at the Pentagon."

"I can't recall meeting anyone there who was actually *for* the war, or the draft, although some were more militantly against it than others."

"My classes bored me to tears, but I had to keep up with the work because to have flunked out of the school would, of course, have lost my deferment. And my work at the library, which was pretty menial, very much like that of a file clerk, bored me to tears too, but of course I had to do that for enough money to live, and it was about the only job that fitted in with my school schedule.

"I thought to myself, 'Here I am, I'm twenty-three, it's one of the most crucial parts of my life, and I'm just marking time, I'm doing busy work. I can't even really think about the future, let alone prepare for it, because I have to spend all my energies and direct my whole life around staying out of the military.'

"I began to feel my life was not only worthless to everyone else, but to myself as well. It was being lived on a purely negative plane."

. . .

"In a sense you could say I'm still being channeled. I hate to admit it, and I certainly couldn't admit it to myself at the time, but the main reason I got married and we had a child right away was that I was just desperate to get out of divinity school. It was a very bad marriage, very destructive to both of us, right from the start, and of course any marriage that one of the partners enters into as I did—even subconsciously—is bound to be bad. Equally, it's a terrible thing to bring a child into the world as a deferment, even if you come to love the child.

"The reason I chose to go back to graduate school was primarily that I knew that eventually I could make enough money to support the child, and can even do it more or less right now. I'm not saying that my field doesn't interest me. It does. But I think that if I hadn't had to consider the child, I would have spent at least a year or so—as I wanted to do during college—studying music, and seeing if I didn't want to be a professional musician, seeing if I had the talent to be one. But because I have the responsibility of the child, I didn't feel I could afford to. So even if I'm in-

---

*Other evaders tell similar stories about different seminaries. One relates that he frankly told the admissions officer of a large divinity school that he was trying to evade the draft. The officer replied that although the seminary had to give first consideration to young men who actually wanted to become ministers, the administrative officials were willing to take as many draft evaders as they had room for.

terested in my field now, I'll never know if I couldn't have been in a field which interests me far more deeply. I'm more or less stuck in the academic world now. I know that this will always bother me.

"I made my mistake in the very beginning, when I decided not to become a C.O., and to play along with the system. I allowed myself to be manipulated, to be directed, and to have the control of my life taken out of my hands, just as I would have, in a more extreme set of circumstances, if I had gone into the military.

"This thing of channeling is rotten all through. It keeps kids in college who don't want to be in college, and aren't getting anything out of college, or at least who could be getting more out of something else. It sends people into these 'social service' projects who don't want to be in them, who do them badly and without talent, and who keep bad projects going without criticism just because they're deferments.

"Basically what's wrong with channeling is the same thing that's wrong with conscription. It doesn't allow you to make a choice based on your own ideas, your own feelings, your own morality. It just demands, and forces on you, blind obedience, blind service. And worst of all, it does so in terms that can trick you into thinking that you ARE making a meaningful choice, or even that you're manipulating the system to your own ends, when it's actually manipulating you. . . ."

SOURCE 50

Another young man described his experience in evading the draft after being classified 1-A:

. . . like a last-minute reprieve for a condemned man, came a call from [a] friend. . . . an uncle in Pittsburgh, with a plant doing defense work, needed a bookkeeper, and promised an absolutely certain deferment.

"It sounded fantastic. I had already done bookkeeping for two summers, for a friend of my father who had a mail-order business. And I would be able to take courses at the University of Pittsburgh at night, toward my Ph.D., so that I could finally go into teaching when I didn't have to worry about the draft anymore. So I called the guy up and made an appointment, and then drove up to Pittsburgh the next day, and of course, it turned out to be a little less fantastic than I had thought.

"My friend's uncle did defense work, all right. He had a small plant employing about twenty people, and maybe three quarters of his production was what they call "room coolers," you know, those things that look like

Source: Franklin Stevens, *If This Be Treason* (New York: David McKay Co., Inc., 1970), pp. 19-20. Reprinted by permission of David McKay Co., Inc.

air conditioners but are actually just fans with a sort of water-cooling system, and of course are much cheaper than air conditioners. The other part
was done under subcontract for a large aviation company. It was through
the aviation company that the owner promised to get my deferment, and
I figured—correctly, as it turned out—that their name was certainly big
enough to command the respect that would make my draft board grant it.

"The catch was that the salary he offered me was really incredibly low.
I mean, when I figured it out, it actually came to be about four cents an
hour above the minimum wage. And when I asked him about this, he just
sort of looked at the wall above my head, and said that he had employed
other young fellows like myself in the past who had found it acceptable
and that after all, there were certain 'fringe benefits,' as he put it.

"I was about to ask him what these 'fringe benefits' were when suddenly it struck me: this guy had been hiring guys like myself who were desperate to stay out of the draft, and willing to accept this miserably, un-
fairly low wage to do it. The 'fringe benefit' was my deferment.

"And of course, I was no different from the rest. I took it."

SOURCE 51

*Still another described the deception to which he and his par-
ents had resorted to avoid service:*

"I'm one of the lucky ones, I guess," said Ron B., a twenty-three-year-old
graduate student. "My parents have disapproved of this war since the
very beginning, so when I—like my older brother—decided I wasn't going
to let myself be drafted, they told me they'd stand behind me all the way,
in whatever course of action I decided to take.

"Well, there was more to it than just their disapproval of the war. My
parents' attitude toward my brother and myself has always been: It's
your life and your conscience, so you have to make your own decisions.
You decide what you think is right for you to do, and as your parents
we'll back you up on it. They're great parents, great people.

"Anyway, I was just finishing UCLA, and I knew I'd get snatched up by
the army within a few months of graduation, so I started really thinking
about what I was going to do. I was absolutely determined not to let myself be drafted. The Vietnam war had revolted me from the very beginning,

SOURCE: Franklin Stevens, *If This Be Treason* (New York: David McKay Co., Inc., 1970),
pp. 56-59. Reprinted by permission of David McKay Co., Inc.

and it seemed to me that refusing to help my country do something corrupt and aggressive like that was a more patriotic act than going along
with it.

"What I really wanted to do was become a C.O. I wouldn't have minded
performing alternate civilian service, in some job where I was helping
people, even if it was something crummy like scrubbing floors in a mental
hospital. But my older brother had applied for a C.O. classification and
because in our family we're not members of any church, and he refused
to base his application on religious rather than ethical principles, he was
turned down. My parents appealed in one court after another, they fought
the thing for two years, and finally he was turned down anyway, and had
to go to Canada, and it cost my parents a small fortune, far more than
they could afford. So I didn't want to put them through that again, drain
them dry financially, when I probably didn't have any better chance of
success than my brother did.

"I thought of going to Canada like my brother, but I guess I'm just not
as principled as he is. I don't want to leave America for good. All my friends
are here, and it's just my home, that's all. And I sure as hell didn't want to
go to jail. I wouldn't be any good to anybody in jail, least of all to myself.

"Finally I decided that the only thing to do was to fake my way out, get
a IV-F any way I could. So I told my parents this, and at first they seemed
disturbed. Then, after they had thought it over for a couple of days, my
mother said to me, 'We've decided we were being hypocritical; there's no
reason why you should have to go to jail or go into exile either, if you
don't want to, because you won't fight a war you think is immoral. The
important thing is to stay out of the Army.'

"Then she just said. 'Do you have any plans as to how you're going to
do it?'

"I said, the only thing I could figure out was to try to convince the
psychiatrist at the examination that I was emotionally disturbed.

"And she said, 'You'll need a letter from a psychiatrist, then. Let me see
what I can do.'

"And as usual, she came through. I was still at school, when I got a telephone call from her saying I had an appointment with this shrink in L.A.
four days later.

"I don't know where she found this guy, but I have a strong suspicion
that she managed to get hold of somebody who was more than willing to
help guys stay out of the army. Because my vist to him was pretty per-
functory. He asked me if something was bothering me, and I said yes,
that the thought of going into the army was bothering me. The he asked
me why, and I said I couldn't stand the idea of being ordered to do something I didn't think I should do, like killing people who are only trying to
run their own country without outside interference. So he said, 'The thought

of taking orders makes you feel you're going to crack up, is that it?' And I said yes. And he wrote me out a note to give to the psychiatrist at the examination. He told me it said that I was too emotionally unstable to be suited to military life, and required psychiatric treatment in the near future.

"I asked him if that meant I actually *had* to start psychiatric treatment. And he smiled and said that he had a very busy schedule, and it might be quite a while before he could fit me in. I got the message. A very nice guy.

"So about six weeks later, I was called down for examination, and I went down there with my heart in my throat, and when I got to the shrink, I gave him the note. And he said to me, 'How long have you been in treatment with this man?'

"And I said, 'I'm supposed to start as soon as he can fit me in.'

"And he said, 'Hmm.' Then he asked me a lot of questions, most of them about my relation to my parents and my teachers. And I lied through my teeth, and talked about how I couldn't stand to live at home any more because my parents kept making demands of me, and trying to run my life, and sometimes I felt such resentment of them that I thought I was going to explode. All these things I thought might make him believe I couldn't take discipline, couldn't stand having demands made on me.

"I didn't really know what I was doing, of course. I mean, I don't know anything about psychopathology except what I read in college, and have heard people talk about. But apparently it did the trick, because after the shrink finished talking to me, he sent me home. No blood test. Everybody had told me that means you're IV-F. And I was, because I got the notification a couple of weeks later.

"But the thing was, I went home feeling sick to my stomach. I felt dirty. I didn't even really feel relieved that I was out, I was so disgusted. I mean, at all those lies. Lies about my parents, who I think are really tremendous people, whom I love.

"When I told them about it, they were just glad I was out. They said I shouldn't feel bad, that I had done the only thing I could do. But I still felt lousy. And I felt even lousier because I had been forced to involve my parents, by getting my mother to find me a shrink who would write that phony letter. And I felt lousy about involving the shrink in my lies, too. After all, if he felt that guys like me shouldn't have to go, what choice did he have when I asked him for help, or rather, when my mother asked him at my request?

"Well, so I'm out. I soiled myself doing it, and managed to soil my parents and that nice shrink, too.

"But the truth of the matter is that I'd do it all over again if I had to. I just don't see any better way.

"It's a hell of a price to pay for doing what you think is right."

SOURCE 52

Allen Morgan recalled his decision to move to Canada in order to avoid military service:

It was hard to get rid of the feeling that I was going to get it, that I was being crushed and munched and there was no way to get out of the way of it. If the Selective Service took away my 2-S classification, then what? Well, I guess I was going to be 1-A and drafted . . . maybe not, maybe they weren't going to reclassify . . . not very likely, why'd they go to all the trouble of getting me to take the physical? . . . so, all right, maybe I can try for a different classification. I went down the list of categories and none of them fitted me at all: 1-Y for a mental—I'm not crazy; 1-O for conscientious objector—I can't prove it; 4-F for not fit—I'm fit; and on and on but there was none for me. There was a place for clergy, a place for aliens, a place for those that have already served (sorry we gave), a place for people in the so-called necessary occupations. A place for the sole surviving son, a place for sons of Draft Board heads, but there was no place for me except 1-A and that was no place at all. And there was no "None of Above," there was no "Sorry, wrong number." The only possibilities for me were 1-A and 2-S, and I was losing my 2-S. Not that it mattered really in the long run. I was graduating from school later in the year anyway. 2-S was just a longer way of saying 1-A.

And there wasn't anything that I could do about it. When you're my age you can't really disagree with the system effectively: you don't know anybody, you don't have any money to buy your way out, you don't have enough of a reputation to bullshit your way out, in short there is no way legally or illegally that you can effectively say, "Hey, I don't believe in this," and then back up that belief with actions. In most states you couldn't even go off and get drunk when you saw yourself getting screwed. You were too young.

And there are thousands and thousands and tens of thousands of guys in the same situation—I'm sure it wasn't personal on behalf of the Selective Service—like the guys getting on the bus, like most of the guys I knew in school all up and down the country, personalities and persons poking their heads up there for the first time and a big voice says, "Who are you?" and they answer back . . . "Me" . . . and the big voice says, "OK, that means you can go into the Army and kill a lot of guys and kick around your friends and take orders from idiots and in general waste a lot of time and" . . . "Wait a minute, I don't want to do that" . . . "Why not?" . . . "I just don't want to, it doesn't sound like something that I would enjoy doing" . . . "Tough shit, it's the law" . . . "Well, who do I see about changing

Source: Allen Morgan, *Dropping Out in ¾ Time* (New York, 1972), pp. 38-41.

the law?" . . . "You can't change the law, son" . . . "Why not?" . . . "Because that's the law." It seems to me to be the same situation as having to join General Motors at the age of nineteen. Now think about that for a minute: you get a note in the mail saying, "Greetings, this is to tell you that you have been selected to put fenders on cars at General Motors and you got to be at the plant tomorrow morning at six and you have to live in special houses that we have built and wear funny clothes and learn how to dismantle Volvos in parking lots at night." I mean the Army is just another corporation when you think about it and it seems to me that I have the right to choose what corporation I want to work for. There's no way that I want to work for the Army corporation. Working conditions aside, they're just bad guys. Let me put it another way: they're trying to hurt people. They are erecting a reality that is causing considerable grief to a considerable amount of people. I mean not only are they a bad corporation but they're constructing a bad product.

Now a lot of people get pissed off at that. "Why everybody's got to go into the Army . . . Everybody always goes into the Army . . . I went into the Army . . . We need an Army . . . What will our neighbors think if we don't put everybody in our Army," and on and on. Well, bullshit to all that. If there was a whole bunch of bad guys running around raping everybody's sisters I'd do something about it, but that just isn't what's happening. It seems to me that our Army is over doing that in someone else's country. "But what about the Communist threat and the Red Chinese threat and the Russian threat and the . . ." Right, I'm hip, if it really does exist and it's not just a lot of political bullshit I'll do my bit . . . sure . . . but I sure am going to wait till they get a hell of a lot closer than Vietnam. Maybe when they're in New Jersey, and only then if they raze Atlantic City first. I want something out of the deal, too.

Now you wonder why all of us young guys are doing peculiar things; well, the reason is that we are all in situations where there are really no choices available that make any sense. In that kind of situation you become free to do all sorts of peculiar things. Like not care, or blow up things, or drop out, or just go away. What do you expect? I mean you make all these very interesting Skinner boxes for people to walk into, you make them very attractive and you get them inside, and then you wonder why they freak out on you? They freak out because they have no meaningful choices to make. If they go right they get shocked, and if they go left they get shocked. So what do they do? They sit down in the middle and turn on. Or some climb out of the box and punch out and leave. A whole bunch of us just sit in the middle and go crazy. . . . What's the matter with mice today, I ask you? They are all sitting in the middle and wetting their pants. Why in my day we went to the other end and got shocked like a man and sometimes we even got food in our hoppers. What is the matter with mice today?

SOURCE 53

*S.A.S., a young black man drafted in 1941, had not had access
to Ron B. — —'s "friendly shrink." He may, or may not, have
developed psychoneurotic disorders while in training. In any
event, he was soon out of the army and back where he wanted
to be. Army psychiatrists wrote his case history:*

S.A.S. was the seventh of sixteen children born to a Negro family in the
deep South. As a child he was healthy and spent much of his time helping
his mother and brothers and sisters work the farm. His father rarely helped,
was often away, and drank rather heavily. S.A.S. attended a country school
for two years and then went to school in town where he completed the
ninth grade at the age of seventeen. Actually he did quite well considering
the fact that his education was frequently interrupted by demands for his
help at home. At about the time he left school his father left his family
for good. S.A.S. worked for about six months as a laborer in a dairy and
then joined the Civilian Conservation Corps where he spent over a year.
Several months as a laborer in a brick yard followed and then he went to
work as a stock boy in a large department store. After about a year on
this job he was drafted into the military service.

Private S. was assigned to the medical detachment at an air base in the
South for his basic training. The soldier did well at first, but quickly developed a thorough distaste for military routine.

Quite suddenly after a month of training he began to behave very pe-
culiarly. He walked over to another soldier's bed in the middle of the
night and asked: "What is 6 over 3 and 3 over 6? What is alert? Why does
a siren blow?" His talk became incoherent at times and he seemed to be
in a daze. During classes he stared into space and apparently heard nothing. Sometimes he walked around with a perpetual grin while proclaiming:
"I am a son of a living God." Later he refused to eat and began to do exactly the opposite of what he was told to do. He complained, "I can't figure
out what's going on around here."

Source: Eli Ginzberg et al. (eds.), *The Ineffective Soldier: Vol. II: Breakdown and Recovery*
(New York: Columbia University Press, 1959), pp. 156-58.

Within a week he was in the hospital. There his speech was so silly and confused that it was impossible to take a case history. The doctors felt, in spite of the fact that they knew very little about him, that his behavior was so consistent with the pattern commonly found in schizophrenic patients of the hebephrenic type that there was almost no chance of error in this diagnosis.

Accordingly, five days after entering the hospital Private S. went before a disposition board and was approved for separation from the service because of psychosis. Almost immediately he began to improve and soon was transferred from the locked ward to the open ward. By the time he was discharged just before Christmas 1942 with eighty-nine days of service he appeared to be very much improved. Nevertheless, he was turned over to the sheriff of his home county and after a jury trial to establish insanity was committed to the state hospital.

On his arrival, there did not appear to be anything wrong with him at all. He was quiet, cooperative, and exhibited no signs of confusion. He seemed to be well-informed for a man of his socioeconomic background and education. For a while the doctors were thoroughly mystified. Then the veteran began to talk to the ward attendants about the Army and how much he detested it. He indicated that he never had been really sick, but had put on an act to obtain a discharge. He was rather proud of his success. After a brief stay, S.A.S. was released and returned to his job as a stock boy.

At the store his supervisors were quite surprised to learn that he had been in a mental institution. He appeared to be quite normal and was a very satisfactory employee. Although his mother applied to the Veterans Administration for a disability pension while he was in the hospital the application was turned down because there was apparently nothing wrong with him. The veteran himself did not push his claim, and his mother later stated that she did not want her son to receive compensation as long as he could support himself.

After about a year he left the department store and worked first for a furniture store and later for a garage. In 1945 he was married. In late 1946 he applied for schooling under the G.I. Bill but was turned down because he lacked by one day the mandatory ninety days of military service. Shortly after this he began work as a mail room assistant and truck driver for a daily newspaper, a job which he still holds.

In 1954 he was supporting a rapidly growing family of five children. He was in very good health and had had no difficulties of an emotional nature. Observing him, one would never believe that he had suffered a severe psychotic breakdown but despite his statements to the attendants at the state hospital it is likely that he had suffered one.

SOURCE 54

Selective Service complaints of draft law violations, per 100 inductions, 1966-1970.

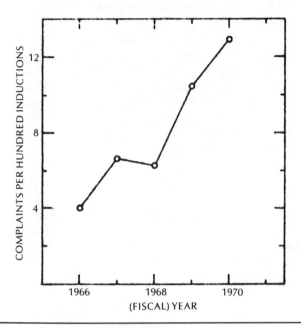

(FISCAL) YEAR

Source: U.S. Department of Defense, 1971; U.S. House Committee on Armed Services, 1970, 12860; U.S. House Committee on Armed Services, 1967, 243; cited in M. Useem, Conscription, Protest, and Social Conflict (New York: John Wiley and Sons, Inc., 1973), p. 127.

SOURCE 55

James W — — described his "draft-motivated" navy enlistment:

I joined the Navy in '66 because I knew I'd get called [up by the army] if I didn't. I was 1-A; no job; no college. And I didn't want to go to no Vietnam. I figured the extra year was worth it if I came out in one piece. And maybe I was right. As it was, the [destroyer] I got assigned to spent a lot of days on "ditch" duty [1,000 yards off the bow of carriers launching planes]

Source: Personal interview, July 1974.

and [antiaircraft] "screen" duty in the South China Sea, but I survived. I didn't *like* spending [all that time] on that can, but it was better than [a year] in the bush as a grunt.

SOURCE 56

"Channeling" continued to operate within the services them-selves. Tim O'Brien described the "pitch" he and his buddies received upon reaching the combat zone in Vietnam:

Then the battalion Re-Up NCO came along. "I seen some action. I got me two purple hearts, so listen up good. I'm not saying you're gonna get zapped out there. I made it. But you're gonna come motherfuckin' close. Jesus, you're gonna hear bullets tickling your asshole. And sure as I'm standing here, one or two of you men are gonna get your legs blown off. Or killed. One or two of you, it's gotta happen."

He paused and stared around like a salesman, from man to man, letting it sink in. "I'm just telling you the facts of life, I'm not trying to scare shit out of you. But you better sure as hell be scared, it's gotta happen. One or two of you men, your ass is grass.

"So—what can you do about it? Well, like Sarge says, you can be care-ful, you can watch for the mines and all that, and, who knows, you might come out looking like a rose. But careful guys get killed too. So what can you do about it then? Nothing. Except you can re-up."

The men looked at the ground and shuffled around grinning. "Sure, sure—I know. Nobody likes to re-up. But just think about it a second. Just say you do it—you take your burst of three years, starting today; three more years of army life. Then what? Well, I'll tell you what, it'll save your ass, that's what, it'll save your ass. You re-up and I can get you a job in Chu Lai. I got jobs for mechanics, typists, clerks, damn near anything you want, I got it. So you get your nice, safe rear job. You get some on-the-job training, the works. You get a skill. You sleep in a bed. Hell, you laugh, but you sleep in the goddamn monsoons for two months on end, you try that sometime, and you won't be laughing. So. You lose a little time to Uncle Sam. Big deal. You save your ass. So, I got my desk inside. If you come in and sign the papers—it'll take ten minutes—and I'll have you on the first truck going back to Chu Lai, no shit. Anybody game?" No one budged, and he shrugged and went down to the mess hall.

Source: Tim O'Brien, *If I Die in a Combat Zone* (New York, 1973), pp. 68-69.

SOURCE 57

Army Enlisted Personnel in Combat Arms, by Component and Education

EDUCATIONAL LEVEL	DRAFTEES		FIRST-TERM REGULARS		CAREER REGULARS	
	%	N	%	N	%	N
Less than high school	41.2	(1,306)	34.9	(2,163)	24.1	(530)
High school graduate	29.1	(1,943)	22.8	(4,588)	23.6	(2,598)
Some college	15.5	(1,064)	15.5	(1,597)	12.7	(715)
Total	28.0	(4,313)	24.5	(8,348)	21.2	(3,843)

Source: 1964 NORC survey, reproduced in Charles Moskos, *The American Enlisted Man* (New York, 1970), p. 203.

SOURCE 58

**Estimated Military Participation Rates, by Education
and Whether Qualified for Service (Men 26 Years Old, 1964)**

CATEGORY	TOTAL	LESS THAN HIGH SCHOOL	HIGH SCHOOL GRADUATE	SOME COLLEGE	COLLEGE GRADUATE
Per cent of total population	51.6	49.9	57.2	59.5	40.3
Per cent of qualified population[a]	74.2	85.5	76.0	74.3	50.0

Source: Walter Y. Oi, in Sol Tax, ed., *The Draft* (Chicago, 1968), p. 225.
[a]Presumed able to pass military mental and physical entrance examinations.

SOURCE 59

Mode of Entry for Those 26–34 in 1964 Who Had Served

CATEGORY	TOTAL	LESS THAN HIGH SCHOOL	HIGH SCHOOL GRADUATE	SOME GRADUATE	COLLEGE
Enlistment	50.3	61.0	53.8	43.2	8.7
Induction	34.1	32.8	35.7	39.8	24.8
Officer programs	5.5	0.0	0.2	3.7	48.9
Reserves	9.4	5.4	9.8	13.0	17.3

Source: H. Wool, *The Military Specialist* (Baltimore, Md.: Johns Hopkins University Press, 1967), p. 106.

SOURCE 60

A 1968 (September–October) national election survey asked respondents whether they or any of their immediate relatives had been in the armed services and stationed in Vietnam over the previous five or six years. There was a substantial association between education, income, and Vietnam experience:

	PROPORTION WITH SELF OR RELATIVE IN			
	VIETNAM (%)	ARMED SERVICES (%)	RATIO	N
Education				
10th grade or less	14.0	24.7	0.57	(393)
11th grade	12.9	25.8	0.50	(248)
12th grade	12.1	30.9	0.39	(528)
At least some college	7.3	27.1	0.27	(439)
Family income				
$4,000 or less	13.5	27.5	0.49	(415)
$4,000 to $7,000	12.9	26.7	0.48	(363)
$7,000 to $12,000	10.9	31.7	0.34	(524)
$12,000 and over	8.8	26.3	0.33	(319)

Source: M. Useem, *Conscription, Protest, and Social Conflict* (New York: John Wiley and Sons, Inc., 1973), p. 141.

SOURCE 61

Recruiting Brochures, ca. 1974

Explore the Pacific Northwest.
Work with the 9th Infantry Division at Fort Lewis, Washington.

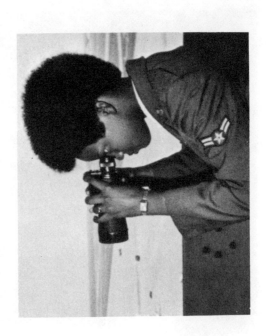

Professions

Girls have jobs . . . women have professions. It's what **you** are that makes the difference. If you've lifted your eyes past the end of your nose and set your sights on a distant horizon, then the United States Air Force is the world for you.

And under our guaranteed enlistment program, your profession isn't determined by chance . . . it's based on your **choice.** The Air Force offers some specialties from which to select **before** you enlist. If you qualify and are select-

ed, it's yours. Simple! Clean! No hassle!

If you already have a skill that the Air Force can use, you might be able to enter into your Air Force specialty, immediately after basic training with a higher skill level. If not, the Air Force will train you.

Either way, the Air Force will assign you where the need is greatest . . . but as a trained specialist, you'll usually get the position you want, regardless of where you're stationed.

2

Training

In 1975 "Leadertown" residents who had served as enlisted men in the 1940s, 1950s or 1960s were asked to assess the effect of military regimentation on their ways of living. Several doubted that they had been affected at all:

1. A Vietnam war-era veteran:
"No, I wasn't changed at all, I was what I was when I was in because I had to be, but I was never a regimented person. There is a place for everything, and everything has its place, but my place is where I put it. I am the way I have always been, but in the army you had to be neat and tidy, so I played their game because it was the only way to get along. If you don't play their game, you end up in jail. These are the rules, there's a right way, and a wrong way, and there's 'my' way, and your going to play it 'my' way."

2. A World War II-era veteran:
"I don't think that the army made a man out of me; for me basic training was fun because I was a sports nut; it was fun for me; I enjoyed it. I never had a dad; I learned to accept responsibility as a youngster, and as far as making a man out of me, I always felt that I was a man when I went in the service."

3. A Korean War-era veteran:
"No, if anything I think it was the opposite reaction, I think I am a less regimented person. The regimentation I did not like at all, and so rather than having the experience of having it rub off on me, I didn't like it; therefore I tended to reject even the slightest hint of regimentation even more so than I did when I was in the army."

Source: Interviews conducted by Thomas Conley in "Leadertown," a working-class section of Pittsburgh, 1975.

But a World War II-era veteran offered a different view:
"I always like to be clean; when I wear a pair of shoes they are always shined. When I go down street to buy a paper, I have to wear a suit all the time, or a sport coat, always wore a tie. Before I went into the service it was different, sloppy, I didn't care how I looked. The army taught you how to dress properly and how to conduct yourself."

SOURCE 63

> *Marine recruit Richard Marks wrote home about boot camp, 1964:*

To Mrs. Gloria Marks,
November 14, 1964

DEAR MOM AND SUE,

Tonight is my second night at Parris Island, and I can honestly say that the Marine Corp. has grounds for calling itself the "best". The training they give, physically and mentally, is by far the hardest imaginable.

Even in these past 24 hours, I have felt more than once that I would like to quit, but then I remember it is only 14 months, and then I have a chance for education.

. . .

Things are hard here, but I think I can make it—I want to. . . .

November 19

For the past three or four days now we have been in the midst of training, and during this time we really grow to love the corp. As we march one of the things we sound off is "I don't want a teenage queen, all I want is an M 14".

While we have been here we have all gained self confidence, because we are all Marines.

At first having a Drill Instructor bark at you was a thing to fear, now a day doesn't seem complete without it.

Source: Gloria M. Kramer, ed., *The Letters of PFC Richard Marks (USMC),* (Philadelphia, 1967), pp. 1-57. Compare John Faris, "The Impact of Basic Training," *Armed Forces and Society* 2 (1975): 115-27.

By the time I see you two again I will have a deep manly voice, and a beautiful tan—not to mention the PFC stripes I am in competition for, or the expert Rifleman's medal. I may not be the best Marine Recruit on Parris Iland, but I will at least be one of the few who tries with all his heart, and one of the few who, [General] "Chesty" Puller willing, makes it off the Island.

                                              . . .

November 20

Also as the day go by we become more, and more proud of ourselves, and the Corp. we serve in. We are no longer boys, and we can no longer be expected to be treated like boys. We are now all Marines. We have one boy here who is 16, but he lied to get in. He is treated the same, and expected to do the same as the ones who are 20 & 21.

All I know is, the more I see of this Marine Corp. the more I like. It takes care of its own. The Marine Corp. is nothing more than a big fraturnety.

Being here is quite an experience—everything here is spoken in terms of how it will be used in combat. It was explained to us that the Marine Corp. has no peace time mission, and that we joined to train to be "Top Notch" the best in the world fighting men.

But it also gives us self confidence, and a feeling of strength inside—we all leave here leaders—better than ever before.

My voice has also changed a little—it has gotten deeper—from all the screaming, and growling we do.

No matter how the Marine Corp. works out for me, I will never regret the time I spent in boot camp. It is only hard for the guys who feel they are too good for it.

                                              . . .

November 22

There are a lot of nice guys here with me, and although we have little time to bull shit, but the chance I do have we get to know each other. We talk about why we enlisted, and what we want. Going through common misery makes us all feel a lot closer.

                                              . . .

5 January 1965

Some of us were talking about home today, and how it will be hard to ajust to it. We figure we will be up at about 5 each morning, run around the block a few times, have breakfast, and at about that time we will ask ourselves what the hell are we doing, and go back to bed. In all honesty though it will be strange to get up after the sun, and not have to jump out of bed at attention and sound off.

My senior drill instructor finally realized I was Jewish and as a result he now calls me "Abey". It is basically all in fun, but if he thought it bothered me he would really ride me. They try to break you in boot camp. We are exposed to all types of physical, and mental challenges. They ride us, as an enemy interrogater might. They try to find out if we are strong enough to be Marines—here in Boot Camp, and in training—where it doesn't matter. Rather here than in combat where someone may be counting on you.

From my letters you might get the idea I am Gung-Ho, well I am. Being down here for three months really has an affect on you.

. . .

22 January 1965

Today we went over to the big Parade Deck, and march to the band music— we were in a Parade. It was the first time we have ever marched to music, and in public—the thrill was just sensational—it is hard to describe. All the civilians were looking at us, and we were Marines.

. . .

29 Jan 1965

As we all sit around here and talk we realize how much we miss our DIs, and Parris Island. The morning we left our DI's, and the Island was a real sad one. Sgt. Wells—the real little Drill Instructor, was in tears at one point—Cpl. Loupin didn't even show up. It was quite a sad day for all of us. . . .

SOURCE 64

> *James Sterba of the* New York Times *interviewed army volunteers in boot camp, 1975:*

"They called me Pillsbury back home because I was so fat," said Ray Moreno, 17, from Clovis, Calif., who had just dropped 25 pounds in basic training. "I was wasted. I mean, at home, we were just screwing around every night getting wiped out. It was boring really. So I enlisted and now I feel good. I feel like something, like I'm part of something."

"I couldn't find a job and the recruiter told me I'd get a bonus and get in shape," said Edward McFarren, 17 year-old from Pittsburgh. "I feel a lot better. It even feels good to have short hair."

Source: New York Times Magazine, June 15, 1975, pp. 46 ff.

SOURCE 65

Attitudinal change (or lack of it) among infantry trainees during World War II:

Proportions in a Panel of 420 Infantry Recruits with Favorable Attitudes When First Surveyed Early in Training and When Resurveyed Four Months Later

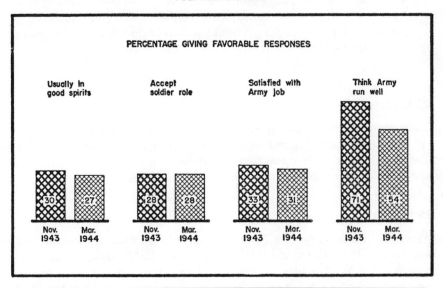

Source: S. Stouffer et al., *Studies in Social Psychology in World War II,* 4 vols. (Princeton, N.J.: Princeton University Press, 1949-50), I, p. 207.

SOURCE 66

A veteran of World War II told an interviewer why he would not work in a factory:

"I've taken orders long enough," one ex-navy radioman said. "I don't want to go back to the goddamned factory. When you've been in the navy, you don't want to go back under those bosses—you feel that way. You want to be more or less on your own, without some foreman giving you orders, telling you what to do all the time. I'd kind of like to get into some electrical work, or radio, or something along that line. I was a radio operator for about two and a half, maybe three, years. Did a little repair work on them, monkeyed around with them. I'd like to take a course in that and then open a radio shop of my own. . . .

Source: Robert Havighurst, *The American Veteran Back Home* (New York, 1951), pp. 108-9.

SOURCE 67

> *A Pennsylvania volunteer, William P. Tomlinson, complained
> to a friend in 1848 of the brutality of the regiment's officers,
> and of the soldiers' sentiments:*

I wish a man of good standing would inform them men at Washington of
the brutality of these officers now in Mexico, but there is no use of a soldier writing to them as no notice would be taken of it, but these are facts
if they do come from a soldier. They have never had any hold of me yet
and I have no reason to lie about it but I have a heart and feeling for my
brother Americans who came out here under arms in defence of their
country and in a foreign country not congenial to our health. But the time
may come and that soon when officers and men will stand on equal foot-
ing. The men seem to form an opinion that some of the officers will soon
depart from this world. . . . A soldiers life is very disgusting. . . .

Source: Tomlinson file, Western Americana Manuscripts, Beinecke Rare Book Library,
Yale University; quoted in Smith and Judah, eds., *Chronicles* . . . (Albuquerque, N.M., 1972),
p. 424, and verified at the Beinecke by the present author.

SOURCE 67a

> *In 1804 Seaman Robert Quinn (or Gwinn) sent an understandably
> pseudonymous letter to his commanding officer, Captain Samuel
> Barron, complaining of conditions and alluding, ominously, to
> the recent mutiny on H.M.S. Hermione:*

The horrid usage that has been carried on in this Ship of late by the principal
officers is enough to turn every Mans Heart to wickedness. We are Kept
on Deck from 3 O'Clock in the morning till 8 at Night. . . . We have been
on deck for several days without one bit of Victuals, and durst not look
for it. We cannot wash a single article for fear of being cut in two. . . . But
the time will come, when you will drive all thoughts of fear out of our
minds. Tyranny is the begining of all mischief. . . . Any Commander or
Captain that had the least feeling or thought, would not suffer this horrid
usage. It is almost impossible for us to live. The *President* is arrived to
such a pitch as to exceed the *Hermione*. . . . [signed] Unhappy Slaves.
[Quinn's authorship of the letter was discovered, and he was branded on
the forehead with the word "Mutinus" and given 320 lashes.]

Source: U.S. Office of Naval Records and Library, *Naval Documents Relating to the U.S.
Wars with the Barbary Powers* (Washington, 1739-1945), 4:203, 219, 227; cited in Christopher
McKee, "Fantasies of Mutiny and Murder: A Suggested Psycho-History of the Seaman in the
U.S. Navy, 1798-1815," *Armed Forces and Society* (forthcoming, Winter 1978).

SOURCE 68

> *Former Tech. Sgt. Willie Lawton recalled the means that some of his comrades used in 1945 to signal their extreme displeasure with their battalion commander:*

"We had an incident in the Philippines that just missed being a bloody war; the 93rd vs. the Dixie Division. This white outfit was there when we arrived. I do not remember the name of the place but it was in the vicinity of the Dole Pineapple Company. Our men had been overseas nineteen months without seeing any women to speak of so when the guys hit the Philippines they went hog wild. The Dixie Division couldn't stand the Filipino girls going for the Negro soldiers. After several days there were small battles. The ultimate finally arrived; the Dixie Division was lined upon one side of the road for about two miles or more and the 93rd was lined up opposite them. Both sides had fixed bayonets, their guns were on-load and unlock. It took the colonels of every battalion from both divisions to get their men and bring the situation under control. They were real busy riding or running up and down that road to keep down outright war.

"The next morning the colonel of my battalion called a meeting of all of the officers and NCOs. He marched us to a field and instead of talking some kind of sense we were severely reprimanded, so we knew where we stood. The thing we kept thinking about was those Dixie boys wouldn't have been caught dead with the Filipino girls back home. Anyway, we were told that anyone would be busted in rank should he become involved with the girls of the country. Neither the officers nor the NCOs liked this directive, and instead of telling the enlisted what we were supposed to we told them exactly what had been said.

"The colonel, being the colonel, was the only person who had a generator to furnish light in his tent at night. That night several men cut loose with their .30 caliber rifles on that light and the upper part of his tent. Man, he came crawling out of that tent screaming bloody murder. The whole thing was settled without another word; he had gotten the message and there was no problem about our mixing with the women who came into our area."

. . .

SOURCE 69

> *A psychologist correlated IQ test scores of soldiers in non-*

commissioned-officer-training programs with their ability to pass such training in 1918:

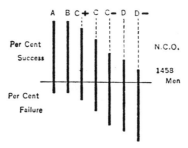

SOURCE 70

Those scoring higher than others on the Army General Classification Test in 1945 tended to have more success in paratroop training:

Relationship Between AGCT Scores and Failures in Paratroop Training

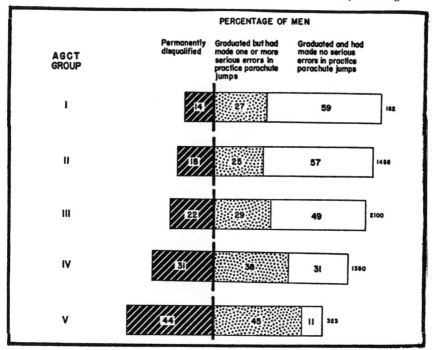

(Based on a Study of Background Characteristics of 539 Recruits in Paratrooper Training, March-June 1945) (Numbers Following Bars = the Numbers of Cases on Which Percentages Are Based)

Source: S. Stouffer et al., Studies in Social Psychology in World War II, 4 vols. (Princeton, N.J.: Princeton University Press, 1949-50), II, p. 218.

SOURCE 71

*Attitudinal scores of students entering Officer Candidate School,
1969, were sorted to compare those who had graduated with
those who had dropped out:*

Differentiation by Selection

GROUP OF 833 ENTERING STUDENTS WHO LATER GRADUATE ARE HIGHER ON THESE SCALES		GROUP OF 328 ENTERING STUDENTS WHO LATER VOLUNTARILY DEPART TRAINING ARE HIGHER ON THESE SCALES	
SCALES	T-TEST RESULTS	SCALES	T-TEST RESULTS
Degree of self-confidence	8.34	Move away from aggressor	−3.07
Prefers supervisory activities	6.43	Values social service	−2.51
Extent of optimism	5.73	Values approval from others	−2.36
Influences by persuasive leadership	5.67	Prefers delegative leadership style	−2.23
Values intellectual achievement	5.19		
Prefers social interaction	4.23		
Values status attainment	4.07		
Prefers activity frequent change	4.05		
Extent of orderliness	3.97		
Degree of perseverance	3.94		
Influences by being self-assertive	3.66		

SOURCE 72

*Bell Irwin Wiley, the historian of the "common soldier" of the
Civil War, described the distress some aristocratic Southerners
felt upon finding themselves subordinate to "vulgarians":*

Sensitiveness to class seems to have been voiced more frequently by the rich than by the poor. George Cary Eggleston recalled an instance in a Virginia company where a young private of superior social standing forced a public apology from a lieutenant of ordinary background who had dared to put him on double duty for missing roll call. A Georgian refused in 1861 to obey an order on the ground that the officer issuing the command was no gentleman. Corporal John Hutchins on being called to task for a minor infraction said to his superior, "God damn you, I own niggers up the country," and when private John Shanks was ordered from the drill field to the guardhouse for inebriation he blurted out to his captain, "I will not do it. I was a gentleman before I joined your damned company and by God you want to make a damned slave of me."

The aversion of aristocratic privates to plebeian officers sometimes extended to men of high rank. A case in point is that of a young Mississippi gentleman whom the fortunes of war in 1864 placed under the authority of Nathan B. Forrest. The chagrined grandee [one Henry St. John Dixon] wrote in his diary:

"The dog's dead: finally we are under N. Bedford Forrest . . . [a circumstance that] I have dreaded since the death of the noble Van Dorn. . . . 'The Wizzard' now commands us . . . and I must express my distaste to being commanded by a man having no pretension to gentility—a negro trader, gambler,—an ambitious man, careless of the lives of his men so long as preferment be en prospectu. Forrest may be & no doubt is, the best Cav officer in the West, but I object to a tyrannical, hotheaded vulgarian's commanding me. . . ."

Occasionally there was a snob, such as a youngster from Natchez [Theodore Mandeville] who refused to join one company because it was composed of commoners, and who, when he finally joined another, looked down his nose at most of his associates. "We are two distinct parties," he said on one occasion, "the Aristocrats and the democrats," and he professed nothing but disdain for the latter. He took offense at his colonel for "putting on airs," ceased saluting him, and swore to call him to task after the war for failure to proffer the recognition due one of his high social standing. His attitude was identical with that of another snob [Henry St. John Dixon] who wrote:

"It is galling for a gentleman to be absolutely and entirely subject to the orders of men who in private life were so far his inferiors, & who when they met him felt rather like taking off their hats to him than giving him law & gospel."

Source: Bell Irwin Wiley, The Life of Johnny Reb (New York, 1943), pp. 337, 338, 344.

SOURCE 73

Social scientists interviewing GIs during World War II found tensions between drafted privates and educated men, on the one hand, regular army "noncoms" and less educated men, on the other:

Draftees

. . . the privates can see what the generals won't admit or do anything about. It doesn't do any good to be bossed by men inferior in every way except length of service. There is a way of limiting this as applied to noncoms. Tests for ratings might show up a lot of our present noncoms. In our company when some training tests were given the noncoms got lower than *any* of the privates. But they are still noncoms and the privates are still privates. Men don't do their best when they know that they won't be promoted for being better than the men over them.

The noncommissioned officers are not efficient enough to operate in war. There are so many who have received stripes and don't know what the score is. Anybody can be an NCO. Under the present Army, no tests are given, you are just told that you have been made corporal, sergeant, or what have you, and that is all.

This new era in the Army brought about by the Selective Service Act should be dealt with accordingly. My First Sergeant knows the NCO's are not too intelligent—he admits this. He also admits that (selectees) are, by far, more intelligent than the Army's regular NCO's. But he says there is nothing can be done about this. My advice is to run an IQ test and let the men who have the most knowledge be the bosses.

Regulars

My own pet gripe is that Selective Service men are treated much better than *we soldiers* [the italics were the writer's own]. They grunt and gripe too much.

I think discipline was relaxed on Selective Service men, from what it was formerly on Regular Army men. Selectees have been allowed to wise off too much. Many of them are too smart for their own good.

Source: S. Stouffer et al., *Studies in Social Psychology in World War II*, 4 vols. (Princeton, N.J.: Princeton University Press, 1949-50), I, pp. 67-68, 75.

The Army is nothing like it use to be say even five years ago. The men are too use to doing their on way. So it is hard to change. Sense the number men [selectees] has to be here the regulars men get put on K.P. over the week-end so the numbers boys can go home. I don't like that cause I was one of the boys that got put on K.P. during Easter. I think I am as good as any man. Number men and regulars should be treated the same way. I mean what is good for the goose is good for the gander.

The social scientists' comment

The frustration felt in not climbing the status ladder faster was, as might be expected, much greater among the selectees—especially the better educated—than among the regulars.

In response to the question, "Is the Army giving you a good chance to show what you can do?" 52 per cent of the regular privates as compared with 30 per cent of the selectee privates responded "Very good" or "Fairly good," while among selectee privates the proportions making these responses, by education were:

College men	14%
H.S. graduates	21
Others	34

The same patterns are found in responses to other questions about job assignment.

SOURCE 74

World War II trainees were shown instructional films designed to impart opinions, information, or attitudinal change. Some trainees regarded the films to be manipulative in nature; others were more positive and saw the films as merely informational. In either case, those with more education were more affected by the films ("learned" more from them) than were those with little or no education:

Source: S. Stouffer et al., *Studies in Social Psychology in World War II*, 4 vols. (Princeton, N.J.: Princeton University Press, 1949-50), II, p. 300.

Mean Effects on Five Opinion Items Broken Down By Educational Status

	"MANIPULATIVE" SUBGROUP (N = 103)	"AMBIGUOUS" SUBGROUP (N = 147)	"INFORMATIONAL" SUBGROUP (N = 121)
Low education men (grade school, some high school)			
Final level (% after)	50.1%	65.8%	64.0%
Initial level (% before)	45.3	53.1	49.0
(% after minus % before)	4.8	12.7	15.0
Effectiveness index	11%	24%	29%
High education men (high school graduate, college)			
Final level (% after)	63.8%	75.0%	73.6%
Initial level (% before)	48.9	55.2	52.9
(% after minus % before)	14.9	19.8	20.7
Effectiveness index	34%	32%	44%

SOURCE 75

World War II GIs who were assigned to jobs of their choice were more satisfied with their duties than were those who were not assigned to jobs of their choice:

Source: S. Stouffer et al., *Studies in Social Psychology in World War II,* 4 vols. (Princeton, N.J.: Princeton University Press, 1949-50), II, p. 300.

Job Satisfaction as Related to Chance to Choose Job Assignment
(Numbers Following the Bars = Numbers of Cases on Which
Percentages Are Based)
(Troops in the United States)

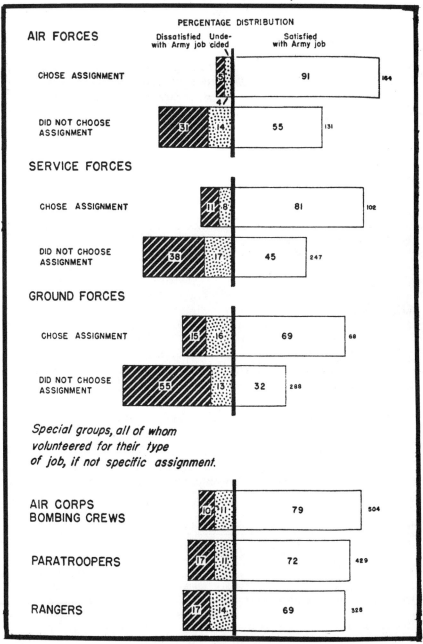

SOURCE 76

Vietnam veterans who were members of the Veterans of Foreign Wars (VFW) (Group I), members of drug addict programs (Group II), or members of the Vietnam Veterans Against the War (VVAW) (Group III) were asked a similar question by a sociologist:

Satisfaction with Job Asignment, by Group

QUESTION: DID YOU GET THE OPPORTUNITY (IF ENLISTED—AS PROMISED) TO SELECT AND TRAIN FOR THE SPECIALIZATION YOU WANTED?

GROUP	YES %	(N)	NO %	(N)	NO PREFERENCE %	(N)	(N)
I	57	(17)	13	(4)	30	(9)	(30)
II	7	(2)	93	(28)			(30)
III	50	(15)	50	(15)			(30)
N		(34)		(47)		(9)	(90)

Source: John Helmer, *Bringing the War Home* (New York, 1973), p. 149. Reprinted with permission of Macmillan Publishing Co., Inc., copyright © 1974 by John Helmer.

SOURCE 77

Most of those who later joined the VFW (Group I) went through training with hometown friends; most of those who later joined the VVAW (Group III) or who were drug addicts after the war (Group II) did not:

Maintenance of Primary Group Affiliation in Basic Training, by Group

QUESTION: IN YOUR TRAINING UNIT HOW MANY PEOPLE DID YOU ALREADY KNOW?

GROUP	SOME %	(N)	NONE %	(N)
I	80	(24)	20	(6)
II	27	(8)	73	(22)
III	20	(6)	80	(24)
N		(38)		(52)

Source: John Helmer, *Bringing the War Home* (New York, 1973), p. 145.

SOURCE 78

A marine advanced infantry trainee commented on the splitting up of his training unit, 1966:

I just came back from chow, and it was something to see—everyone asking where the other was going. This separating the company is a hard blow to take. It is like losing your brothers—we have all been together for such a long time, and now on the eve of a big operation we all get split up.

Source: *Letters of PFC Richard Marks,* ed. Gloria M. Kramer (Philadelphia, 1967), p. 174.

SOURCE 79

Former Sgt. Lester Simons had been raised in Ann Arbor, Michigan, had attended an integrated high school, and had participated in numerous integrated athletic events in the year prior to his induction. His unit was sent to Arkansas for training in 1942:

"On maneuvers we were in a wooded area. We had rifles but no ammunition, not even bayonets. Our officers had their 45s, and that was all the protection we had in an area that was getting more hostile every minute. It was decided that we would move about twenty miles down the road. As we marched along counting cadence, to our new destination, a group of mounted farmers came out of nowhere, or so it seemed. Their spokesman told our lieutenant to 'Get those god-damned niggers off of the white highway and march 'em in the ditch.' The ditch he spoke of had several inches of water in it; water mocassins' playground. Our lieutenant objected and told them if they weren't careful the area would be placed under martial law (which should have been done in the beginning). The rednecks rode him down with their horses, then pistol-whipped him—one of their own color! The lieutenant was later given a medical discharge because of this beating; they damned near killed him.

"While this was happening a truckload of white MPs, who were armed, sat in their truck and offered no assistance to this white officer. More horse-riding dirt farmers were coming; we could see them in the distance burning our one truck with our supplies. A company was on a parallel

Source: Reprinted from *The Invisible Soldier: The Experience of the Black Soldier in World War II,* copyright © 1975 by Mary P. Motley, ed., by permission of the Wayne State University Press. Excerpt is from p. 46.

road about five miles over and they too were set upon by these male witches on their broomsticks.

"About thirty to forty of our guys took the packs off their backs and were gone. When I heard about this I turned my platoon over to the next sergeant and told him I was heading back to Fort Custer. He said he was going back north also. It ended up with four sergeants, two corporals, and a private leaving for God's country. . . ."

SOURCE 80

J.G.S. came from a background similar to that of Sergeant Simons, and, like Simons, experienced racism while in the service during World War II. He developed psychoneurotic disorders, was hospitalized, and was eventually discharged. Army psychiatrists recorded his case history and noted his successful recovery upon his return to a less discriminatory and racist atmosphere:

J.G.S. was born and raised in a small Northeastern town. A member of one of the few Negro families in that area, he experienced little discrimination and was generally accepted as an equal by his schoolmates. He completed junior college at the age of twenty with a very good scholastic record and thereafter held jobs as a public stenographer and chief clerk with the draft board. Just before his twenty-second birthday, he enlisted in the Army. Until then he had had only very limited contact with the manifestations of prejudice against his race. He had deliberately sought out an environment in which he could expect to find people, both Negro and white, who would not feel that he should act differently just because he was a member of a minority group. In this way, he was able largely to avoid discrimination and devloped cultural values much closer to those of the white middle class than to those of his fellow Negroes in the South.

In the Army, however, J.G.S. found himself treated differently from other soldiers because he was a Negro. He had no choice as to where or with whom he worked. He was constantly and directly exposed to a set of values which differed radically from his own and to the manifestation of these values in discrimination, segregation, and rigidly prescribed patterns of behavior. He received his basic training in the South; later he was sent to clerical school and then assigned as a clerk, specializing in courts-martial, to an anti-aircraft artillery group.

Intelligent and relatively well educated, he was promoted rapidly and

Source: Eli Ginzberg et al. (eds.): *The Ineffective Soldier: Vol. II: Breakdown and Recovery* (New York: Columbia University Press, 1959), 105–8.

became a technician fourth grade in less than a year. Nevertheless, he was in constant conflict with many of his officers, especially those from the South. He resented any system which assigned Negroes to segregated units and on many occasions found himself in serious disagreement with his fellow Negro officers and enlisted men who accepted a second-class status. As a court stenographer he saw or heard about many instances of discrimination, which affected him in a very personal manner. Furthermore, as an educated Northern Negro he was considered by many of his white officers a troublemaker. Several times he was threatened with court-martial for treason. He was forbidden to give books to other soldiers and just before going overseas his commander denied him a pass to go to his home which was nearby; instead he received a two-hour lecture designed to make him give up his "liberal" values and accept his status as a Negro.

Early in his Army career the soldier began to develop psychiatric symptoms. During basic training he went on sick call several times with nausea, headaches, tenseness, and stuttering. While in clerical school he consulted a psychiatrist, but was not hospitalized. The symptoms continued after he joined the anti-aircraft group and became quite severe after his outfit left its former location in the Deep South and went overseas to North Africa. At times his stuttering was so incapacitating that he was unable to speak at all.

The morale of the outfit was poor primarily because of the discord between the white officers and Negro enlisted men. In May 1944, however, after about a year of overseas duty, the organization was disbanded because of reduced need for anti-aircraft protection, and J.G.S. was placed in charge of a quartermaster laundry receiving office. For two months until the replacement depot closed he supervised both white and Negro enlisted men. There was no difficulty and his headaches, nausea, and stuttering improved considerably. He was next sent to Italy and spent another two months working on courts-martial before being assigned to clerical duty with an Infantry division. Although he saw only intermittent combat, his symptoms now became quite severe. Again he was involved in a good deal of strife with white officers. Morale among the Negro troops was low and many resented being led by officers who seemed to hate them as much as the enemy. In addition there was frequent strife between Negro and white soldiers in rear areas. All this had a marked effect on J.G.S. and he spent almost a month at one time in the hospital because of his stuttering. Nevertheless, he was able to return to duty and served until returned to the States in the spring of 1945 after more than two years overseas.

Back in this country and on furlough, he became extremely disturbed over any evidence of discrimination, especially against Negro soldiers, who he felt deserved better. At that time he decided that he would never marry because he did not want a child of his exposed to the discrimination that he had experienced. On returning to camp he was hospitalized with a severe speech impediment and consant headaches. Several months later he was discharged.

Shortly after leaving service the veteran began receiving treatment for his speech disorder through the Veterans Administration while working as a government clerk in the Northeast. Free once again to avoid people who might be prejudiced against him because of his race, he gradually improved. By late 1947 when the treatment was terminated, he was making a good adjustment. He had married and had one child; he was happy in his home life. He had started taking courses with a view to obtaining a degree in business administration. By 1950 he was well on the way to accomplishing his educational objectives, although the necessity of holding a full-time job to support his family left him little time for studies.

3

The Tour of Duty and Combat

SOURCE 81

> *Private E. J. Ellis of the Louisiana infantry told his mother of what he had learned in the army, June 1862:*

"This war has done me good in many ways—It has taught me patence and endurance & 'to labor & wait'. . . . it has learned me to be less particular in a great many things—when I see dirt in my victuals, I take it out and eat on—If I taste it, I swallow & eat on. . . . If my bed is hard & my head not high enough. I content myself with the idea that it might be worse & go to sleep. . . . I think I have seen the dark side of soldiering and although it is tolerably hard, yet there aint any use of calling it intolerable."

Source: Bell Irwin Wiley, *The Life of Johnny Reb* (New York, 1943), 130.

SOURCE 82

> *Private J. Madison Pierce, writing from camp in 1898 to the editor of the Cleveland Gazette, commented on the unfamiliar tasks the volunteers found themselves, of necessity, performing:*

To-day is wash day in camp. It is an amusing sight to see some of our boys, who have never washed a handkerchief, bent double over tubs. Some of them, more industrious than others, "take in" washing. Very desirable husbands they will make when they return to civil life, won't they?

Source: Willard B. Gatewood, comp., *"Smoked Yankees" and the Struggle for Empire* (Urbana, Ill., 1971), p. iii.

SOURCE 83

> *Lt. Louis Ranlett, who had risen "through the ranks" of the AEF,*
> *chatted with his men about "the curious change of habits made*
> *by a few months of life in the army," 1918:*

Late Sunday afternoon we left Nancy and marched away along the road that follows the Moselle Canal through Maxeville, the home of a widely advertised beer, to Frouard, a small village, scattered like countless others along both sides of a single main street.

The march was a pleasant one, for the road was shaded with large trees, the sun was low, and the pace was easy. I had my first opportunity to become acquainted with some of the men in my platoon. Sergeant Beaudry, I found, came from Uxbridge, Massachusetts; Sergeant Bohon lived nearer home in Cambridge; Corporal Scopolitis had enlisted from Boston. Corporal Cobb conversed with me for some time and we both "reminisced" about the curious change of habits made by a few months of life in the army. I recall particularly that the subject of bathing came up, as it did so frequently in France, and that we both remarked on our different attitudes toward baths at home and abroad. When they were easy to get, they were not in demand; when there was barely enough water to drink, every one clamored for a swim.

Source: Louis Ranlett, *Let's Go!* (Boston, 1927), pp. 150-51.

SOURCE 84

> *Private Jim — — — wrote home "after the first day in Vietnam,"*
> *1967:*

HOME,

After the first day in Vietnam, I can honestly say this beats a gas oven for heat. It got so hot, I had trouble believing it. It was so stifling that any movement just lowered the floodgate of sweat, and you found yourself as wet as it you had walked in a shower.

To resupply this water you'll drink four or five quarter-sized canteens a day, or so we did the first day.

...

There is nothing to worry about. All in all, I am enjoying what I am doing. There is the excitement, the companionship of friends, and the atmosphere

Source: Glenn Munson, ed., *Letters from Vietnam* (New York, 1966), pp. 12–13.

of a unit in the field. Don't feel undue distress. I laugh and joke too much each day to feel right in being the recipient of a lot of anxious moments. You raised a hard-nosed soldier, so don't worry about him.

Give my regards to everyone.

Son,

Jim

SOURCE 85

Harry Watkins recalled that army life in the 1840s had led him to drink "to keep [his comrades] company":

I never acquired the use of tobacco in any shape, but I was in danger of becoming a devotee at the shrine of Bacchus. To drink seemed *so manly.* All my companions drank and I drank to keep them company. The dangers and difficulties which the old soldiers risked to satisfy their insane craving for strong liquor is well-nigh incredible. Smuggling liquor into camp is termed "Running the Mail." Among the "Mail runners," I held chief position. It was *sport* to me. How often have I scaled the walls of old Fort Snelling and, in company with one or two others, travelled through deep snow to an old log hut on the left bank of the river five miles above the fort. No weather, cold or stormy, could keep back our Mail once we had resolved to run it through. The hut where we procured the liquor was kept by a Canadian Frenchman who realized a fortune from his traffic with the soldiers and Indians. The stuff he sold was the most villainous "fire-water" that man ever had the courage to swallow, a compound of turpentine and alcohol requiring a copper lined throat and a stomach of gutta percha. For this deadly compound, which couldn't have cost more than ten cents, the villain charged from three to five dollars a gallon. To obtain it the soldiers would overdraw their Government allowance of clothing and sell it for anything they could get. The punishment for those caught "Running the Mail" would have done credit to the Inquisition. One form was condemning a man to carry ten six-pound balls packed in his knapsack and strapped upon his back, *for fifteen days and nights every alternate two hours.*

Source: Francis Prucha, *Broadax and Bayonet* (Madison, Wis., 1953), p. 48.

SOURCE 86

Carleton McCarthy, a genteel veteran of Confederate army service, rhapsodised about the beneficent effects of the tour of duty upon "a pure and noble boy":

Source: Carleton McCarthy, *Soldier Life in the Army of Northern Virginia* (Richmond, 1882), compiled by Philip Van Doren Stern in *Soldier Life in the Confederate Army*, pp. 377-83.

Let us consider the effect of camp life upon a pure and noble boy; and to make the picture complete, let us go to his home and witness the parting. The boy is clothed as a soldier. His pockets and his haversack are stored with little conveniences made by the loving hands of mother, sister, and sweetheart, and the sad yet proud hour has arrived. Sisters, smiling through their tears, filled with commingled pride and sorrow, kiss and embrace their great hero. The mother, with calm heroism suppressing her tender maternal grief, impresses upon his lips a fervent, never-to-be-forgotten kiss, presses him to her heart, and resigns him to God, his country, and his honor. The father, last to part, presses his hand, gazes with ineffable love into his bright eyes, and, fearing to trust his feelings for a more lengthy farewell, says, "Good-by, my boy; God bless you; be a man!"

Let those scoff who will; but let them know that such a parting is itself a new and wonderful power, a soul-enlarging, purifying, and elevating power, worth the danger, toil, and suffering of the soldier. The sisters' tears, the father's words, the mother's kiss, planted in the memory of that boy, will surely bring forth fruit beautiful as a mother's love.

As he journeys to the camp, how dear do all at home become! Oh, what holy tears he sheds! His heart, how tender! Then, as he nears the line and sees for the first time the realities of war, the passing sick and weary, and the wounded and bloody dead, his soldier spirit is born; he smiles, his chest expands, his eyes brighten, his heart swells with pride. He hurries on, and soon stands in the magic circle around the glowing fire, the admired and loved pet of a dozen true hearts. Is he happy? Aye! Never before has he felt such glorious, swelling, panting joy. He's a soldier now! He is put on guard. No longer the object of care and solicitude he stands in the solitude of the night, himself a guardian of those who sleep. Courage is his now. He feels he is trusted as a man and is ready at once nobly to perish in the defense of his comrades.

He marches. Dare he murmur or complain? No; the eyes of all are upon him, and endurance grows silently, till pain and weariness are familiar and cheerfully borne. At home he would be pitied and petted; but now he must endure or have the contempt of the strong spirits around him.

He is hungry — so are others; and he must not only bear the privation, but he must divide his pitiful meal, when he gets it, with his comrades; and so generosity strikes down selfishness. In a thousand ways he is tried, and that by sharp critics. His smallest faults are necessarily apparent, for in the varying conditions of the soldier every quality is put to the test. If he shows the least cowardice he is undone. His courage must never fail. He must be manly and independent, or he will be told he's a baby, ridiculed, teased, and despised. When war assumes her serious dress, he sees the helplessness of women and children, he hears their piteous appeals, and chivalry burns him till he does his utmost of sacrifice and effort to protect and comfort and cheer them.

It is a mistake to suppose that the older men in the army encourage vulgarity and obscenity in the young recruit; for even those who themselves indulged in these would frown on the first show of them in a boy and without hesitation put him down mercilessly. No parent could watch a boy as closely as his mess-mates did and could, because they saw him at all hours of the day and night, dependent on himself alone, and were merciless critics who demanded more of their *protégé* than they were willing to submit to themselves.

The young soldier's piety had to perish ignominiously, or else assume a boldness and strength which nothing else could so well impart as the temptations, sneers, and dangers of the Army. Religion had to be bold, practical, and courageous, or die.

In the Army the young man learned to value men for what they were and not on account of education, wealth, or station; and so his attachments, when formed, were sincere and durable, and he learned what constitutes a man and a desirable and reliable friend. The stern demands upon the boy, and the unrelenting criticisms of the mess, soon bring to mind the gentle forbearance, kind remonstrance, and loving counsels of parents and homefolks; and while he thinks, he weeps, and loves, and reverences, and yearns after the things against which he once strove, and under which he chafed and complained. Home, father, mother, sister— oh, how far away; oh, how dear! Himself, how contemptible ever to have felt cold and indifferent to such love! Then, how vividly he recalls the warm pressure of his mother's lips on the forehead of her boy! How he loves his mother! See him as he fills his pipe from the silk-embroidered bag. There is his name embroidered carefully, beautifully, by his sister's hand. Does he forget her? Does he not now love her more sincerely and truly and tenderly than ever? Could he love her quite as much had he never parted; never longed to see her and could not; never been uncertain if she was safe; never felt she might be homeless, helpless, insulted, a refugee from home? Can he ever now look on a little girl and not treat her kindly, gently, and lovingly, remembering his sister? A boy having ordinary natural goodness, and the home supports described, and the constant watching of men, ready to criticise, could but improve. The least exhibition of selfishness, cowardice, vulgarity, dishonesty, or meanness of any kind, brought down the dislike of every man upon him, and persistence in any one disreputable practice, or habitual laziness and worthlessness, resulted in complete ostracism, loneliness, and misery; while, on the other hand, he might by good behavior and genuine generosity and courage secure unbounded love and sincere respect from all.

Visits home, after prolonged absence and danger, open to the young soldier new treasures—new, because, though possessed always, never before felt and realized. The affection once seen only in everyday attention, when he reaches home, breaks out in unrestrained vehemence. The warm embrace of the hitherto dignified father, the ecstatic pleasure beaming in the mother's eye, the proud welcome of the sister, and the wild enthusiasm even of the old black mammy, crowd on him the knowledge of their love and make him braver, and stronger, and nobler. He's a hero from that hour! Death for these, how easy!

The dangers of the battlefield, and the demands upon his energy, strength, and courage, not only strengthen the old, but almost create new, faculties of mind and heart. The death, sudden and terrible, of those dear to him, the imperative necessity of standing to his duty while the wounded cry and groan, and while his heart yearns after them to help them, the terrible thirst, hunger, heat, and weariness — all these teach a boy self-denial, attachment to duty, the value of peace and safety; and instead of hardening him, as some suppose they do, make him pity and love even the enemy of his country, who bleeds and dies for *his* country.

The acquirement of subordination is a useful one, and that the soldier perforce has; and that not in an abject, cringing way, but as realizing the necessity of it, and seeing the result of it in the good order and consequent effectiveness and success of the Army as a whole, but more particularly of his own company and detachment. And if the soldier rises to office, the responsibility of command, attention to detail and minutiae, the critical eyes of his subordinates and the demands of his superiors, all withdraw him from the enticements of vice, and mold him into a solid, substantial character, both capable and willing to meet and overcome difficulties.

The effect of outdoor life on the physical constitution is undoubtedly good, and as the physical improves, the mental is improved; and as the mind is enlightened, the spirit is ennobled. Who can calculate the benefit derived from the contemplation of the beautiful in nature, as the soldier sees? Mountains and valleys, dreary wastes and verdant fields, rivers, sequestered homes, quiet, sleepy villages as they lay in the morning light, doomed to the flames at evening; scenes which alternately stir and calm his mind, and store it with a panorama whose pictures he may pass before him year after year with quiet pleasure. War is horrible, but still it is in a sense a privilege to have lived in time of war. The emotions are never so stirred as then. Imagination takes her highest flights, poetry blazes, song stirs the soul, and every noble attribute is brought into full play.

...

And, strange to say, it was not whose who suffered most and lost most, fought and bled, saw friend after friend fall, wept the dead and buried their hopes — who became bitter and dissatisfied, quarrelsome and fretful, growling and complaining; no, they were the peaceful, submissive, law-abiding, order-loving, of the country, ready to join hands with all good men in every good work, and prove themselves as brave and good in peace as they were stubborn and unconquerable in war.

Many a weak, puny boy was returned to his parents a robust, healthy, *manly man*. Many a timid, helpless boy went home a brave, independent man. Many a wild, reckless boy went home sobered, serious, and trustworthy. And many whose career at home was wicked and blasphemous went home changed in heart, with principles fixed, to comfort and sustain the old age of those who gave them to their country, not expecting to receive them again. Men learned that life was passable and enjoyable without a roof or even a tent to shelter from the storm; that cheerfulness was compatible with cold and hunger; and that a man without money, food, or shelter need not feel utterly hopeless, but might, by employing his wits, find something to eat where he never found it before; and feel that, like a terrapin, he might make himself at home wherever he might be. Men did actually become as independent of the imaginary necessities as the wild beasts. And can a man learn all this and not know better than another how to economize what he has, and how to appreciate the numberless superfluities of life? Is he not made, by the knowledge he has of how little he really needs, more independent and less liable to dishonest exertions to procure a competency?

SOURCE 87

But Bell Irwin Wiley's account of "the life of Billy Yank" included these passages from the letters of men troubled by "the wickedness" that had possessed many of their comrades:

"I will be a perfect Barbarian if I Should Stay hear 3 years," wrote a Vermonter from camp near Burlington in June 1861, while a Minnesotan who marched with Sibley against the Indians in 1863 noted in his diary a short time after the expedition got under way: "I must confess that I have seen but little of the wickedness and depravity of man until I Joined the Army." In similar vein, an Illinois soldier reported from Corinth, Mississippi, after Shiloh: "If there is any place on God's fair earth where wickedness 'stalketh abroad in daylight,' it is in the army. . . . Ninety-nine men out of every hundred are profane swearers . . . hundreds of young men . . . devote all their leisure time to [gambling]."

Countless other Yanks serving in widely scattered commands testified to the prevalency of evil and the degenerating influences of army life.

Source: Bell Irwin Wiley, *The Life of Billy Yank* (New York, 1943), p. 247.

Alfred Davenport, a city-bred Easterner not overly pious or easily shocked, wrote his homefolk from near Baltimore in December 1861 that camp was "a hard school" and that scores in his regiment had been "ruined in morals and in health for they learn everything bad and nothing good." A year later he reported from Fredericksburg: "The more vulgar a man is, the better he is appreciated and as for morals . . .[the army] is a graveyard for them." Still later he observed: "If you think soldiering cures anyone of wild habits it is a great mistake, it is like Sending a Boy in the Navy to learn him good manners. We have Drummer Boys with us that when they came at first could hardly look you in the face for diffidence but now could stare the Devil out of contenance and cant be beat at cursing, swearing and gambling."

In like tone Private Delos W. Lake of the Nineteenth Michigan wrote in 1864 from Middle Tennessee to a brother about to become a soldier: "The army is the worst place in the world to learn bad habits of all kinds. there is several men in this Regt when they enlisted they were nice respectable men and belonged to the Church of God, but now where are they? they are ruined men."

Source 88

> *Charles Bardeen, a young Union fifer, recorded his gambling experiences in his diary in 1863 and commented on them after the war:*

April 17. Pleasant. Played Bluff at night for the first time, winning 65 cts.
April 18. Pleasant. Still win at Bluff.
April 19. Pleasant. Lent Baldwin 2.00 and Lydston $1.00. Inspection of Knapsacks by Gen. Sickles.
April 20. Pleasant. Still win at Bluff.
April 21. Pleasant. Lost at Bluff as I was too green to see that the cards were stacked. I suppose my readers are surprised that I do not omit these references to gambling, but I am telling what did happen, not what ought to have happened. I had in me something of the gambling spirit. I was fond of all games, and of cards with the rest.

. . .

What had been a pastime, indulged in only because I could get no other game going, became a study. I played whenever I could get a chance, for money if we had it, "on pay day" if we hadn't.
Aug. 20. Pleasant. Played Bluff as usual. Came out a little ahead.

Source: C. Bardeen, *A Little Fifer's War Diary* (Syracuse, 1910), pp. 176-79, 262-64, 275;

Aug. 21. Pleasant. Did not play much today. Shower in P. M.

Aug. 22. Pleasant. We were paid off today. I made considerable playing Bluff. $27.00 at Draw Poker.

. . .

Lost 5.00 at Sweat in the morning but won it back again at Bluff. I seem to have uniform good success at Bluff this payday.

Aug. 29. Rainy. Was on Orderly. Sent $5.00 as present to Georgie.

Aug. 30. Pleasant. Had Sunday Inspection.

Lost $10.00 at Bluff & Sweat & set up a board winning more than I lost. Paid $25.00 to Hull for watch.

. . .

Aug. 31. Pleasant. Had Inspection and Mustering in. Started a sweat table and won 19 dollars but lost it in the P. M.

Sept. 1. Pleasant. Won $20.00 at Bluff in A. M. A Full hand, two Flushes. I held the Full. In P. M. won twenty dollars at Sweat. Got a $30.00 Draft.

. . .

Sept. 18. Rainy. Played Bluff all day.

Sept. 19. Rainy. Was on Orderly. Made 12.00 in a half hour in P. M. Sent $40.00 home.

Sept. 20. Pleasant. Played no Bluff today. Sunday Inspection as usual.

Sept. 21. Pleasant. Won about $22.00 counting 29.00 that McRea owes me. Lost 22.00 by careless playing. $10.00 on one hand.

Sept. 22. Pleasant. Played but won little and came out about square.

Nov. 14. Pleasant. Made $25.00 at bluff. Held 4 kings, 4 sixes twice, and 4 fives. In the forenoon a Rain came up at our Parade and it rained very hard all aft.

Nov. 15. Pleasant. The rain cleared off at 9 A. M. Heavy firing ahead and ordered to be ready to move.

Nov. 16. Pleasant. Moving a humbug. Won some at Bluff.

Nov. 17. Pleasant. Drills commenced. Cards as usual.

Nov. 18. Pleasant. Won some at Bluff. Tried at a Raffle but did not win.

Nov. 19. Pleasant. Won pretty well at Bluff. Am fifty dollars ahead.

Nov. 20. Pleasant. Made about eleven dollars at Bluff which I paid for Cady's place (42) at a Raffle. I was tied by Leander and in shaking off got (15) which beat him and the watch was mine. Worth $50.00.

Nov. 21. Rainy. Raffled my watch, won the twenty-five dollars clear. Have over a hundred now.

Nov. 24. Rainy. Lost my night's rest by eating beans before I went to supper last night. Orders to move and after we had got on line and were wet through, they were countermanded. Lost $20. at Bluff.

Nov. 25. Pleasant. Set up a sweat board among the Excelsiors, and after getting about $50. ahead was "cleaned out", having vest torn and losing all my money. Big thing.

Dec. 31.
The year that has passed was passed by me in the Army. I bear witness to its contaminating effects. Many an evil habit has sprung up in me since Jan. 1st 1863. God grant that the year in which we now have entered may not be so.

SOURCE 89

> *Captain Arthur Carpenter, a farmer's son who had enlisted in the Union army in 1861, compared "camp life" with the duties and routine of a recruiting officer, in which capacity he was serving by 1866:*

"I don't like this business much. I would rather be in the Field Bleeding & dying for my Country. . . . Camp life agrees with me better than any other. The free and open air with the coarse but substantial food is the principle [sic] thing for promoting health—I sleep with my windows open, & wash myself all over in cold water every Sunday."

Source: Carpenter to his parents, 1866, quoted in T. Bright, "Yankees in Arms," *Civil War History* 19 (September 1973): 209.

SOURCE 90

> *Private Richard Marks warned his family that he had learned a new vernacular in marine training, January 1965:*

I must warn you that my language has become most foul, and at times things slip out—so please bear with me if I should slip, but after being with all men for 2 months or more straight without the benefit of any comforts, a person tends to turn a little savage, and uncouth. We often talk about going home on leave, and having some of our ill gotten expressions slip out at the wrong place and time—now we laugh, but if I should happen it would be most embarassing.

Source: Letters of Richard Marks, ed. Gloria M. Kramer (Philadelphia, 1967), p. 50.

SOURCE 91

> A French prostitute, interviewed by an investigator from the
> AEF, remarked that "Americans had changed in love-[making]
> from what they were at first, and now make love much like the
> French." "An Officer," writing in the Paris edition of the Chicago
> Tribune in late 1918, remarked:

"Some fellows don't realize that a big disappointment is waiting for them
at home. Girls they thought were wonderful once will turn out to be gold
bricks and camouflage artists socially. . . . If only to be good is the American girl's idea of life, we will let her alone, so that she can be as good as
she pleases. [Discriminating soldiers] will go out with their little French
girls when they want a really interesting evening."

Source: D. Wecter, When Johnny Comes Marching Home (Cambridge, Mass., 1944), pp.
332-33.

SOURCE 92

> Pfc. William Backer of Shenandoah, Virginia, wrote to a friend
> from France in December 1918:

We all went over the top that Knight and do most every Knight when I get
back I will explane what over the top means. We have Bucko Madamozels
over here and I am getting so much French that I cant hardly speak English.
I feel like an old man now. ha. ha.

Source: Fred Baldwin, "The American Enlisted Man in World War I," unpublished Ph.D.
dissertation, Princeton University, 1964, p. 233.

SOURCE 93

> Lt. Jack Wright, a young Harvard graduate who was a pilot in
> the AEF, maintained that his "self-confidence" had:

. . . [grown] with the help of war—the great electrifier, that banishes all
stiff conventionality and stimulates passions, imaginations, free thinking

Source: Wright, A Poet of the Air (Boston, 1918), p. 46; quoted in C. Genthe, American War
Narratives (New York, 1969), pp. 68-69.

and free acting, till the land of war becomes a land of living poems and poets' dreams of anything you want to make—so supple and various does war make a country.

SOURCE 94

Over 1,000 veterans of World War II, Korea, and Vietnam were asked a number of questions by staff of the Opinion Research Corporation in 1969:

Benefits of Military Service

"HERE IS A LIST OF BENEFITS VETERANS SOMETIMES SAY THEY HAVE GAINED FROM MILITARY SERVICE. PLEASE READ THROUGH THE LIST AND PICK AS MANY OR AS FEW STATEMENTS THAT DESCRIBE THE BENEFITS YOU FEEL YOU GAIN FROM YOUR MILITARY SERVICE."

	TOTAL	ARMY VETERANS WW II	KOREA	VIETNAM	VIETNAM VETERANS IN COLLEGE
Intangible Rewards					
Satisfaction of serving my country	79%	82%	78%	64%	62%
Chance to travel and see the world	72	71	76	68	67
Sense of accomplishment	41	40	43	39	49
Character Development					
Developed sense of responsibility	63	61	66	62	57
Discipline	62	63	67	46	47
Self-confidence	56	56	59	53	56
Social Benefits					
Helped me to get along better with people	61	61	62	61	53
Personal lifetime friendships	42	40	41	50	45
Helped me socially	23	22	25	24	15
Civilian Career Benefits					
GI benefits for education	48	41	57	63	92
Became a more effective supervisor	31	30	32	35	41
Helped me to get a job in civilian life	18	18	17	16	12

("None" and "no opinion" responses omitted)

Source: Opinion Research Corp., *The Image of the Army* (Princeton, N.J., 1969), pp. 73, 77.

Effect on a Man's Character

"IN GENERAL, DO YOU THINK SERVICE IN THE ARMED FORCES HAS A GOOD OR BAD
EFFECT ON A MAN'S CHARACTER?"

	TOTAL	ARMY VETERANS			VIETNAM VETERANS IN COLLEGE
		WW II	KOREA	VIETNAM	
Good	79%	80%	80%	72%	65%
Bad	4	4	2	13	10
Other answers	14	13	16	11	20
No opinion	3	3	2	4	5

"WHY DO YOU SAY THAT?"[a]

	TOTAL	ARMY VETERANS			VIETNAM VETERANS IN COLLEGE
		WW II	KOREA	VIETNAM	
Percent who say army service has a *good* effect on a man's character	79%	80%	80%	72%	65%
Maturity	27%	24%	33%	31%	31%
Discipline	22	26	19	10	9
Responsibility/independence	20	19	21	20	15
Learns how to get along with people	18	19	16	12	12
Learns and acquires general experience	7	6	6	10	13
Acquires training, special schooling, and education	4	5	3	1	0
Improves personal well-being, habits	4	5	2	4	2

(Top mentions)

---

[a]Open, free-response question.

SOURCE 95

According to sociologist Robert Havighurst, "Eric" had been known in his Midwestern home town as a lacklustre, insecure youth before entering the Army during World War II. But he had flourished in the service and was a self-confident, successful young man when interviewed in 1949:

"The way I feel about it, there are a couple of good angles for it. I wouldn't take anything for my service life. Probably the most valuable thing I got out of it was learning a great deal from associations with fellows my own age. You see, until I got into the service I had hardly been outside Midwest, and I had very little to do with anybody but just hometown boys. Not that there's anything wrong with the fellows around here, but if you stay in one place all your life, you live within a very restricted sphere. I suppose you'd call that being provincial in the way you look at things. Well, when I was in the service, I found myself living among fellows from all over the country, some from New York City, some from the South, some from way out west. Well, I picked up a lot of ideas from them, not only what the United States was really like—I mean the whole country—but about how to live my own life and to get more out of it. It's pretty hard to explain just what I mean there. You know, you talk with one fellow and he's planning to be a doctor; you talk with another and he's planning to be a carpenter, and somebody else wants to be an aviator. Well, when you talk these things over with them and get their slant on things, it sort of opens up your horizons for you; you start thinking in broader terms than you did before. I came out a lot more ambitious than I was before I went in. Well, maybe not more ambitious, really; but with a lot more real knowledge of what I wanted to do. I think it might have been even more valuable for me if I had followed up with college work; I don't know about that. I thought about that for a while, but I decided to take advantage of the GI Bill of Rights and learn something about refrigeration."

Source: Robert Havighurst, *The American Veteran Back Home* (New York, 1951), p. 188.

SOURCE 96

Three other World War II veterans from the same midwestern town offered views regarding the effect of military service upon them, views that differ sharply from each other:

Source: Robert Havighurst, *The American Veteran Back Home* (New York, 1951), pp. 171, 175.

"It gives you a bigger, broader perspective, I think. I didn't get out of the States because the time I went into the service, I had only one good eye. Just the same, I spent some time down in the south, down in Mississippi, and I had over a year up in New England. I was down in Texas for a while and out in California for a few months. Altogether I guess I was stationed in seven different states during the service. Well, you travel around like that and see so much, you know more what other people are doing. I guess what it really does is get you out of your rut that you've got into living in a little town. It sort of shows you what a big thing our country is. You meet a lot of people and see new things to do and new ways of doing things. It broadens you a good bit, I think."

"I can't see that it's been especially worth while for me, except for the experience of traveling and being in the war. I couldn't say that I learned anything from it. I got some sea stories to tell, that's about all. We get Bill Robertson and some of the fellows over here, with a little beer thrown in, and we keep going till four o'clock in the morning about the South Pacific. Yeah, it was all right, that way. A lot of things happened to us that we'll never forget; but as far as learning anything that would help me out now, I can't see it. It's one of those things — I wouldn't want to do it over but I wouldn't want to have been left out of it."

"Well, the way I look at it, it was just so many years lost, that you just quit livin'. I couldn't say that I lost out on very much because of it, but I certainly couldn't say that I gained anythin' from it. It might just as well not have happened; I wish to hell it hadn't."

SOURCE 97

> "John," a Navaho youth, was drafted in 1941. He wrote to a friend after several months of military service:

This army business is getting pretty strick all the time, but I have been in this outfit for a long time that I don't mind a bit. I got used to this army pretty good, where I can do things without having much trouble. I learnt many things both bad and good. I think I drink about twice as much whisky then when I was home . . . please tell my mother that she don't have to worry about me. Because I am now full grown man — and I know how to take care of myself.

Source: Egon Vogt, "Navaho Veterans," in Papers of the Peabody Museum of American Archaelogy and Ethnology, Harvard University 41 (1951): 50.

SOURCE 98

Some 300 discharged veterans in seven midwestern cities were asked by interviewers in December 1944 to indicate the kinds of changes they had experienced while in the service:

Undesirable changes (47% of all):

More nervous, high-strung, restless, jumpy, tense, can't concentrate, want to be "on the go"	41%
More irritable, short-tempered, quarrelsome, belligerent	17
Sadder, more solemn, depressed, lacking pep, "older," no longer carefree	10
Harder, more bitter, cynical, critical, self-centered	,9
More dependent, have trouble making their own decisions	8
More withdrawn, less social, shy	7
"Dumber," intellectually narrower, less well-informed	2
Wilder, less moral, more given to drinking and gambling	2

Desirable changes (32% of all):

Intellectually broadened, think deeper, understand things or people better	16
Quieter, more settled, less given to running around or drinking	13
More independent, responsible, ambitious	12
More affectionate, appreciative, considerate	8
More spartan, more self-controlled, able to endure difficulties and discipline	5
More social, like being with people more	4

Source: S. Stouffer et al., *Studies in Social Psychology in World War II,* 4 vols. (Princeton, N.J.: Princeton University Press, 1949-50), II, p. 632.

SOURCE 99

Bruno Bettelheim and Morris Janowitz correlated the responses given by ninety-four World War II veterans (to the question: "Who gained as a result of our winning the war?") with the degree of prejudice ("tolerant" to "outspoken and intense") that these veterans had displayed in their responses to other questions:

Source: Bruno Bettelheim and Morris Janowitz, *Dynamics of Prejudice: A Psychological and Sociological Study of Veterans* (New York, 1950), p. 73.

"Who Gained Through the War?"

	TOLERANT		STEREOTYPED		OUTSPOKEN AND INTENSE		TOTAL	
	No.	%	No.	%	No.	%	No.	%
Collective symbols, including veteran	14	34	11	52	6	19	31	33
Nobody	19	46	5	24	4	12	28	30
Specific symbols, excluding veteran	8	20	5	24	22	69	35	37
Total	41		21		32		94	

SOURCE 100

A National Opinion Research Corporation survey of veterans and nonveterans in February 1947 asked whether "the war generally made life better or worse" for them:

	VETERANS	NONVETERANS
Life worse	48%	35%
Life changed, but don't know whether better or worse	6	3
Life better	24	9
No change	21	52
No answer	1	1
	100%	100%

Source: S. Stouffer et al., *Studies in Social Psychology in World War II,* 4 vols. (Princeton, N.J.: Princeton University Press, 1949-50), II, p. 633.

SOURCE 101

Captain John Lowe visited a church in Mexico, in 1847, and wrote home:

This is Sabbath afternoon. . . . To get out of the noise of the camp, I this morning rode up to the City and went to Church; there were several churches open, two of which I attended. They were beautiful, heavy buildings but rather tawdry and tinselled in the inside; the floors were of marble in small diamond slabs, small organ galleries and few seats. One thing in particular pleased me much and that was, *the equality of all ranks before the altar of God.* For here I saw kneeling on the marble pavement for more than 15 minutes, the haughty Castillian in whose veins flowed the pure blood of the Cortes, the yellow Aztec, the stupid Indian, and the decrepid negro, altogether, side by side; the distinction of races, of color, of wealth, of rank was disregarded or unknown and they all seemed to regard each other, at least in the Sanctuary, as equal before God. In one instance (and I am satisfied it was of common occurence) I saw a beautiful young, fair, Spanish girl, evidently of the higher class, kneeling, and just in front of her, was an old negro beggar in the same attitude, while at the side of the negro was a Castillian gentleman and his little son (about Tom's age) all devoutly offering up their prayers to Almighty God without even a thought of "Negro pews" or "poor seats." And then I wished that it were so in my own, my native land, where we boast that all men are *free and equal.*

Source: G. Smith and C. Judah, eds., *Chronicles of the Gringos* (Albuquerque, N.M., 1969), p. 410.

SOURCE 102

Recently discharged white World War II veterans commented on Jewish and black comrades-in-arms:

There were some Jews [in the Army] that were real white men and they were swell, but back here they are a separate race all by themselves.

I saw what these [black truck-driving] boys did on the Burma Road. I had closer contact with them in the hospital and all. It explodes a lot of things

Source: S. Stouffer et al., *Studies in Social Psychology in World War II,* 4 vols. (Princeton, N.J.: Princeton University Press), II, p. 638.

you hear. You realize they have the same abilities — they just haven't had any breaks.

SOURCE 103

Other military personnel, during the Korean War, commented on the black soldiers they had come to know while serving in some of the first fully integrated units:

(Trainee): When I first came in, most of the men in our outfit were from Oregon, and a lot of them didn't like being with colored boys. But once they got with them it was all right. A lot of us never lived around them in Oregon. Where I lived they didn't even allow them in the city. They wouldn't be here if they didn't have to be, same way with us. I have changed my thinking. I've never lived around them. What I've heard wasn't so good. But I didn't see anything. They're just the same as we are.

(Second lieutenant from North Carolina): After all, I was born in the South. I wouldn't care to go to a social function with them. I can treat them just as nice as anybody. But everybody has the right to pick his own friends. [Do you feel the same about the man you said you liked?] No. Not for him. I'd go anywhere for him. Yes, I do feel different about him. I guess I got to know him better. I grew to like him a lot. Maybe if I got to know more, I would like them more. I never dealt with too many except for work. This guy slept next to me in school. I got to know him real well. [Do you feel the same toward him as toward a white fellow?] Yes. [But there is still a difference?] I don't know. Not with him. As I said before, I never dealt with any. He's an all around nice fellow. Just the same as an ordinary guy you get to like. [Do you think of him as of a colored man?] No, I don't think so. I feel the same about him as about a white man anywhere.

(Captain): I had all the reason in the world to be against the nigger, and my being from Tennessee didn't help any. But you are listening to a man who has had a complete change of mind. It all began with my being thrown in the same job in Germany with a Negro captain, who in civilian life had been a professor of history in a southern university. I started out being pretty cool with him, but we were together over two years, and during that time, I am proud to say, that man gave me an education in race relations. I can truthfully say that there is one of the finest men I have ever met.

Source: Leo Bogart, ed., *Social Research and the Desegregation of the U.S. Army* (Chicago, 1969), pp. 222–23, 225.

SOURCE 104

Groups of integrated and segregated Quartermaster Corps personnel were asked to respond to questions about the long-term consequences of integration, 1951:

Question: "As Time Goes on, Do You Think That Colored People in the United States Will Have More Opportunities Than They Have Today, Fewer Opportunities, or About the Same as Now?"

	QUARTERMASTER			
	WHITES IN ALL-WHITE UNITS	WHITES IN INTEGRATED UNITS	NEGROES IN INTEGRATED UNITS	NEGROES IN ALL-NEGRO UNITS
They will have more opportunities	50%	79%	92%	87%
It will be about the same as now	43	19	7	12
They will have fewer opportunities	7	1	0	0
No answer	0	1	1	1
N(100%) =	(68)	(99)	(73)	(144)

How Quartermaster Troops Answered the Question: "As Time Goes on, Do You Think That White and Colored People in the United States Will Get Along Better Together Than They Do Today, Not as Well as They Do Now, or About the Same as Now?"

	QUARTERMASTER			
	WHITES IN ALL-WHITE UNITS	WHITES IN INTEGRATED UNITS	NEGROES IN INTEGRATED UNITS	NEGROES IN ALL-NEGRO UNITS
Answers:				
They will get along better together	13%	68%	85%	82%
They will get along about the same as now	65	23	13	15
They will not get along as well as now	22	7	1	2
No answer	0	2	1	1
N(100%) =	(68)	(99)	(73)	(144)

Source: Leo Bogart, ed., Social Research and the Desegretation of the U.S. Army (Chicago, 1969), pp. 176, 353, 355.

Question: "In Civilian Life in the U.S., How Do You Think It Works out When White and Colored People Sit Together in the Same Sections on Buses and Trains?"

	QUARTERMASTER			
	WHITES IN ALL-WHITE UNITS	WHITES IN INTEGRATED UNITS	NEGROES IN INTEGRATED UNITS	NEGROES IN ALL-NEGRO UNITS
It works out better than any other arrangement	1%	19%	62%	30%
It works out about the same as any other arrangement	31	43	27	51
It does not work as well as some other arrangement	68	37	10	17
No answer	0	1	1	2
N(100%) =	(68)	(99)	(73)	(144)

SOURCE 105

> *Three World War I "doughboys" from Virginia wrote home from Europe about the "backward" people they found there:*

"Tell Bertha that I am going to buy her a pair of wooden shoes that they wear here. Ha. Ha. They certainly are awful things to have on your feet but I guess as long as they don't know any better it is all right."

"Aint they backward? . . . This is some country over here. About 500 years behind times."

"Actually the people are too slow to go fast asleep."

Source: Fred Baldwin, "American Enlisted Man," unpublished Ph.D. diss., Princeton University, 1964, pp. 184-85.

SOURCE 106

> *Three "Leadertown," Pennsylvania, veterans learned "to appreciate this country more":*

Source: Personal interviews in a working-class section of Pittsburgh, 1974, conducted by Thomas Conley. (Tapes deposited with author at University of Pittsburgh.)

A Korean War-era veteran

"I found that this country does a better job than I ever thought it did. From being in Mexico, and seeing how bad that country is run, it helped to appreciate this country more."

A World War II veteran

"Before the war, I took the United States for granted. After being in Europe, and seeing how the average person lived, this is really an outstanding country."

Another World War II veteran

"I always thought we had the best, and I still do. I learned to appreciate this country more."

SOURCE 107

Comparable groups of veterans and nonveterans in a midwestern town were asked in 1949: "Would you say that you are more satisfied or less satisfied with the American Government [now] than you were in 1941?"

Satisfaction with Government by 48 Veterans and 24 Nonveterans

	MORE SATISFIED		NO CHANGE		LESS SATISFIED	
	NO.	%	NO.	%	NO.	%
Veterans	28	59	16	33	4	8
Nonveterans	3	13	13	55	8	32

[One of these veterans compared America with what he had seen in Japan in 1945:]

"We have got one of the best governments in the world. You get over in the other countries, and you see what we've got here. In Japan it's all hand work. I spent three months in the naval barracks over in Tokyo, and I saw a lot of it. The people over there have to dig their fields with their

---

Source: Robert Havighurst, *The American Veteran Back Home* (New York, 1951), pp. 227-28.

bare hands, and they don't have any of the good things we've got—electricity, bathrooms, refrigerators. They live almost like animals. I saw a little girl on the streets over there. She was about the age of my little girl, here. The minute one of the policemen came around or one of the soldiers, she ran out of sight like a rabbit. Well, that's no way to have to bring up your children. No sir, I'm sold on our government!"

SOURCE 108

Another midwestern veteran, of the European theater, told an interviewer in 1948 that he had learned something from being overseas:

"Of course, that experience in the army isn't the kind of thing you'd like to go through again and there were parts of it I didn't like, but on the other hand it adds to experience that most of us don't get more than once in a lifetime and perhaps not even then. I was in England and France and Belgium and Germany and I had a couple of furloughs that I was able to spend over in Switzerland. Not only did I enjoy those experiences but they opened up my eyes to a lot of things I had never known before, and like I said, I wouldn't trade the experience for anything. I think the experience of traveling around made me realize how much more fortunate we are than those people over there. You see the way those people live and you realize that this is the best country in the world."

Source: Robert Havighurst, *The American Veteran Back Home* (New York, 1951), p. 170; Compare Havighurst, p. 224.

SOURCE 109

Two more veterans from the same midwestern town had more hatred than pity for Europeans:

"England? My God! You never saw so many perverts in your life. It's full of them. And France, I'd say, is a country without morals. They aren't

Source: Robert Havighurst, *The American Veteran Back Home* (New York, 1951), p. 221. Compare Daniel Glaser, "Sentiments of American Soldiers Abroad Toward Europeans," *American Journal of Sociology* 51 (1946): 433-38.

perverted or anything else — they just don't give a damn. I never saw anything like it. The country is full of disease. And the French are the most
two-faced people you ever saw. They'll be nice to you to your face, and
as soon as you turn around they'll be swearing at you in French. I don't
have any use for them, frankly."

"I'd just love to clean hell out of the frogs and the English. Those English
and French are a bunch of phonies. They will try to screw you every chance
they get. The French are the worst, though. They charged us ten prices for
everything, and you couldn't do anything about it or you'd be court-mar-
tialed. As for the Italians, they didn't have brains enough to get mad at."

SOURCE 110

Source: S. Stouffer et al., *Studies in Social Psychology in World War II,* 4 vols. (Princeton,
N.J.: Princeton University Press), II, p. 629.

Respect for Allied War Effort, as Related to Contact with Allied Nationals, by Education

(Enlisted Men Returned from Overseas Theaters, Surveyed in Redistribution Stations in the United States, March, April, and May 1945) (Numbers following the bars = numbers of cases on which percentages are based)

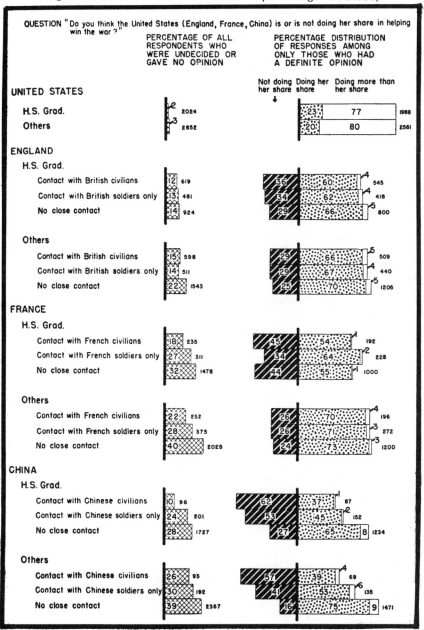

SOURCE 111

> *A GI with a college education confessed his lack of "tolerance"*
> *for the Vietnamese he had seen:*

"Since my sister-in-law is Japanese, I have met many Japanese 'war brides' back in the states. They sure are a world apart from the Vietnamese. The Japanese are so clean, polite and considerate.

One would seem to think that a man of my education would understand and tolerate the dynamics of "cultural relativity" but I find it so hard to tolerate these people. Intolerance certainly runs contrary to my general personality, but [I] simply have so little tolerance for these people. Going back to the 'gooks,'. . ."

Source: David Sartori to Edward Paterson, July 1968, State Historical Society of Wisconsin Manuscript Division; quoted at length in Stanley Kutler, ed., *Looking for America* (San Francisco, 1976), p. 428.

SOURCE 112

> *Korean War casualties have been correlated with family income*
> *levels as follows:*

MEDIAN INCOME ($)	CASUALTY RATE/10,000 OCCUPIED DWELLING UNITS
Under $2500	14.6
2500–2999	10.8
3000–3499	9.1
3500–3999	8.6
4000–4499	7.5
4500–4999	6.6
5000–5499	5.8
5500 and over	4.6

Source: M. Useem, *Conscription, Protest, and Social Conflict* (New York: John Wiley and Sons, Inc., 1973), p. 139. Compare J. Segal in *Social Issues* (September 1957); and *U.S. News & World Report* (February 20, 1953), pp. 18 ff.

SOURCE 113

> *Among GIs from the Chicago area during the Vietnam War*
> *socioeconomic status, but not race, was significantly associated*
> *with one's becoming a casualty in the field:*

Source: Badillo and Curry, "Social Incidence of Casualties," *Armed Forces and Society* 4 (1976): 403.

**Standardized Regression Coefficients for Casualties and Military
Participation as Related to Predictor Variables:
Cook County Communities (n = 101)**

	SIZE OF AGE-ELIGIBLE MALE POPULATION	SOCIO-ECONOMIC STATUS	RACIAL COMPO-SITION	MILITARY PARTICI-PATION	R^2
Casualties[a]	0.66[b]	−0.32[b]	−0.06	0.03	0.61[b]
Military participation	0.68[b]	−0.18[b]	0.13[c]	—	0.56[b]

[a]Based on both all Army casualties from 1964 to mid-1968, and all casualties (regardless of branch of service) from mid-1968 through 1972.
[b]Significant at .001 level of statistical significance.
[c]Significant at .05 level of statistical significance.

SOURCE 114

> John Faller, a veteran of Andersonville prison, described the
> long-term consequences of the poor diet made available to him
> and his comrades by the Confederates, circa 1890:

We were all more or less afflicted with scurvy, and some of us were very
bad. Our teeth became loose, and in many cases would drop out. Toby
Morrison's legs began to swell and turn black. One day we dug a hole in
the sand, and buried him up to his waist, and tramped the sand tight about
him and left him in that position for hours. We were told by an old sailor
that that would draw the scurvy out of him. I don't know whether it did
him any good or not, but he was very lame when we left Andersonville to
go to another prison. He lived through it all and thinks he is a pretty good
man yet.

Comrade Sites was afflicted with scurvy, and sinews of his limbs were
drawn up so that he had to walk on his toes. He would put a little piece of
wood under the ball of the foot and tie a string around it, which would
relieve the pain to some extent. He, too, managed to get home alive.

J. Humer was left at Andersonville when we left in the fall on account
of not being able to walk. The only meat he got to eat after we left was
the half of a rat and he says he enjoyed it very much. He, too, managed
to get home alive in July 1865. Broken down in health, he has since died.

Comrades McCleaf and Natcher were left back in Andersonville. McCleaf
died shortly after. Natcher lived to get home but died a few years after
the war from the effects of the imprisonment.

Source: M. Flower, ed., *Dear Folks at Home* (Carlisle, Pa., 1963), pp. 140-41.

Jack Rhoads managed to pull through, after living on low diet for so long. He now lives in the country; and enjoys a good square meal, and has no more use for cow feed and water as he called it.

Comrades Harris and Elliot, after starving and almost dying for many months, and partaking of the same hospitalities in the South as we all did, managed to reach home alive. If there is anything good to eat around, they prefer it to corn meal or [Captain] Otto [Wirz's] vegetable soup.

While at Florence, Cuddy, Landis, Adams, Hefflefinger, Schlusser and the Walker boys died, and later Hal Eby died on reaching our line. Holmes died at Annapolis before reaching his home. Harkness, Meloy, McCune, Natcher, Ruby, Humer have died since the war. Of those surviving today are Comrades Burkholder, Constercamp, Elliott, Faller, Gould, Harris, Morrison, Otto, Rhoads, Sites, Stoey and Vantelburg.

SOURCE 115

> Pfc. John Conroy, a Guadalcanal veteran, wrote to his father from a hospital in late 1942:

"I have been shell-shocked and bomb-shocked. My memory is very dim regarding my civilian days. . . . Of course I'm not insane. But I've been living the life of a savage and haven't quite got used to a world of laws and new responsibilities. So many of my platoon were wiped out, my old Parris Island buddies, that it's hard to sleep without seeing them die all over again. Our living conditions on Guadalcanal had been so bad—little food or hope—fighting and dying each day—four hours sleep out of 72— the medicos here optimistically say I'll pay for it the rest of my life. My bayonet and shrapnel cuts are all healed up, however. Most of us will be fairly well in six months, but none of us will be completely cured for years. . . ."

Source: D. Wecter, When Johnny Comes Marching Home (Boston, 1944), pp. 545-46.

SOURCE 116

> Two barely literate privates from Alabama wrote home during the Civil War, describing their horror at what Bell Irwin Wiley called their "Baptism of fire":

"Martha . . . I can inform you that I have Seen the Monkey Show at last and I dont Waunt to see it no more I am satsfide with Ware Martha I Cant

Source: Bell Irwin Wiley, Life of Johnny Reb (New York, 1943), pp. 32-33.

tell you how many ded men I did see . . . thay ware piled up one one another all over the Battel feel the Battel was a Six days Battel and I was in all off it . . . I did not go all over the Battel feeld I Jest was one one Winge of the Battel feeld But I can tell you that there Was a meney a ded man where I was men Was shot Evey fashinton that you mite Call for Som and there hedes shot of and som ther armes and leges Won was sot in the midel I can tell you that I am tirde of Ware I am satsfide if the Ballence is that is one thing Shore I dont waunt to see that site no more I can inform you that West Brown was shot one the head he Was sent off to the horspitel . . . he was not herte very Bad he was struck with a pease of a Bum"

"We have had every hard fite a bout ten miles from Chat ta nooga on Chick a mog ga creak in gor ga . . . i com out safe but it is all i can say i have all ways crave to fite a lit[tle] gust to no what it is to go in to a bat tle but i got the chance to tri my hand at last anough to sad isfi me i never wan to go in to an nother fite any more sister i wan to come home worse than i eaver did be fore but when times gits better i will tri to come home thare has ben agrate meney soldiers runing a way late ly but i dont want to go that way if i can get home any other way."

SOURCE 117

Thomas Cole was eighteen when he ran away from slavery in northeastern Alabama and stumbled inadvertently upon a Union field force in 1863. He was "drafted" on the spot. Some seventy years later he spoke of the experience:

I eats all the nuts and kills a few swamp rabbits and cotches a few fish. I builds the fire and goes off 'bout half a mile and hides in the thicket till it burns down to the coals, then bakes me some fish and rabbit. I's shaking all the time, 'fraid I'd git cotched, but I's nearly starve to death. I puts the rest the fish in my cap and travels on that night by the North Star and hides in a big thicket the next day, and along evening I hears guns shooting. I sure am scared this time, sure 'nough. I's scared to come in and scared to go out, and while I's standing there, I hears two men say, "Stick you hands up, boy. What you doing?" I says, "Uh-uh-uh, I dunno. You ain't gwine take me back to the plantation, is you?" They says, "No. Does you want to fight for the North?" I says I will, 'cause they talks like Northern men. Us walk night and day and gits in General Rosecrans' camp, and they

Source: B. Botkin, ed., *Lay My Burden Down,* rev. ed. (Chicago, 1958), p. 199.

thunk I's the spy from the South. They asks me all sorts of questions and says they'll whip me if I didn't tell them what I's spying 'bout. Finally they 'lieves me and puts me to work helping with the cannons. I feels 'portant then, but I didn't know what was in front of me, or I 'spects I'd run off 'gain.

I helps sot them cannons on this Chickamauga Mountain, in hiding places. I has to go with a man and wait on him and that cannon. First thing I knows — bang! bang! boom! — things has started, and guns am shooting faster than you can think, and I looks round for the way to run. But them guns am shooting down the hill in front of me and shooting at me, and over me and on both sides of me. I tries to dig me a hole and git in it. All this happen right now, and first thing I knows, the man am kicking me and wanting me to holp him keep that cannon loaded. Man, I didn't want no cannon, but I has to help anyway. We fit till dark, and the Rebels got more men than us, so General Rosecrans sends the message to General Woods to come help us out. When the messenger slips off, I sure wish it am me slipping off, but I didn't want to see no General Woods. I just wants to git back to that old plantation and pick more cotton. I'd been willing to do 'most anything to git out that mess, but I done told General Rosecrans I wants to fight the Rebels, and he sure was letting me do it. He wasn't just letting me do it, he was making me do it. I done got in there, and he wouldn't let me out.

White folks, there was men laying wanting help, wanting water, with blood running out them and the top or sides their heads gone, great big holes in them. I just promises the good Lord if He just let me git out that mess, I wouldn't run off no more, but I didn't know then He wasn't gwine let me out with just that battle.

SOURCE 118

> *David King, an American volunteer serving with the British at the Battle of the Somme in 1916, wrote to a friend in the United States:*

July 25th, 1916.

DEAR GERALD,

. . . We are moving up again shortly. At present we are in wooden huts about seventeen miles from the front. The band is giving a concert, and over the music you can hear a continual booming — the most devilish bombardment I have ever heard. It makes you feel as if you were at a comic opera, with a storm gathering, while the villagers stroll about the plaza. It would be funny if we had not been there before and did not

Source: David King, *L.M. 8046: The War Diary of a Legionnaire* (London, 1929), pp. 156-61.

know what all the cannonading meant. I hope I get plugged this time for better or worse. I'm tired of being the lone, last survivor of gory battlefields, the only human, civilized eyewitness, so to speak. God! how those guns are roaring! I have never heard anything like it before. Wish we would hurry up and get into it. Funny—I'll be nervous as a marmosette now till I get right into the first line, and they start bursting over us. Always the same—almost trembling till the riot starts, and then feeling like a kid going home for Christmas vacation. . . .

July 28th.
. . . The flag was decorated this morning, so we should be on our way ere long! I'm pleasantly confident that I'm going to be wounded this time. My God, it's about time—two years without a rest is enough for any man. . . .

11 a.m., Aug. 13th (?)
By golly, they wanted to send us out again. But the lieutenant sent us back. My Lord, those guns are busy. They are beginning to strafe our part of the line now. They move up and down the line, concentrating, and giving each a bit of music for a while, and then move on. This war gets worse and more terrible every day, Gerald. I don't see how flesh and blood stands it. It makes me sick when some bloated profiteer sits in his armchair in Paris and talks about going on to the limit. If those people had to go through sixteen hours' shelling, and didn't die of heart failure, we would have peace to-morrow. And don't you believe all those hardy poilu yarns. They are spun by men in the reserve who spend all their time in quiet parts of the line, where they have shelters forty feet deep and get about ten field-gun shells a day. I think this war must be getting on my nerves, for every day I get more and more fretful, and I used to like these affairs. . . .

SOURCE 119

Two GIs fighting in Italy during World War II sent poems to the GI's official newspaper, Stars and Stripes:

Prospect

And in the days to come,
Unbelievably distant still,
Someone is sure to ask—
What was it like?
And I shall stare at him
Vacant of eye

Source: *Puptent Poets of the "Star and Stripes, Mediterranean,"* compiled by Cpl. Charles Hogan et al. (Italy, 1945), pp. 74, 106.

Sluggish to catch the meaning of his question
But in my heart, the past will rip apart
Indignant gashes; fear will bleed again
My hand will move
To brush aside the madness
Recalled to consciousness.
My lips will close
In bitter line upon the caustic word
And all of me will turn the overtones
Of curious watching into frozen shame—
The pent up silence of a zero hour.

— Pfc. Hans Juergensen-Steinhart

Are You Nervous in the Service?

Are you nervous in the service, Mr. Jervis?
Do you wish that you were anywhere but here?
As the shells begin a-squealing
Do you get that empty feeling
That your life has been shortened by a year?
There are times at night when "butterflies" are fallin'
That you really wonder what it's all about.
Then a shell comes helter-skelter
And you dive for nearest shelter,
And once more you curse the dirty, lousy Kraut.
Are you nervous in the service, Mr. Jervis?
Are you frantic—don't know quite just what to do?
Well, please don't let it getcha,
For you'll find, if time will letcha,
That, though you're nervous, I am nervous, too!

— Pvt. Eddie Bendityky

SOURCE 120

Dominick Yezzo recorded his thoughts in a diary in Vietnam, 1968:

Nov 19

No letters today. I wanted to hear from Jennifer so badly.
The pressure doesn't only tax me when we get hit, but thinking of what

Source: Dominick Yezzo, *A G.I.'s Vietnam Diary, 1968–1969* (New York, 1974), unpaginated.

might happen is, I think, my biggest burden in this war. Just as right this moment I realize all too well that I'm a born worrier. My insides will probably age many years during my twelve month stay in Vietnam.

I'm asking God to watch over my family, not to allow any combat, and to carry me through my duties now, and help me to explore my potential after I return from the military. I also often ask for an end to this bastardly war, and all wars now and to come. . . .

Nov 22

Again, again, again. Will it ever end? Once in broad daylight at 6:00 P.M. (mortars). Then rockets at 2:30 in the morning. I'm half crazed with fear. It's affecting me much worse then the others. I can't eat, don't sleep, can't study anything. I'm not normal under the strain. I'll never be able to write down what I feel now. I can't explain the horror. It's locked up in me, and it hurts. After the rockets came in, I went into the bunker and stayed there all night. God, please come.

Got a beautiful package from Mom and Dad. I love my family so very much. I want to go home to that security now.

Have K.P. on Saturday, November 23.

I'm looking for some way to get out of all this. I'm completely wrecked.

Nov 23

Spent today with much misery and worry. Even during the night I'm sweating.

Was on K.P. today. The new first cook is a bastard. I left early, about 5:00. I just walked out to help the guys build our new bunker complex; I think mainly I was afraid to be far from any protection.

I'm going to go to the priest for some help. I'm toying with my mind, thinking of absurd ways to get out of all this.

Spoke with Doc this evening about my problem. My grave problem! He advised me to see an army psychiatrist. He said that it was possible for me to have a nervous breakdown. He suggested that I get help. He's so good that way. At first, the word "psychiatrist" shook me up, but maybe one of them can straighten me out. I know I can't go on living like this. Slept in the bunker again tonight.

Nov 24

Today is Sunday. I made an appointment with the chaplain this morning before Mass. During Mass I offered Communion to my parents and family. Also for myself and all in Vietnam, and for an end to the war. . . .

I know that my problem is worry and its eating me up. I also know that when the enemy fire starts coming in, everyone is just as scared as I am. But with me, the fright lasts even when it's over. I'm just as scared during the day as I am when we get hit at night. I can't forget about it.

Nov 25

Saw the priest today. We spoke lightly of fate and human life. I feel somewhat better. If I get hit there's nothing I can do about it. There's no way out. . . .

Nov 26

I'm totally defeated. No defense left in me. I don't know where to turn.

Good letter from Frank and Wayne today. I love my brothers very much. Frank has made me feel good with things he's told me.

I want out of this so badly. Been so very depressed and that's also making me homesick. . . .

SOURCE 121

Plasma samples drawn from airmen who had just returned from Vietnam combat missions, and from two other sample groups, were analyzed and compared, 1968:

Plots of the Z indices — adjusted log, for seven plasma phospholipid fractions and the plasma cortisol levels for normal subjects, individuals under combat stress, and the stress of schizophrenia. Individual points which are misclassified are encircled.

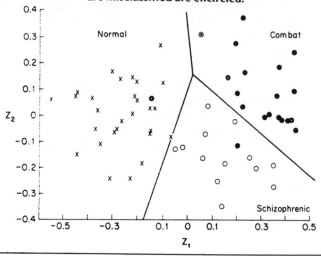

Source: Peter Bourne, ed., *Psychology and Physiology of Stress* (1969), p. 212. Compare Mitchell Berkun, "Urinary Responses to Psychological Stresses," paper read at 1962 Society of Psychophysiological Research Meeting, Denver, Colorado.

SOURCE 122

Newsman Ernie Pyle and a GI friend watched troops passing by Italy in 1944 "after a seige in the front line":

Their clothes were muddy, and they were heavily laden. They looked rough, and any parade-ground officer would have been shocked by their appearance. And yet I said, "I'll bet those troops haven't been in the line three days."

My friend thought a minute, looked more closely as they passed, and then said, "I'll bet they haven't been in the line at all. I'll bet they've just been up in reserve and weren't used, and now they're being pulled back for a while."

How can you tell things like that? Well, I based my deduction on the fact that their beards weren't very long and, although they were tired and dirty, they didn't look tired and dirty enough. My friend based his on that too, but more so on the look in their eyes. "They don't have that stare," he said.

A soldier who has been a long time in the line does have a "look" in his eyes that anyone who knows about it can discern. It's a look of dullness, eyes that look without seeing, eyes that see without conveying any image to the mind. It's a look that is the display room for what lies behind it— exhaustion, lack of sleep, tension for too long, weariness that is too great, fear beyond fear, misery to the point of numbness, a look of surpassing indifference to anything anybody can do. It's a look I dread to see on men.

And yet to me it's one of the perpetual astonishments of a war life that human beings recover as quickly as they do. For example, a unit may be pretty well exhausted, but if they are lucky enough to be blessed with some sunshine and warmth they'll begin to be normal after two days out of the line. The human spirit is just like a cork.

Source: Ernie Pyle, *Brave Men* (New York, 1944), p. 270.

SOURCE 123

GI cartoonist Bill Mauldin describes (in two media) the stress combatants feel: ". . . the unutterable relief as you sink down for a ten-minute break, spoiled by the knowledge that you'll

Source: Bill Mauldin, *Up Front* (New York, 1944), p. 47. Drawings copyrighted 1944, renewed 1972, Bill Mauldin; reproduced by courtesy of Bill Mauldin.

have to get up and go again—the never-ending monotony of
day and weeks and months and years of bad weather and wet
clothes and no mail—all this sends as many men into the psy-
chopathic wards as does battle fatigue."

"I'm depending on you old men to be a steadying influence for the replacements."

SOURCE 124

Anxiety Symptoms Reported by Combat Troops
(Based on a Survey of 1,766 Combat Veterans in Italy, April 1944)

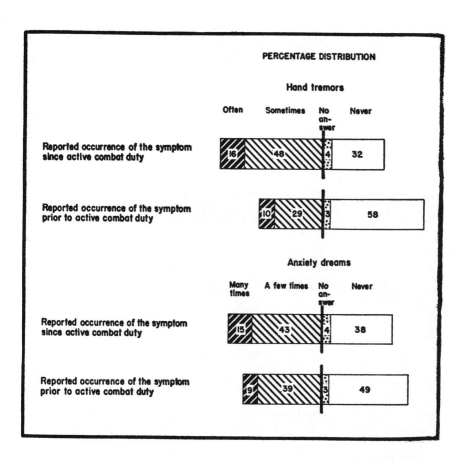

Source: S. Stouffer et al., Studies in Social Psychology in World War II, 4 vols. (Princeton, N.J.: Princeton University Press, 1949-50), II, p. 204.

SOURCE 125

**Degree of Reported Bodily Expression of Fear in Battle, in
Relation to Various Sources of Stress, in Combination.**

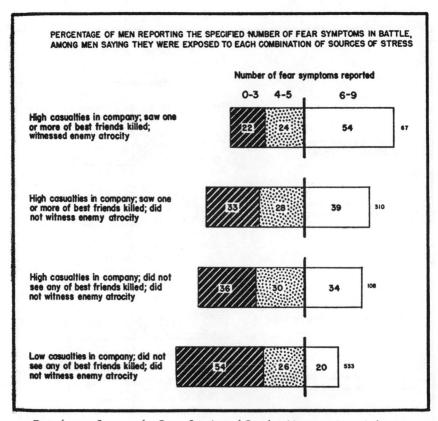

Data from a Survey of a Cross Section of Combat Veterans in an Infantry
Division in the South Pacific, March 1944 (S-100). (Numbers following the
bars = Numbers of Cases on Which Percentages are based.)

Source: S. Stouffer et al., *Studies in Social Psychology in World War II,* 4 vols. (Princeton,
N.J.: Princeton University Press, 1949-50), II, p. 81.

SOURCE 126

Fifteen-Item Neuropsychiatric Screening Adjunct Scores of Flying Personnel With and Without Combat Flying Experience

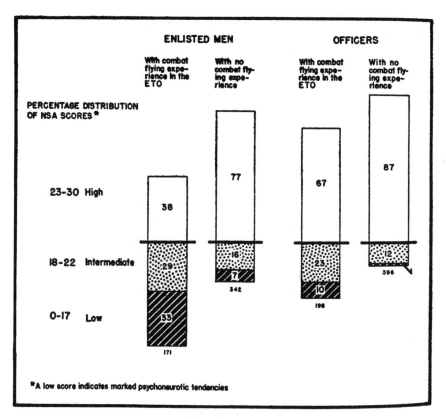

(Based on a Survey of Officer and Enlisted Air Crew Members in One Very Heavy Bombardment, B-29, Wing in Training in the United States, May 1945)(Numbers at the Bottom of the Bars = Numbers of Cases on Which Percentages are based.)

Source: S. Stouffer et al., Studies in Social Psychology in World War II, 4 vols. (Princeton, N.J.: Princeton University Press, 1949-50), II, p. 376.

SOURCE 127

Relationship Between Amount of Combat Experience and Sleep Disturbance

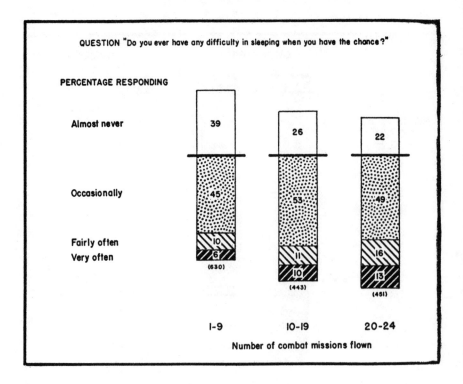

(Based on a Survey of Flyers in Heavy Bomber Crews in the European Theater, June 1944) (Numbers in Parentheses at the Bottom of the Bars = Numbers of Cases on Which Percentages Are Based.)

Source: S. Stouffer et al., *Studies in Social Psychology in World War II,* 4 vols. (Princeton, N.J.: Princeton University Press, 1949-50), II, p. 374.

SOURCE 128

**Relationship Between Sick-Call Rate and Number of Combat Missions
Flown Among Heavy Bomber Crews**

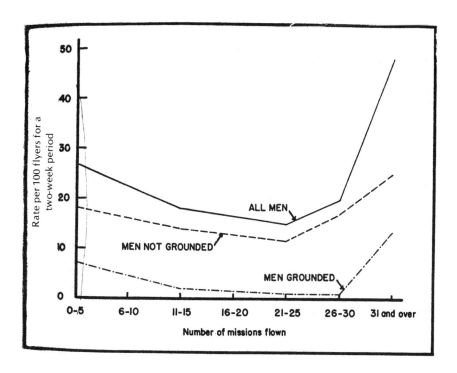

The data are based upon statistics from the Office of the Air Surgeon on
all members of heavy bomber crews in the European theater during June
1944. Sick-call rates cover the two-week period of June 3 to June 16, 1944.
Men who had flown 31 or more missions are included in this chart in order
to show sick-call behavior after the tour of duty was completed.

Source: S. Stouffer et al., *Studies in Social Psychology in World War II,* 4 vols. (Princeton,
N.J.: Princeton University Press, 1949-50), II, p. 381.

SOURCE 129

GIs with psychiatric illnesses and other GIs were asked questions about their childhood and family background, 1944:

Reported Childhood Fears as Related to Neuropsychiatric Breakdown Among Troops in the United States (January 1944)

QUESTION: "Below is a list of things commonly feared by children. Some of them are important in medical histories, but nothing is known about how often the average person has been afraid of these things. *Check one answer after each thing listed to show how much you yourself were afraid of it when you were a kid.*"

| | PERCENTAGES CHECKING "NOT AT ALL"[a] | | |
	CROSS SECTION	PSYCHO-NEUROTICS	DIFFERENCE
Being on high places	43	23	20
Being shut up in a room or closet	55	35	20
Thunderstorms	54	34	20
Falling	40	21	19
Sharp knives	46	27	19
Being with girls	60	41	19
Strangers	59	41	18
Walking by a graveyard at night	44	28	16
Large animals	45	30	15
The Devil	58	43	15
Family quarrels	42	28	14
Being laughed at by other boys	39	26	13
Being left alone	42	30	12
Getting bawled out	25	14	11
Being called on to recite in class	30	19	11
Thoughts of death	45	34	11
Number of cases	*3,729*	*613*	

[a]Other check-list categories were "Very much" and "A little."

"So far as you know, has anyone in your family had a nervous breakdown? (Do NOT include yourself if you think you had a nervous breakdown.)"

	"BEST ADJUSTED"	CROSS SECTION	PSYCHONEUROTICS
Yes	12%	22%	46%
Don't know	13	18	29
No	75	60	25
	100%	100%	100%

Source: S. Stouffer et al., *Studies in Social Psychology in World War II,* 4 vols. (Princeton, N.J.: Princeton University Press, 1949-50), II, pp. 138, 134.

SOURCE 130

> *A psychiatrist commented in 1946 on one World War II veteran's use of his "war experiences and the anxiety connected with them" as a "screen and defense to cover up the individual conflicts which became reactivated in the highly charged emotional atmosphere of the period of readjustment. . . . It is the same with combat fatigue or war neurosis":*

He returned home after four years of service. He was the second of four siblings. His sister, two years older, married when he was drafted, which was before Pearl Harbor. He was then only twenty and he did not mind being drafted. On account of the depression and the financial situation in the family, he had worked hard and felt dissatisfied. He hoped the Army would give him a "break." He had two younger brothers. The next younger was always ambitious and wanted to study medicine. After finishing high school he managed to take some premedical courses while working evenings. The "kid-brother" was still in school. Ed, our patient, felt that he really got the "breaks" in the Army when he was put into the medical corps. He was trained to be a technician. He wrote enthusiastically to his brother, who meanwhile, when he came to be of draft age, was put into the ASTP as a medical student. Ed felt that everything was alright between them. Then he went overseas where he saw much hard fighting and gave plasma to many severely wounded men. The "medics" have a hard life and, except for the gratefulness of the men they helped and their own good conscience, they receive little recognition. As things became harder in the Italian campaign, he felt more and more frustrated; the young doctors, although much older than he and his brother, reminded him of his brother very much. He envied them, of course, but he also liked them and he had no obvious difficulty in adjusting to them. Finally he developed trench-foot and was sent back to the States and discharged from the Army. His brother was then in his last year of medical school. His father was getting along well financially and he was told that he had time to make up his mind about his future. However, this was more easily said than done. Although he was having a good time, meeting and dating girls, his sleep became more and more disturbed; he yelled in his sleep and he awoke very tired. He told his family that he went through the battle of Salerno during the night—only it was worse. Sometimes he dreamed that he was shot, carried away and operated on. Other times he dreamed that some other man was in an awful condition and he was trying to help him and could not. There were endless variations of painful scenes and he

---

Source: Therese Benedek, *Insight and Personality Adjustment—A Study of the Psychological Effects of War.* Copyright 1946 The Ronald Press Company, New York. Excerpt is from pp. 92-94.

carried the mood of them with him all day. He was angry with himself because he felt that he might become an "NP"; he became quite irritable and finally his brother brought him for consultation.

After he talked about his dreams in vague terms and about his dissatisfaction that he did not really know what he would like to do, the therapist could bring him easily to talk about his brother. Then the envy and competition, the hatred toward him poured out as from a vessel filled to the brim, not in an orderly fashion. He did not say, "I envy my brother because he is going to be a doctor, a medical man, an officer." No, here came the anger that the government, the Army paid for his brother's medical education while he worked for $64 a month. In this anger was repeated the original envy of the new-born sibling who took away his mother's attention. It was followed by the doubt as to whether he was as capable as his brother; perhaps everybody was justified in giving him up as a worthless individual and putting all their love, money and expectations on the brother. His hostility pulsated between two poles — between himself and his brother. Here the primary hostility between brothers came to the surface — "Who is better, he or I?" "Whom does my mother love, me or him?" And this basic question and doubt took many forms. The therapist's confidence that nothing unforgivable would happen if he recognized his feelings toward his brother gave him the courage to face his hostility. Yet back in his mind, there lived the notion that so many men had died, that death does not count much; only he did not know whether he or his brother should die. The primary hostile conflict with the brother was reawakened by the actual situation in which it seemed to him that he was losing and the younger brother was winning in the competition. The frustration of the present situation increased his hostility. Instead of facing the conflict which was rooted in him since early childhood, he projected his anxiety on to the war situation, for war is a good rationalization for any horror and hostility.

SOURCE 131

A psychiatrist described a "typical" case of "pseudocombat fatigue syndrome," around 1968:

This 22-year old LCPL USMC with 2 years of active duty and 4 months of service in Viet Nam was hospitalized aboard *Repose* after he "froze" while under enemy fire. At the time of admission he was grossly anxious, trem-

Source: Robert E. Strange, "Hospital Ship Psychiatric Evacuees," in P. Bourne, ed., *The Psychology and Physiology of Stress* (New York, 1969), pp. 83-84.

ulous, and agitated. His speech was in explosive bursts, interrupted by periods of preoccupied silence; he reported only vague memory for his combat experiences of recent weeks and the incident which had precipitated his evacuation from the field. He was immediately treated with chlorpromazine in a dosage schedule similar to that of Case I, and 24 hours later his symptoms had remarkably improved. He was calm and communicative, and history could be obtained. This indicated longstanding problems with emotional and impulse control which had caused difficulties in social, family, and school relationships. He enlisted in the Marine Corps after impulsively quitting high school; and his 2 years of service had been marked by frequent emotional upheavals, marginal performance of duty, and a total of nine disciplinary actions for a variety of minor offenses. His initial 2 months of Viet Nam duty had been comparatively peaceful. As his unit made more contacts with the enemy over the next 2 months, however, he grew increasingly apprehensive, and this became more severe after he received a minor shrapnel wound. On the night prior to hospitalization, he was involved in a brief but intense fire fight, and he "froze" in a state of tremulous dissociation. He was sedated, maintained in the field overnight, and then evacuated to the hospital ship in the morning. There his treatment program was very similar to that of Case I, utilizing both chemotherapy and group and individual psychotherapy; he showed early good results with almost complete initial disappearance of anxiety symptoms. It was noted that some tremulousness and apprehension recurred, however, whenever new casualties arrived aboard or when combat ashore was visible or audible from the ship. He then demonstrated acute exacerbation of symptoms when confronted with the prospect of possible return to duty, and he was finally evacuated out of the combat zone with the diagnosis of emotionally unstable personality after 10 days of hospitalization.

Source 132

Another Vietnam-era army psychiatrist described the background of a psychiatric case from the combat zone:

Henry was a 21-year-old enlisted man who had been in Viet Nam for some 7 months prior to his referral. He was a member of an airborne unit that had been engaged in fairly heavy combat since its arrival. Four weeks prior to his referral, the company had been surrounded while on a search

---

Source: Gary Tischler, "Combat Zone Patterns," in Peter Bourne, ed., *The Psychology and Physiology of Stress* (New York, 1969), pp. 37-38.

and destroy operation. A saturation bombing of the area was requested. After the bombing, the enemy withdrew and the company returned to base camp. The cost, however, had been heavy. A number of Henry's close buddies had been killed or wounded. Henry did not remember talking very much about the buddies upon his return to base camp. He was all caught up with the realization that he had emerged unscathed. Besides, he was to leave on R & R the following week. The unit did not engage in combat during that week. Henry had a good deal of time to contemplate what he would be doing when he got to Thailand. His description of R & R was of a complete surrender to pleasure. There were girls and "booze." The days and nights were quiet. He had no thought of killing or being killed. However, R & R lasted only 5 days. As the time came to return to Viet Nam, he noticed that his heart was beating more rapidly, that he was sick to his stomach, and that he was restless and "all tied up in knots." Upon return, he heard that the unit had a new CO who was reputed to be a "bastard" and a "glory-hound, John Wayne type." The actual return to the unit was a lonely affair. There had been another mission in his absence. Casualties had again been high. Of the squad to which he was assigned, he was now the only "old timer." I felt like a stranger in my own home, and that home didn't look so good either." He began to get suspicious of the new men. He thought that they were talking about him and planning to steal the things that he had brought back from Thailand. The next evening, Henry picked up an M-16. He pointed it at one of the new men, accused the man of wanting to laugh at him, and threatened to shoot. A number of men jumped on him. He was subdued and evacuated shortly thereafter.

SOURCES 133 and 134

Psychiatrists serving with the army and the Veteran's Administration offered these case histories of World War II psychiatric casualties, and indicated their condition a decade after the combat stress had been experienced:

The youngest of five children, U.V. left his parents' Midwestern farm shortly after completing two years of high school and secured employment as a carpenter's helper in a nearby town. Married in 1937, he continued working at this trade until inducted late in 1942. Assigned to an

Source: Eli Ginzberg et al., eds. *The Ineffective Soldier, Vol. II: Breakdown and Recovery* (New York: Columbia University Press, 1959). Excerpt is from pp. 231-32.

anti-aircraft unit, he participated in the Normandy invasion and in the campaign across northern France. He was in good health and his character and efficiency ratings were "excellent."

After about two months of combat he was knocked unconscious by the blast of an aerial bomb. Because he complained of headaches, dizziness, and a "roaring in the ears," the aid station transferred him to the evacuation hospital where his condition was at first described as "mild." However, his headaches grew worse, and his dizziness was accompanied by spells of nausea and vomiting. U.V. developed increasing nervous tension, had battle dreams, and jumped at any loud noise. Five months of hospitalization in England failed to reveal any organic basis for his persistent headaches but he showed no improvement. He was evacuated to the United States where his hospitalization continued for another seven months in general and convalescent hospitals. Finally, shortly before V-J Day, he was given a medical discharge with a diagnosis of psychoneurosis, acute, severe, anxiety state.

U.V. went back to the family farm and tried to return to the carpentry trade but could not make it. He could not tolerate the noises nor could he climb ladders. Unable to work, he puttered around the farm, and received as his only cash income the 70 percent disability compensation which the Veterans Administration had awarded him. Successive examinations failed to reveal any improvement in his emotional state. He started a liberal arts course at a junior college but soon dropped out. He was not considered suitable for training under Public Law 16 until he improved.

Over the next few years he worked occasionally at odd jobs but never for long. He had difficulties in securing jobs because he detailed his symptoms and his disabilities to any prospective employer. At times, he was able to work reasonably well but either he quit or his temporary work had ended. One employer reported (in 1950) that the veteran was "an excellent painter and carpenter but that he doesn't seem able to work. He frequently blew up on a job and went to pieces." His wife had left him and later divorced him.

He is still rated as 50 percent disabled by the Veterans Administration and the last information (1953) indicates that for the past several years he had been earning some money by working as a part-time contact man for the local post of a veterans' service organization. But his supervisor reports that he could never qualify for a service representative since he appears to be incapable of assuming responsibility. Even with close supervision he had not been doing very well since he made more promises to veterans seeking help than he could possibly fulfill. In communal activities, he would start out on a new project with great enthusiasm but soon tired and moved on to something else.

* * *

Plumber. Is employed by a plumbing contractor as a master plumber; has been with present employer 2 years. Employer knew of veteran's disability at time of hiring. Works a 40-hour week, more when necessary. Reports that his relationships with supervisor, coworkers and customers have been very good. Likes his work and is satisfied with its pay and security. Does not want to assume the responsibilities of operating a business of his own.

Prior to World War II service, veteran had completed 2 years of high school vocational education and an apprenticeship program in plumbing and had worked as a plumber. Following discharge, did not seek work for a year. Then returned to his trade. Has worked for numerous contractors, with only very brief periods of unemployment between jobs.

Initial VA rating for psychoneurosis, anxiety state, moderately severe, has been continued. Veteran has history of fearing closed places, having "smothering spells" during which he gasps for breath, develops palpitation, and perspires profusely. He attributes these feelings to having been hemmed in an engineroom aboard ship during 2 years of combat duty.

Veteran is married and has children.

Source: Department of Veteran Benefits, U.S. Veteran's Administration, *They Return to Work: The Job Adjustment of Psychiatrically Disabled Veterans of World War II and Korea* (Washington, D.C., 1963), p. 137.

SOURCE 135

A psychiatrist offered this "case history" of a World War II Air Corps veteran whose disorder stemmed from his sense of guilt:

Born to a very religious Midwestern family, P.P.T. started attending church at an early age. As well as being the religious center of his community, the church was also a major factor in much of its social life. As he grew up, graduating from high school and taking his first job, he came to accept the religious precepts as basic to his way of life. He attended services twice a week and participated actively in church affairs. Religion was his guide as well as his solace. To flout its doctrines was to flout not only his God and his family, but the whole community of which he was a part. After leaving school P.P.T. worked for four years as a truck driver and construction laborer before entering the Army at age of twenty-two.

During the first nine months of his service career he was shifted rapidly

Source: Eli Ginzberg et al. (eds.), *The Ineffective Soldier: Vol. II: Breakdown and Recovery,* New York: Columbia University Press, 1959. Excerpt is from pp. 113-15.

from one air field to another—Florida, Utah, Colorado, Washington, Oregon, Nebraska. By the time this training was completed he was qualified to work as a gunner on the large bombers and had attained the rank of sergeant. Although this was not the type of duty he would have chosen he accepted it. Next he was sent to England and joined a bomber squadron that had already amassed an impressive record in raids over France and Germany. His first mission was an easy one, but after that it was very difficult. The flak was almost always heavy and enemy fighters were everywhere. His pilot was killed on one raid, his bombardier on another. Once they just barely made it back to England after losing three engines and putting out a fire in the cockpit.

P.P.T. was frightened, but even more, he felt terribly guilty. Every time his plane went up its only purpose was to drop bombs on defenseless people. His job as a gunner was to kill enemy fliers and he did his job. But it seemed all wrong to him. This was contrary to his religion and everything that he had learned prior to entering the Army. He felt that he was guilty of participating in a never ending series of heinous crimes for which his family, his community, and his God must always condemn him. He became jittery, could not sleep, and vomited frequently. Yet he kept going and completed his twenty-five missions in a commendable manner. Seven months after leaving the United States he was on his way home again.

After a furlough, he returned to duty still completely obsessed with guilt. If anything, his state was worse than when he had been in combat. He didn't want to do anything, could not eat or sleep and had the sensation that ants were crawling all over his body. Hospitalized, he poured forth his preoccupations to the doctor: "There was the raid the day before Christmas. We had to go. I didn't want to kill those poor people. . . . I shot down a man, a German. I feel guilty about it. We shouldn't kill people. Here they hang people for that. . . . I guess that is what bothers me most. I killed somebody. . . . I think about that German I shot down. I know it was him or me, but I just can't forget that I saw him blow up. Up to then it was just an airplane. Then I realized that there was a man in the plane. . . . I keep trying to think that it is all behind me, but I can't. I just think about it and get upset. I can't read or go to classes without thinking about it. You have fighters coming at you in bed and you can't do anything about it. I keep dreaming about it. I just can't help it." The doctor tried to convince him that he had only been doing his duty, but to no avail, and he was finally discharged virtually unimproved by his hospital stay.

Within two months of leaving the Army P.P.T. started work in a steel plant. At first he found it difficult to work; he was plagued with frequent thoughts and dreams of combat. He did not go to church or associate with his old friends. Gradually, however, he began to participate in community activities and finally started going to church again. By 1948, although still rather restless and suffering from insomnia, he had almost fitted himself back into his old pattern of life. He enjoyed his job, went hunting and fishing for recreation, and was thinking of getting married. He felt far less guilty than he had when he returned from Europe. Later he married and had two children. He feels very much a part of his community again and has, as he sees it, returned to a religious way of life.

SOURCE 136

A young Confederate officer and two enlisted men commented on the hardening effect of seeing the physical remains of battlefields day after day:

"I felt quite small in that fight the other day when the musket balls and cannon balls was flying around me as thick as hail and my best friends falling on both sides dead and mortally wounded Oh Dear it is impossible for me to express my feeling when the fight was over & I saw what was done the tears came then free oh that I never could behold such a sight again to think of it among civilized people killing one another like beasts one would think that the supreme rule would put a stop to it but wee sinned as a nation and must suffer in the flesh as well as spiritually those things wee cant account for."

"Up on the bluff we saw the first dead Yankee—he lay stark and cold in death upon the hillside among the trees in the gloom of the gathering twilight; the pale face turned towards us, upon which we looked with feelings mingled with awe and dread. We had heard and seen many new and strange things that day. Later on in the war, we could look upon the slain on the battlefield with little less feeling than upon the carcass of an animal. Such are some of the hardening effects of war. I don't think we were again as badly scared as on that day; I was not, I am sure."

"I saw the body [of a man killed the previous day] this morning and a horrible sight it was. Such sights do not affect me as they once did. I can not describe the change nor do I know when it took place, yet I know that there is a change for I look on the carcass of a man now with pretty much such feeling as I would do were it a horse or hog."

Source: Sgt. W. H. Morgan, *Personal Reminiscences of the War of 1861-65* (Lynchburg, Va., 1911), p. 62; Bell Irwin Wiley, *The Life of Johnny Reb* (New York, 1943) pp. 32, 35.

SOURCE 137

Green Berets, veterans of Vietnam, spoke of their impressions of bloodshed in combat:

Case 217

Did you ever go deer hunting? You lead. It's just a lucky shot. Felt like having a party. Just a freak, lucky shot. . . .
  It was a lot of fun.
  . . . was never nauseous. No, from the heat, yes, not from what I saw. . . .
Enjoyed Vietnam. Always something to do, twenty-four hours a day.

Case 221

I just felt more relaxed [in Vietnam] and free of mind. There wasn't no pressure on me and I enjoyed relaxation even on operations. I enjoyed it. No money problems. No women problems. I just felt comfortable there. . . .
  They killed the kid trying to get her to talk . . . so they just killed her too
. . . didn't bother me a bit. . . .

Source: D. M. Mantell, *True Americanism: Green Berets and War Resisters* (New York: Teachers College Press, 1975), p. 168.

SOURCE 138

Samuel L. Clemens was a member of a small company of Confederate volunteers in 1861. He later recalled the first "action" he and his comrades saw after having been warned one evening of the approach of Union troops:

It was late, and there was a deep woodsy stillness everywhere. There was a veiled moonlight, which was only just strong enough to enable us to mark the general shape of objects. Presently a muffled sound caught our ears, and we recognized it as the hoof-beats of a horse or horses. And right away a figure appeared in the forest path; it could have been made of smoke, its mass had so little sharpness of outline. It was a man on horseback, and it seemed to me that there were others behind him. I got hold

Source: Mark Twain, "The Private History of a Campaign That Failed," in *The American Claimant and Other Stories* (New York, 1899), pp. 276-79.

of a gun in the dark, and pushed it through a crack between the logs, hardly knowing what I was doing, I was so dazed with fright. Somebody said "Fire!" I pulled the trigger. I seemed to see a hundred flashes and hear a hundred reports; then I saw the man fall down out of the saddle. My first feeling was of surprised gratification; my first impulse was an apprentice sportsman's impulse to run and pick up his game. Somebody said, hardly audibly, "Good—we've got him!—wait for the rest." But the rest did not come. We waited—listened—still no more came. There was not a sound, not the whisper of a leaf; just perfect stillness; an uncanny kind of stillness, which was all the more uncanny on account of the damp, earthy, late-night smells now rising and pervading it. Then, wondering, we crept stealthily out, and approached the man. When we got to him the moon revealed him distinctly. He was lying on his back, with his arms abroad; his mouth was open and his chest heaving with long gasps, and his white shirt-front was all splashed with blood. The thought shot through me that I was a murderer; that I had killed a man—a man who had never done me any harm. That was the coldest sensation that ever went through my marrow. I was down by him in a moment, helplessly stroking his fore-head; and I would have given anything then—my own life freely—to make him again what he had been five minutes before. And all the boys seemed to be feeling in the same way; they hung over him, full of pitying interest, and tried all they could to help him, and said all sorts of regretful things. They had forgotten all about the enemy; they thought only of this one forlorn unit of the foe. Once my imagination persuaded me that the dying man gave me a reproachful look out of his shadowy eyes, and it seemed to me that I would rather he had stabbed me than done that. He muttered and mumbled like a dreamer in his sleep about his wife and his child; and I thought with a new despair, "This thing that I have done does not end with him; it falls upon *them* too, and they never did me any harm, any more than he."

In a little while the man was dead. He was killed in war; killed in fair and legitimate war; killed in battle, as you may say; and yet he was as sincerely mourned by the opposing force as if he had been their brother. The boys stood there a half-hour sorrowing over him, and recalling the details of the tragedy, and wondering who he might be, and if he were a spy, and saying that if it were to do over again they would not hurt him unless he attacked them first. It soon came out that mine was not the only shot fired; there were five others—a division of the guilt which was a great relief to me, since it in some degree lightened and diminished the burden I was carrying. There were six shots fired at once; but I was not in my right mind at the time, and my heated imagination had magnified my one shot into a volley.

The man was not in uniform, and was not armed. He was a stranger in the country; that was all we ever found out about him. The thought of him got to preying upon me every night; I could not get rid of it. I could not drive it away, the taking of that unoffending life seemed such a wanton thing. And it seemed an epitome of war; that all war must be just that—the killing of strangers against whom you feel no personal animosity; strangers whom, in other circumstances, you would help if you found them in trouble, and who would help you if you needed it. My campaign was spoiled. It seemed to me that I was not rightly equipped for this awful business; that war was intended for men, and I for a child's nurse. I resolved to retire from this avocation of sham soldiership while I could save some remnant of my self-respect. These morbid thoughts clung to me against reason; for at bottom I did not believe I had touched that man. The law of probabilities decreed me guiltless of his blood; for in all my small experience with guns I had never hit anything I had tried to hit, and I knew I had done my best to hit him. Yet there was no solace in the thought. Against a diseased imagination demonstration goes for nothing.

SOURCE 139

> Three GIs wrote home from Vietnam of their thoughts upon knowing they had killed enemy personnel:

DEAR NANCEE,

I received your letter yesterday evening, and it was good to hear from you again. I am fine—just a little beat. I had guard duty last night, so I am tired. We had some visitors when I was on guard the other night. About 30 V.C. tried to get into our compound. You see, what we mainly guard are helicopters. Anyway, a few tried to blow up some copters. I saw them about 20 feet from where I was. I fired a few rounds in their direction, so I might have hit one. You see, the next morning they had an investigation of the area in which I saw the V.C., and they found traces of human blood.

When I was getting off the ship, I said a silent prayer for God not to make me try to kill anyone. Because He's the only one who has the right to take a life—after all, He put us here. He can take us when He wants.

But Nancee, it was either him or me.

Sincerely,

Eddie

Source: Glenn Munson, ed., Letters from Vietnam (New York, 1966), pp. 53, 73, 123.

HI, GRAM,

It was good to hear from you. I was so glad to hear from home. It felt good. My arm was giving me a little trouble this week, but okay today. Tell everyone I said hi. My back is giving me some trouble. Say, do you know when I got shot I cried, and I grabbed my gun and rifle and said *dear God don't let me die,* then I started to yell and cry and stood up. I was shooting all over, then he shot back, and I saw where he was at. I killed him. When he fell from the tree, I ran to him. I was bleeding and I was shaking very bad. When I saw him, I don't know what came over me, but I emptied all I had in him, some 87 holes they found in him. After an hour or so, I was okay. It's no fun shooting a person, and now whenever I see a person who is a Vietnamese I think of that time out there, and I start shaking and I don't know if I should kill them or what. Say, how I wish I was home. It's no fun out here. I feel lost and all alone out here so far from home. I am not doing too good. Please take care of yourself, okay? And please say a prayer for me that I get back okay. I tell you it's bad out here.

. . .

DEAR MARILYN AND LOWELL,

Hi! How is everything going for the two of you and the kids? Just fine, I hope. Everything is going pretty good for me here at the present time.

Since the last time I wrote, a few new things have been happening. Since the last time, I've turned from a nice quiet guy into a killer. That raid I told you about that they kept canceling came off on the thirtieth, but my platoon didn't go. The next one was on the fifth, and we weren't supposed to go, either. About ten o'clock that morning we got the word to get ready.

We went in by helicopter, and after reaching shore we set up outside a village. My lieutenant after a while asked for eight guys to go on a combat patrol with him, and I of course volunteered to go.

We were supposed to search an area that was cleared earlier, but they weren't sure if any Vietcong were left or not.

While we were walking along, a shot just missed the lieutenant, and everyone hit the deck. Just before it happened, I was looking up into the trees and saw the muzzle flash from the rifle. After we hit the deck, the lieutenant yelled and asked if anyone saw him. I was raising my rifle up towards the tree just then, and I said "yeah" as I pulled the trigger. I have an automatic rifle and fired about 14 or 15 rounds into the tree where I saw the flash, and the Vietcong came falling out.

I always wondered what it would feel like to kill someone, but after it happened I didn't feel any different. It didn't bother me a bit, and I sort of felt good about it. I didn't feel proud because I killed him, but proud that I didn't freeze up when the time came. I figured his next shot might have been at me and I beat him to it.

That was the only thing that happened around me, and the next morning everyone went back to the ships. We had a couple of guys killed and some wounded, but just how many I don't know.

Well, I guess that is about it for now, so I'll close for the time being. Take care of yourself for now and don't work too hard. I'll write again soon.

All my love,

Mike

SOURCE 140

A Confederate soldier ended a letter containing a long, familial poem with this note:

"Molly thar were several other verses but having to write it by moonlight and with a pensil I can not read them this morning I hav composed meny such sens I have bin from home and as I walked my post at knight this will show you that not withstanding my long absens from home and has seen so much murder I still have the same tender feelings that I evar had."

Source: Bell Irwin Wiley, The Life of Johnny Reb (New York, 1943), p. 215.

SOURCE 141

A well-to-do Californian volunteer in the British army during World War I commented on the transitory character of combat's horrors:

I, who am over here for the good of my soul and the greater success of allied arms, have got to go through a number of extremely unpleasant experiences and become thoroughly familiar with all the sides that go to make up the "Romance of War"; and for me these things are good and threaten no danger to the mind, because a very few seconds after you are . . . turned sick by the sight of some uncleared remains of a late battlefield, you have forgotten about it, and while the item undoubtedly left a permanent subjective impression, its effects on the *objective* mind of you and on your good health and spirits is *nil*.

Source: Harry Butters, Harry Butters, R.F.A. (New York, 1918), p. 231; quoted in C. Genthe, American War Narratives (New York, 1969), p. 44.

SOURCE 142

Marine Lt. John Doyle speculated in a letter to his father, written on Guadalcanal in November 1942, on the effect of the combat experience on his personality and values:

What has it done to me? What does it mean to me?

I know that I have not become cruel or callous. I am sure that I am hardened. If a man cannot produce, I'll push him into the most degrading, menial task I can find. A man that shrinks from duty is worse than a man lost. He should be thrown out of the entire outfit. He's not fit to live with the men with whom he is not willing to die. Death is easy. It happens often.

The toughest part is going on, existing as an animal. Wet, cold and hungry many times, a man can look forward only to the next day when the sun, flies and mosquitoes descend to devour him.

Few men fear bullets. They are swift, silent and certain. Shelling and bombing are more often the cursed bugaboos.

Source: Harry Maule, ed., *A Book of War Letters* (New York, 1943), p. 185.

SOURCE 143

Sgt. Floyd Jones, a black artilleryman in World War II and veteran of "the Battle of the Bulge," recalled his decision to "set [my army experience] outside of the mainstream of my life":

"From the very beginning, when I realized there was going to be a conflict in which I would participate, I determined I was not going to allow myself to be warped by war. Therefore the time I spent in service was something I set outside of the mainstream of my life. I did my time with but one thought; in spite of hell I was going to return just as I left physically and mentally. While I was in the army I was a soldier, not an interested spectator, asking no quarter and giving none. When I stepped out of my uniform for the last time I stripped off the last vestige of army life and took up my life, to a great extent, where I had dropped it. . . .

"The time I spent in service was one of the greatest experiences I ever had. I saw much of the world I would most certainly would not have seen otherwise. I did not see the victims of the war that an infantryman, or a front line man, would encounter. I saw devastation but not the victims. I am sure this helped me remain an actor who would eventually remove his makeup and become himself once more. . . ."

Source: M. Motley, ed., *Invisible Soldier* (Detroit, 1976), pp. 177-78.

SOURCE 144

Two GIs expressed their horror in poetic form during World War II:

Battle

The blackness was in me,
Such fate and fury as I had never known:
Complete amnesia from love and spring,
And tenderness of home.
Surging through me, I could feel it rise
And lift me with it.
I was free, to lust for blood,
And I could use my hands
To tear and smash . . .
My eyes to sight for killing!
The noises, whistling, wooming
In the blackness
Became a part of me,
Spurred my passion, lashed me on,
Became fused with my mind's unwholesomeness:
I would caress, with savagery,
And put them all in hell forever.
I willed to butcher as they had butchered,
Destroy as they destroyed.
I sobbed aloud as no man has ever cried:
Someone screamed, maybe me. I could smell
Powder, burnt flesh, maybe mine . . .
I think I died then.
I don't want to remember any more . . .
God knows—I wish I could forget.

—Sgt. S. Colker

Home from War

Who can say at war's end
"We are lucky living men?"
After so much of us has died
How can we be satisfied
That we, the so-called living men,

Source: Puptent Poets of the "Stars and Stripes, Mediterranean" (Italy, 1945), pp. 18, 109.

Will find a way to live again?
For when a man has daily faced
The brute within him, low, debased,
Can he look forward to the light,
Wipe out the memories of the fight
Forget the strange erotic bliss
That comes with some cheap purchased kiss?
Ah, no! And it will be his fateful lot
To live on and find that he lives not
Though like the living we'll behave
We'll be the dead without a grave.

— Cpl. Anthony Carlin

SOURCE 145

Pfc. Richard Marks wrote to his family from Vietnam June 1965, of his fear that he had "just grown up too fast" in combat:

When we finally get out of this it will be quite awhile to reajust to normal life, of not jumping at each sound, and just living like an animal in general. Values even change—a human life becomes so unimportant, and the idea of killing a V.C. is just commonplace now—just like a job. In a way it all scares me more than being shot at.

I am a regular combat veteran now, and I have all the hair raising stories to go with it, and I am only 19 years old. I have just grown up too fast, I wonder when it is all going to catch up to me and kick me in the teeth, and it is bound to happen.

Source: *The Letters of Richard Marks Pfc., USMC,* ed. Gloria M. Kramer (Philadelphia, 1967), p. 85.

SOURCE 146

A black Vietnam veteran from Pennsylvania talked about his moment of horror:

Ya know, some of the fellows in Vietnam, they become hardened; ah, they develop a crustation or something that affords them the benefit of not having their conscience bother them. Now these guys might go out to the field. They might kill women, children.

Ya know, I cannot do this. I tried to develop this shield of force or whatever it was, and I really tried hard. I talked to guys who had; guys who could laugh at this, to try and formulate some way ya know, to help myself, so I could live, and on several occasions when I said I killed or was responsible for the death of my fellow man.

But, um, there's one time that really stands out in my mind, that I feel contributed greatly to my having to spend six months in a psychiatric ward. I was out on patrol and came to a village and the Cong had been there and they had killed about everyone. The ones that they hadn't killed were dying and there was one child there, and they hadn't harmed her; she was a very small child. And one of the officers said that she could inform the Cong, and that we were waiting for them we knew they'd be back because they'd left supplies there.

And he wanted this child killed, and as I looked at him I could see that this really meant something to him (to have her killed); and it was going to help him believe in what he was doing.

I could see that in his face. It was like it was unspoken. And I didn't want to help him. I didn't mind helping my fellow man, but I didn't want to help him with that. But what can you do when someone puts a gun to your head (or in your hand).

So, I killed the child. . . . and a couple of weeks later, as a result of this, my head blew up. I lapsed into a psychosis or something like this. When I was in the psychiatric ward I once saw my chart and it had "schitzophrenic reactions."

I really felt as though when I was in the ward that I was an invalid. Ah, I had no physical handicap whatsoever, but some vital, ah, ah, basic, ah, central or part of my mind was affected to the extent that I really couldn't manage.

I finally left that talk about killing that person, that girl, I don't really have that much trouble providing I stay away from mirrors. But if I go out every face is a mirror, ya know what I mean?

I don't know what I see but I'll just say this, that it immediately transports me back to Vietnam. And I relive what happened over there.

I wanted to burn Pittsburgh and possibly Philly. But it's not that I'm adverse to war, it's just that I had changed so much and Pittsburgh hadn't.

Source: Robert Jones (producer), *The War Comes Home* (New Film Co., 1972). I am indebted to Pat Merwin and Jeff Lewis for bringing this to my attention, and to Jack Hayes and Robert Jones for permission to reproduce this veteran's words.

SOURCE 147

Nonveterans and veterans from Connecticut who had been drafted responded in the mid-1960s to questions designed to sort them out on a "Belligerent-Conciliatory" axis. They were then further distinguished by level of education, annual income, and type of job:

Attitudes of Drafted Veterans Compared with Nonveterans by Education, Income, and Job (in Percentages)

	EDUCATION					
	13+ YEARS		10-12 YEARS		0-9 YEARS	
	DRAFTEE	NONVETERAN[d]	DRAFTEE	NONVETERAN	DRAFTEE	NONVETERAN[c]
Belligerent	20	29	42	26	41	19
Intermediate	40	50	32	37	26	48
Conciliatory	40	21	23	36	26	28
No answer	0	0	3	2	7	5
Total	(10)	(38)	(31)	(65)	(27)	(94)

	ANNUAL INCOME[a]					
	OVER $10,000		$6-10,000		UNDER $6,001	
	DRAFTEE	NONVETERAN[d]	DRAFTEE	NONVETERAN[b]	DRAFTEE	NONVETERAN
Belligerent	27	24	52	25	26	24
Intermediate	64	47	15	47	39	38
Conciliatory	9	26	27	27	30	33
No answer	0	3	6	1	4	5
Total	(11)	(38)	(33)	(89)	(23)	(63)

TYPE OF JOB

	PROFESSIONAL		WHITE COLLAR		BLUE COLLAR	
	DRAFTEE	NONVETERAN[d]	DRAFTEE	NONVETERAN	DRAFTEE	NONVETERAN[c]
Belligerent	0	24	33	23	44	23
Intermediate	25	53	50	40	24	46
Conciliatory	75	24	17	35	26	27
No answer	0	0	0	2	7	4
Total	(4)	(17)	(18)	(60)	(46)	(120)

[a]Seven men omitted because incomes are unknown.
[b]Significant at .01 level of confidence.
[c]Significant at .05 level of confidence.
[d]Significance not tested because of small n.

Source: Nancy Edelman Phillips, "Militarism and Grass-Roots Involvement in the M-I Complex," *Journal of Conflict Resolution* (December 1973): 646.

SOURCE 148

Vietnam veterans responded to hypotheticals put to them by psychologists in 1971 concerning the appropriateness of violence. Their responses were then individually totalled and grouped by degree of combat exposure:

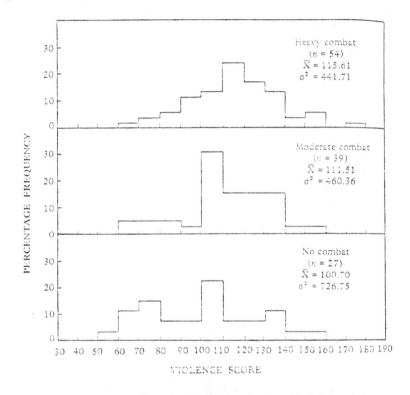

Note: A higher violence score indicates a greater expressed belief that violent responses to the hypotheticals be appropriate

---

Source: David Brody and Leon Rappoport, "Violence and Vietnam," *Human Relations* (1973): 746.

SOURCE 149

A Vietnam veteran who, despite his words, had displayed some violent traits before enlisting and volunteering for Airborne

---

Source: Interviews with "Leadertown" veterans, conducted by Thomas Conley, 1975.

*training, answered a question that asked him to compare him-
self on a "violence scale" before and after service in the following fashion:*

"More violent! Before I went into the service I was definitely against violence. Because I'm a smaller dude, as far as fist fights were concerned, I
wasn't much for it. I would go across the street to avoid the necessary
contact where I would have to display violence. After a time in the service, with the people I was around, with the fact that if Charlie came over
the wire I was going to kill him, with the training that I had, I turned
into a quite violent person. I didn't get to use all the violence when I was
in Vietnam, and when I came home, I wanted to use it. I find myself still
a little more violent than whenever I was younger."

SOURCE 150

*Percentage distribution of army stockade prisoner and overall
army enlisted achievement test scores below 90 (low), 1954-64:*

	1954	1956	1958	1960	1962	1964
Prisoners	63.3	62.9	49.0	42.0	37.7	32.3
All enlisted	32.0	27.0	17.0	16.0	16.4	14.8

Source: Stanley Brodsky and Norman Eggleston, eds., *The Military Prison* (Carbondale, Ill.,
1970), p. 149.

SOURCE 151

*A GI on furlough during World War II found himself talking
about his comrades-in-arms to excess among friends and family:*

"Here I am back home," he suddenly remarked, "home where I've been
longing to come—where I had so many questions to ask—and all I talk

Source: Willard Waller, *The Veteran Comes Back* (New York, 1944), pp. 30-31.

about is the army! I've been thinking about nothing but all of you, but I keep talking about the rest of the army guys."

[Shortly after returning to duty, he wrote to his wife:]

"All the time I was with you, I had the most curious feeling that I was waiting to go back—to go "home" to Camp X——. Now I realize why. I'm really home now, hard as it is to say this. But that's what happens, it seems, when you join the army. You don't feel that you belong anywhere else—you can't, when you're in a uniform. The army seemed strange when I first got into it, but now everything else *but* the army seems strange."

SOURCE 152

> *A veteran of the fight at Monte Cassino recalled a party his company had managed to hold one night in 1944 after having been pulled out of the front lines for a rest:*

Allen and I, staggering a little, with arms around each other's shoulders, went out together, still singing as we crossed the moonlit field to our tent. When we stopped, we could hear from back in the hall the loud singing, the cry of voices and shouts in the night, and I am glad that we did not stay to the end of this drunken affair. There were no fights, though, and no ugly drunks, just a lot of noise, a lot of staggering, a few men violently sick outside, and then, as the last of the men found their way back to their tents, quiet settled down once more on our moonlit valley. Lying in bed with my head going round in circles, I could hear some of the men trying to find their beds in the dark. There were occasional shouts from different parts of the encampment, and now and again a snatch from a song. The men would look after each other, I knew, and I felt a warm sense of companionship with them. It had been a drunken party—what else for a group of men in this situation?—but it had not been a brawl. The men would value this comradeship later in the misery that lay ahead of them, and perhaps after the war was over they would remember it as the one good feature of their military service. In the drunken gaiety of that party we had for a moment felt closer to each other, and almost happy. Yet in retrospect the affair was pathetic: drunken songs in the moonlight, a moment of camaraderie standing out in the dreary landscape of war. For this was only a short respite from the fighting, as we all knew, and for some of us there was just a little of life left.

Source: Harold Bond, *Return to Cassino* (New York, 1964), p. 164.

SOURCE 153

William Logan, a black trooper in the 9th Cavalry Regiment, wrote to the Savannah Tribune from the Philippines of a moment of hardship in the field that he shared with a white Alabaman:

After you march a day over here you will make the soft side of a mahogany board for a bed; this lad with his raincoat said when he was in Alabama that he hated a colored man but since the Spanish-American War he loves a colored man. He was in the Rough Riders. He said he would never forget the day when the colored 10th U.S. Cavalry charged San Juan Hill and saved his life. He said to me the only way I can show my love for a colored man tonight is to let him cover with half my raincoat. He and I covered our heads to keep the mosquitoes from eating us up.

Source: Willard B. Gatewood, comp., "Smoked Yankees" and the Struggle for Empire (Urbana, Ill., 1971), p. 291.

SOURCE 154

Attitudes Toward Serving in a Company Containing Negro and White Platoons Among Men Who Have Done So and Men Who Have Not

(Europe, June 1945) (Numbers Following the Bars = Numbers of Cases on Which Percentages Are Based.)

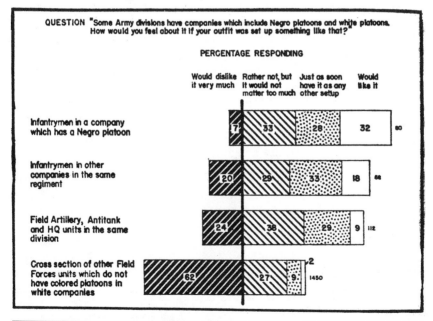

Source: S. Stouffer et al., Studies in Social Psychology in World War II, 4 vols. (Princeton, N.J.: Princeton University Press, 1949-50), I, p. 594.

SOURCE 155

White GIs who had served in units with black GIs during World War II commented on such integration:

A platoon sergeant from South Carolina: When I heard about it, I said I'd be damned if I'd wear the same shoulder patch they did. After that first day when we saw how they fought, I changed my mind. They're just like any of the other boys to us.

A Company commander from Nevada: Relations are very good. They have their pictures taken together, go to church services, movies, play ball together. For a time there in combat our platoons got so small that we had to put a white squad in the colored platoon. You might think that wouldn't work well, but it did. The white squad didn't want to leave the platoon. I've never seen anything like it.

Source: S. Stouffer et al., *Studies in Social Psychology in World War II,* 4 vols. (Princeton, N.J.: Princeton University Press, 1949-50), I, p. 592.

SOURCE 156

White GIs serving in integrated units and others in segregated units commented on fighting ability of black soldiers, Korea, 1951:

**Rating by White Infantrymen in Integrated and All-White Units
of U.S. Black Soldiers as Fighters**

		PERCENTAGE SAYING, "BLACK SOLDIERS ARE JUST ABOUT AS GOOD"
Among		
White infantrymen in all-white units	(N = 195)	31%
White infantrymen in integrated units	(N = 1024)	50%

Source: Leo Bogart, ed., *Social Research and the Desegregation of the U.S. Army* (Chicago, 1969), p. 127.

SOURCE 157

> Black and white GIs from integrated units in Korea commented
> on their reactions to integration:

(Negro EM, QM company): Just as I said before, mixing is the best thing
for the Army because there are many advantages. From my knowledge of
white people at Fort Sill and back in Florida, I didn't have a very favorable
opinion of them. If this is not to be quoted in my name [Of course not!] I
hate white people. Now if all white people were like the white boys in this
company it wouldn't take long before everybody would get along swell.
Of course you know I can only speak from what I have seen in the past
month. If the colored and white get along together the same way from
now on, I'm all for mixed units.

(Negro infantryman): Well, I ain't never had much to do with white folks.
I come from Florida. When I learned that I was coming to a white outfit,
I thought sure that I wouldn't like it. But these 'fay [white] boys ain't so
bad to get along with. I find them no different from other folks. They treat
me all right. I sleep and eat with them. None have said anything out of
the way about my race. This here mixed unit is OK with me.

(Battalion commander [white]): The regimental commander decided
that he would take all the colored soldiers out of the white battalions
except the weapons companies. It was interesting that many of the soldiers who were being transferred didn't want to go . . . I happened to witness a rather unusual incident. This battalion was leaving the demonstration area and the — —th battalion (all-Negro) was marching into the area.
And a number of our men started yelling "Hey Joe!" at one big colored
man who had been in this battalion for a while. And this great big colored
man was marching down the road with tears in his eyes. He was actually
crying, he was so miserable.

(Two white infantrymen): (1): One man's like another man to me. Only
thing was, I didn't think a colored boy could put up much of a fight. They'd
been pushed around so much, all the fight was taken out of them, 'cept
when they was fifty together and had knives.
(2): Boy, you sure have learned different!
(1): I sure did.
(2): Well, I never liked the colored folks. Always thought they'd bug out
on you as well as smile at you. But if these boys are an example, I know
better now.

Source: Leo Bogart, ed., Social Research and the Desegregation of the U.S. Army (Chicago,
1969), pp. 138-41, 167.

(White EM, divisional HQ): I'm not going to have a colored guy up to my house to meet my sister any more than I would have before the War, just because the guy was in the damned Army. Of course if he's wearing a — — — Division shoulder patch I'd consider him my buddy, same as any other guy from the — — — Division.

[How about this colored boy in the tent here?] Oh, that's different. He's just like any of the other boys. I'd take him home. I wouldn't think of treating him any different. He's a buddy of mine.

(Infantryman [white]): Then there's the folks and the way they feel about it. They'd think I'd gone off my rocker. And how about the girls. No girl'd go out with me if I hung around with the black boys. They'd think I was screwing the black bitches. And boy, I wish I was now.

[But how about the colored guys you know right here?] That's different. I owe them something for sticking with me. They're swell guys and I wouldn't let them down. I'd do anything for them. . . . But even so, maybe, I'd have to be careful.

SOURCE 158

Among white GIs in integrated units in Korea, those with more contact with blacks before entering the service were more likely to respond positively to nondiscriminatory personnel policies than were those with little or no contact, demonstrating, once again, the importance of preservice experiences and attitudes:

		PERCENTAGE OF WHITE INFANTRYMEN IN INTEGRATED UNITS WHO SAY NEGROES "SHOULD BE ASSIGNED AS INDIVIDUALS WITHOUT REGARD TO COLOR"
Among men who, in civilian life, had:		
Little or no contact with Negroes	(N = 435)	36%
Some contact with Negroes	(N = 362)	45
Much contact with Negroes	(N = 287)	64

Source: Leo Bogart, ed., *Social Research and the Desegregation of the U.S. Army* (Chicago, 1969), p. 134.

SOURCE 159

Feeling That a Battle Was Not Worth the Cost, in Relation to Time in Combat
(Enlisted Infantrymen in Line Companies, Italy, April 1945)

QUESTION: "WHEN YOU WERE FIGHTING A PARTICULAR BATTLE, DID YOU EVER HAVE THE FEELING THAT IT WASN'T WORTH THE COST?"

PERCENTAGE OF MEN GIVING EACH ANSWER AMONG

	PRIVATES AND PFC'S WHO HAVE BEEN IN COMBAT FOR					NONCOMS WHO HAVE BEEN IN COMBAT FOR			
	LESS THAN 2 MONTHS	2 THROUGH 3 MONTHS	4 THROUGH 6 MONTHS	7 THROUGH 8 MONTHS	9 MONTHS OR MORE	LESS THAN 4 MONTHS	4 THROUGH 6 MONTHS	7 THROUGH 8 MONTHS	9 MONTHS OR MORE
Yes, almost always	17 } 58	22 } 63	22 } 77	17 } 72	24 } 77	12 } 49	12 } 69	16 } 74	14 } 89
Yes, sometimes	41	41	55	55	53	37	57	58	75
No, never	13	10	11	14	12	7	14	15	3
Undecided	23	24	11	14	10	39	14	10	8
No answer	6	3	1	a	1	5	3	1	—
Total	100	100	100	100	100	100	100	100	100
Number of cases	101	180	587	252	195	143	151	89	110

[a] Less than 0.5 per cent.

Source: S. Stouffer et al., *Studies in Social Psychology in World War II*, 4 vols. (Princeton, N.J.: Princeton University Press, 1949-50), II, p. 154.

SOURCE 160

> *A medical corpsman in Vietnam, David* — — — *recalled his
> struggle for "survival":*

"I thought I was there to help people, but I soon learned that the only real
goal anybody had was survival.

I became like the rest of them. I was forced to suspend the values and
the traditions I spent twenty-two years of my life learning, because they
were obstacles to my survival.

I counted on having my values and my identity as an American reaffirmed
when I returned."

Source: Chuck Noell and Gary Wood, *We Are All POWs* (Philadelphia, 1975), p. 39.

SOURCE 161

> *"Ronnie Anderson" had been a janitor, a laborer in a foundry,
> and a miner before service in World War II. He became a ser-
> geant and reenlisted after the war. His mother talked to an inter-
> viewer about him in 1948:*

It seems as though Ronnie's had the army in his blood ever since he was
knee-high to a grasshopper, I guess. He always used to be crazy about
guns—even when he was just a little kid six or seven years old. Anything
to do with guns was wonderful. It used to worry me sometimes, but then I
guess you'd say he just had a knack for it. And then when he was hardly
out of his teens he was scoutmaster of the troop here, you know. He was
crazy about both of them, guns and scouting. I guess he bought every kind
of clothes they had in the scouts. He even bought the scoutmaster top
coat. Seemed foolish, but he just wanted to get everything they had in
scouting—knives, clothes, all sorts of equipment—everything. Ronnie
just seemed to live for that scout troop.

. . . He's decided to reenlist, you know. I had a feeling when he got
home that's what he had in mind. He didn't say much about it, but I sort
of figured that's what he was going to do. He's done very well in the army
—he seems to enjoy the life very much. He says he's learned more in the
army than he did in high school. He went from sergeant right up to top
sergeant, you know. They say—of course I don't know—but they say
that's almost impossible in the army, but Ronnie did it. He said that he
was going to make the jump, that he didn't want any rating after sergeant
but top sergeant, and that's what he got. He was with the 33rd Division on
Luzon. They awarded him the Bronze Star.

Source: Robert Havighurst, *American Veteran Back Home* (New York, 1951), p. 124.

SOURCE 162

Proportions Promoted, as Related to Previously Expressed Attitudes, Holding Education and Age Constant by Standardization, 1943–44

	SAMPLE A		SAMPLE B		SAMPLE C	
	AMONG PRIVATES IN SEPT. 1943, PERCENTAGE BECOMING PFC'S BY JAN. 1944		AMONG PRIVATES IN NOV. 1943, PERCENTAGE BECOMING NCO'S BY MAR. 1944		AMONG PFC'S IN NOV. 1943, PERCENTAGE BECOMING NCO'S BY MAR. 1944	
Think fair to be drafted	24	*(242)*	27	*(186)*	81	*(76)*
Others	19	*(122)*	20	*(116)*	63	*(30)*
In good physical condition	24	*(114)*	40	*(80)*	80	*(50)*
Others	18	*(231)*	20	*(210)*	77	*(42)*
Seldom worry about combat injury	21	*(236)*	29	*(201)*	80	*(78)*
Others	24	*(140)*	16	*(110)*	75	*(24)*
Expect to do O.K. in battle	25	*(270)*	32	*(189)*	81	*(74)*
Others	15	*(103)*	15	*(127)*	70	*(26)*
Think Army's control not too strict	29	*(216)*	28	*(143)*	81	*(54)*
Others	12	*(159)*	22	*(168)*	74	*(48)*
Think AWOL serious	28	*(237)*	28	*(182)*	79	*(79)*
Others	14	*(128)*	20	*(126)*	79	*(17)*
Think officers interested in EM	26	*(193)*	29	*(178)*	80	*(55)*
Others	16	*(182)*	19	*(135)*	73	*(44)*

Source: S. Stouffer et al., *Studies in Social Psychology in World War II*, 4 vols. (Princeton, N.J.: Princeton University Press, 1949-50), I, p. 152.

SOURCE 163

*World War II GIs were asked a number of questions about their
childhood in training camps, and later, after some had distinguished themselves in the service, others had displayed marked
psychoneurotic traits, and still others had absented themselves
without leave (AWOL), the responses of these groups to the
aforementioned questions were compared:*

Reported Childhood Experiences as Related to Adjustment in the Army

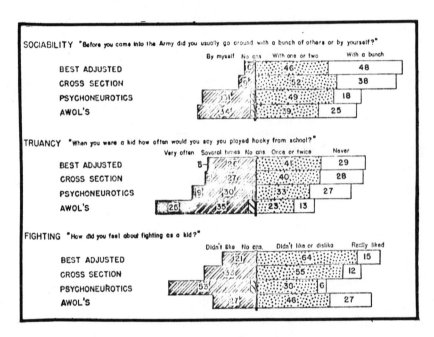

Source: S. Stouffer et al., *Studies in Social Psychology in World War II,* 4 vols. (Princeton,
N.J.: Princeton University Press, 1949-50), II, p. 133.

SOURCE 164

Recruits of the mid- and late 1950s, scoring in the top 20 percent
(I) and next three quintiles (II, III, and IV) on the Armed Forces
Qualification Test, were compared by Defense Department
analysts on a number of "success" standards:

Mental Aptitude and Military Performance

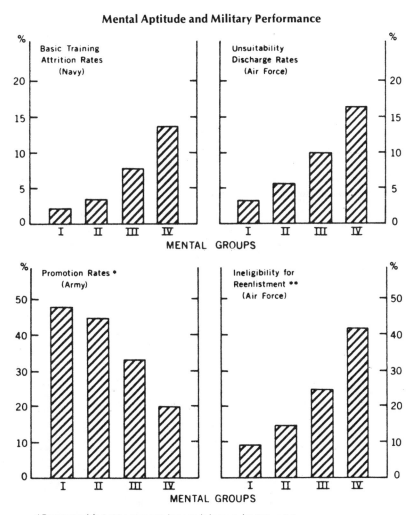

*Percent with 4–10 years service attaining grades E-5 or E-6.
**Percent of initial enlistments in FY 1956–58 not eligible for reenlistment after first
term.

Source: Harold Wool, *The Military Specialist* (Baltimore, Md., 1968), p. 84.

SOURCE 165

Enlisted men with varying levels of commitment to a military career, and civilian men nineteen to twenty-four years of age were asked a number of questions by University of Michigan sociologists in the late 1960s. Note especially the differences between the responses of first-term enlisted men who planned to reenlist and those who did not:

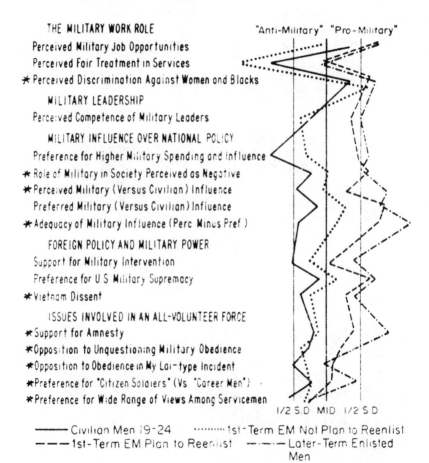

THE MILITARY WORK ROLE   "Anti-Military"   "Pro-Military"
Perceived Military Job Opportunities
Perceived Fair Treatment in Services
✷ Perceived Discrimination Against Women and Blacks

   MILITARY LEADERSHIP
Perceived Competence of Military Leaders

   MILITARY INFLUENCE OVER NATIONAL POLICY
Preference for Higher Military Spending and Influence
✷ Role of Military in Society Perceived as Negative
✷ Perceived Military (Versus Civilian) Influence
Preferred Military (Versus Civilian) Influence
✷ Adequacy of Military Influence (Perc Minus Pref)

   FOREIGN POLICY AND MILITARY POWER
Support for Military Intervention
Preference for U.S Military Supremacy
✷ Vietnam Dissent

   ISSUES INVOLVED IN AN ALL-VOLUNTEER FORCE
✷ Support for Amnesty
✷ Opposition to Unquestioning Military Obedience
✷ Opposition to Obedience in My Lai-type Incident
✷ Preference for "Citizen Soldiers" (Vs "Career Men")
✷ Preference for Wide Range of Views Among Servicemen

                                                  1/2 S.D   MID   1/2 S.D

————— Civilian Men 19-24   ············· 1st-Term EM Not Plan to Reenlist
— — — 1st-Term EM Plan to Reenlist   — ·· — ·· — Later-Term Enlisted
                                                             Men

NOTE: Center line shows midpoint on each measure; other lines show ½ S.D. for all civilians on each measure. Measures marked with an asterisk have been reversed; the "pro-military" side of the chart indicates a low score for the measure.

Mean Scores of Civilian Men 19–24 and Three Navy Groups

Source: Jerald Bachman and John Blair, "Citizen Force or Career Force," *Armed Forces and Society* 2 (November 1975): 85.

SOURCE 166

Army officer candidates in the 1960s were asked a number of questions upon admission to Officer Candidate School (OCS). The responses of those who eventually left the Army were later compared with the responses of those who chose to remain:

Differentiation by Retention in Army

GROUP OF 184 MEN WHO YEARS LATER REMAIN IN ARMY ARE HIGHER IN THESE SCALES AT TIME OF ENTRY INTO TRAINING		GROUP OF 599 MEN WHO YEARS LATER DEPARTED FROM THE ARMY ARE HIGHER IN THESE SCALES AT TIME OF ENTRY INTO TRAINING	
SCALES	T-TEST RESULTS	SCALES	T-TEST RESULTS
Prefers Supervisory Activities	3.88	Values Intellectual Achievement	−2.27
Believes in Moral Absolutes	2.90	Values Approval from Others	−2.13
Extent of Orderliness	2.66	Prefers Problem Analysis	−2.07
Prefers Activity Frequent Change	2.46	Move Away from Aggressor	−1.96
Influences by Persuasive Leadership	2.44		
Degree of Perseverance	2.43		
Values Role Conformity	2.19		
Prefers Mechanical Activities	2.18		
Believes in External Controls	2.17		

Source: Peter Petersen, *Against the Tide* (New Rochelle, N.Y., 1973), p. 150.

SOURCE 167

**Comparison of 358 Men Who Remained in Army with 919 Men Who
Departed: Extent of Their Belief in Moral Absolutes***

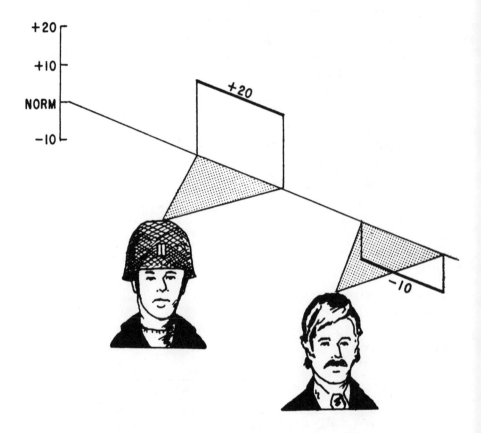

*Persons scoring high believe that moral principles come from an outside power
higher than man; and that it is most important to have faith in something. Individuals
scoring low believe that moral principles are not absolute and unchanging but
depend upon circumstances.*

Source: Peter Petersen, *Against the Tide* (New Rochelle, N.Y., 1973), p. 182.

SOURCE 168

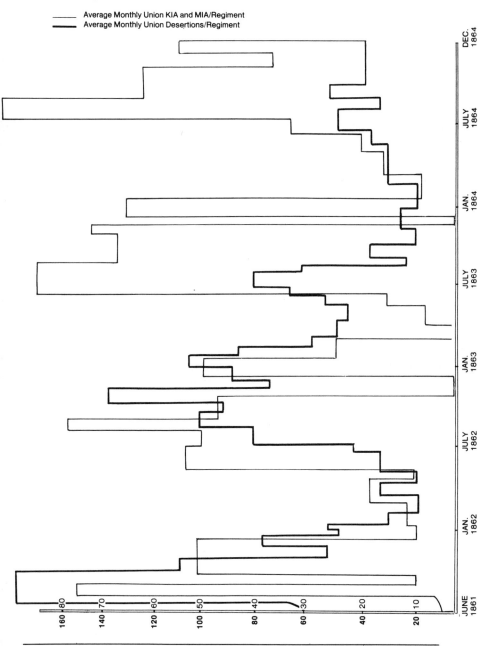

——— Average Monthly Union KIA and MIA/Regiment
▬▬▬ Average Monthly Union Desertions/Regiment

Source: Compiled from tables in U.S. Sanitary Commission, *Statistical Investigations in the Military and Anthropological Status of American Soldiers,* by B. A. Gould (New York, 1869), pp. 590-97.

SOURCE 169

Austin Hodge, a Marine Corps deserter and war resister, addressed a group gathered in a church in 1976 on the eve of his surrendering himself to authorities after living "underground" for seven years:

"I have given up my home, my family, my wife and son, moved from city to city, taken countless menial jobs because in my heart I could not support a war so incredibly hideous that it was far beyond my capacity as a human being to conceive. [I am turning myself in because I want to confront the military with my moral opposition to the war and to actively join in the struggle for amnesty for my fellow exiles.]

You live from minute to minute. You can't be honest with friends. You can't stay in one place. You can't have a job for more than three months. . . . My father [a retired Navy Chief Petty Officer] has been my greatest supporter all along."

Source: Unitarian Universalist *World* 7 (March 15, 1976): 1.

SOURCE 170

Percentage of U.S. Army Using Drugs in the Last Twelve Months (1971) by Place of Service

SERVICE LOCATION	TYPE OF DRUG				
	MARIJUANA (%)	OTHER PSYCHEDELIC DRUGS (%)	STIMULANTS (%)	DEPRESSANTS (%)	NARCOTIC DRUGS (%)
Continental U.S.	41.3	28.4	28.9	21.5	20.1
Europe	40.2	33.0	23.0	14.0	13.1
Viet Nam	50.9	30.8	31.9	25.1	28.5
Other S.E. Asia	42.0	23.2	24.7	18.1	17.6
Total Army	42.7	29.4	28.0	20.4	20.1

Source: Drug Abuse in the Military: Hearing Before the Subcommittee on Drug Abuse in the Military of the Committee on Armed Services, United States Senate, Ninety-second Congress, 1972, p. 127; cited in Savage and Gabriel, "Cohesion and Disintegration . . .," *Armed Forces and Society* 2 (1975): 351.

SOURCE 171

Pfc. Dominick Yezzo's war diary in Vietnam indicates the function that marijuana performed in his efforts to cope with the tension of the last few days in the combat zone:

Aug 4

A few rounds came in this evening, but not as close to my position as it has been recently. The war is at a general lull right now; this means that Charlie is setting up once again for maximum damage. There have been large enemy concentrations spotted on operations a few klicks [kilometers] from here outside of Phouc Vinh! It's in the air for another ground attack.

I have seven days left here with my unit.

I'm going to miss Sergeant So when I leave here. He has been a great deal of help to me in trying times.

I smoked pot last night and became really mellow and placid. I enjoyed music from my radio, and thinking and grooving. I slept well for a change, too. Woke up this morning feeling eager and ready to face the day.

Lately, though, I haven't been sleeping well at all. I've been having WAR nightmares. I wake up screaming No, No!! I dreamt that a rocket just hit my bunker and the thing caved in on me.

Hold on, folks, I'm coming.

Source: Dominick Yezzo, *G.I.'s Diary* (New York, 1974), unpaginated.

SOURCE 172

"John Kohn," a field wireman in Vietnam, was arrested on a narcotics charge after leaving the service. He commented on the relationship between Vietnam and drugs in his experience:

"Before I went to Vietnam I felt an innocence. I didn't use drugs, and didn't want to. I had a peaceful mind. But since then I have had to struggle with myself and my people. I feel myself to be disoriented. . . . My mother said that her son had not come home because I had a mustache and a different point of view."

Source: Questionnaire prepared and administered by Pat Merwin, a Marine Corps veteran of Vietnam, in the Pittsburgh area, 1975.

SOURCE 173

Vietnam veteran Gary Wood spoke of the ways that some of his comrades "work[ed] out [their] survival:"

"I only know one Medal of Honor type who isn't dead. And his head is messed up.

"He used to run with a motorcycle gang down around Philly. A judge sentenced him to Vietnam after he killed a guy. As soon as he got back, he started dealing dope, and he ended up in jail again.

"Most people dealt with Vietnam by getting juiced, or zonked, or by daydreaming about 'the World.' 'The World' was anyplace except 'Nam.

"Each guy had to work out his survival in his own individualistic way. We all understood that ground rule. We avoided trashing each other, but we didn't buddy up either.

"I did daydreaming."

Source: C. Noell and G. Wood, *We Are All POWs* (Philadelphia, 1975), p. 40.

SOURCE 174

Clyde Blue, a black veteran of world War II, recalled drug use en route to the Burma theater:

"In the [Suez] canal there are places dug out so one ship can pull aside to allow another to pass. Little native boats are out in the canal all the time and when a ship pulls over they come right along side your ship and peddle their wares. They must have been selling drugs because we were all potted pretty soon. I am referring to the smoking kind only, the thing we use to call a reefer. The whites over there stayed loaded, scotch, gin, and rum; half of that red color is not suntan. The poor natives can't afford liquid intoxicants so they get high on their native grass, which grows wild. They use it and they sell it. I should say it is not the cut junk you buy in the states, it is pure. When we left the ship no problems, no hangovers, no addicts.

Source: Reprinted from *The Invisible Soldier: The Experience of the Black Soldier of World War II*; copyright © 1975 by Mary P. Motley, ed., by permission of the Wayne State University Press. Excerpt is from p. 130.

SOURCE 175

Incidence and Frequency of Drug Use Among Vietnam Enlisted Returnees, Oakland Overseas Processing Center—1-13 March 1971 (1,010 Vietnam Enlisted Separatees—E-1-6, Age 26 or Below)

	BEFORE VIETNAM		DURING VIETNAM		CURRENT (LAST 30 DAYS)	
Marihuana: total users	45.80%	(461)	58.50%	(592)	37.10%	(374)
Amphetamines: total users	14.00	(141)	16.40	(165)	5.76	(58)
Barbiturates: total users	11.32	(114)	15.46	(156)	7.04	(71)
Acid (LSD, peyote, and the like): total users	12.67	(127)	9.54	(96)	4.16	(42)
Heroin or morphine: total users:	6.17	(62)	22.68	(228)	16.15	(163)
Opium: total users	7.75	(78)	19.59	(196)	9.14	(92)

Source: J. Helmer, *Bringing the War Home* (New York, 1973), Table 2-15.

SOURCE 176

> *Private Herman Clarke wrote to the hometown folks in Oneida, New York, from the front lines in December 1864 and commented on the political views that soldiers had acquired:*

You many enquire then why there were not more Democrats home [on leave to vote]. The reason is they are a very scarce article in the Army at present. The past six months have made a great change politically in the Army. Men who a year ago were bitterly against the [Lincoln] Administration have failed to find even sympathy, much [less] encouragement in any other party. You may say they haven't received these from the Administration. I think they have. At least they haven't received open opposition from it, and they have from all other parties. The ground the Democratic party took in the Vallandigham affair disgusted every soldier. He was as much a traitor as Jeff Davis, and have your constitutional rights and liberties become so sacred that such a rebel cannot be arrested and taken out of town until some Justice of the Peace has decided whether he is loyal or not? Oh, fudge! Where is the loyalty and patriotism of the North? I

Source: Harry Jackson and Tom O'Donnell, eds., *Back Home in Oneida: Herman Clarke and His Letters* (Syracuse, N.Y., 1965), p. 116.

don't believe there is any. Vallandigham ought to have been hung with a tarred rope, and there are others north nearly as bad.

Now perhaps you think I am an Administration man, but it is not so. I know how things worked last winter at Washington, and I don't think they have changed much. But I do think the Democratic party has gone back on the soldiers. A year ago the soldiers thought the Democrats were their only friends, but the New York riot and the figuring of some men in evading the draft has changed the feeling greatly. And in regard to hiring Negro soldiers, I don't know a man so fond of soldiering that he is not willing to let the Negroes have the honors if they want them at $7 per month. And every one who has ever seen them acknowledges that they are the soldiers for this climate.

SOURCE 177

> *A GI in the field in Vietnam reacted to "the boys that are burning their draft cards":*

Hi Mom, Dad, and all,

I just received your letter. The days are getting longer, so it seems. It won't be too long and I'll be back home again. I'm so anxious to get back home that it isn't even funny. I'm so happy that Dad ordered my car, and I can't wait to see it. Thank you, Dad, I'm so very proud of you and really, Dad, you're the greatest.

It's hard to sleep, eat, or even write any more. This place has definitely played hell with us. It's been a long hard road, Mom and Dad, and I think I've proved myself so far. I know you all have a great confidence in me, and I know I can do any job assigned to me. I've engaged with the Vietcong and Hard Core so many times, I lost track of them. I've got a right to boast a little cause I know I was right in hitting the licks, just like other good Marines have done and are doing and always will. We've put long hours of sweat and blood in this soil, and we will do our best to get these people freedom. Also protect America from Communism.

I only wish I could do something to encourage the boys that are burning their draft cards to stand up and take their responsibilities for their country, family, and friends. You can't defeat Communism by turning your backs or burning your draft cards. Anyone who does it is a disgrace and plain yellow. They haven't got the guts to back up their fathers and forefathers before them. Their lives have gone to waste if the sons today are too afraid to face the facts.

. . .

Source: G. Munson, ed., *Letters from Vietnam* (New York, 1966), p. 106.

There, I've said what has been on my mind! I hope this doesn't bore you, but I just had to put it down on paper.

Mom, Dad, and kids, whenever the national anthem is being played, whether over TV, radio, or at a game, *please, please,* stand up. Show your patriotism. After all, I am not fighting for nothing.

Am I?!!

We've got to have a flag, also; do we have one?

Dad, try in every way, whether little or big, to push a little of the patriotism kick into Bob and Ron! *Please!* Also religion.

GO TO MASS . . .

Goodbye for now, and God bless you all.

I love you all.

Doug

SOURCE 178

> *A pilot who had been a captive of the North Vietnamese explained how his political awareness and support for President Johnson rose dramatically:*

"I didn't like Lyndon Johnson or agree with much that he did, but when I was shot down and became a prisoner of war I became the biggest Johnson supporter you've ever seen. He was my commander in chief and everything he did was absolutely right."

Source: Roger N. Williams, "The Vietnam Veteran: Prisoners of War," *Penthouse* (August 1974): 114.

SOURCE 179

> *William Jennings, a World War I veteran, described two incidents to sympathetic comrades at the first Massachusetts convention of the American Legion in 1919:*

"Two weeks after I came back [from Europe] I went into a labor union in Boston and saw fifteen or twenty young men, all naturalized and Americans, playing cards. I asked them: 'What are you fellows doing here? Why aren't you in the service and wearing the uniform of your country?' 'The

Source: D. Wecter, *Johnny Comes Marching Home* (Boston, 1944), p. 350.

hell with the country,' one of them cried. 'Make hay while the making is good.' Coming back from work one morning I was sitting in the car opposite two of these slackers. 'How much did you make last week?' 'Forty dollars.' 'I did better than that, but it is too damn bad that the war won't last a couple of years longer, and then I would be on easy street.' But thank God I had the strength to knock his head through the window. [Much applause and cheering.]"

SOURCE 180

Three World War II GIs, writing to an American Veterans' Committee organizer in the final days of the war, spelled out the political lessons they had learned:

A Corporal

All of us here grope for some solid means which would transfer the helm of the future into our hands, some device which would break for all time the rhythm of war, the strangle hold of inept standards and powerful, anonymous control. When the soldier gets back, he shall want more than a pat on the back and a drink or two. He shall want to be an eager partner in the reconstruction, who has learned much, who can give much and who is afraid of nothing.

A Sergeant

"We're not fighting simply for the 'old order of things,' as some national manufacturers would have us believe. It was the 'old order of things' which insured us unemployment in the millions, people hungering for food while land was being plowed under at the request of the government. If we can produce plenty for a mammoth military machine in wartime then we can certainly produce plenty for an economy of peace. The latter is what we want, what we can do, and we must notify our legislators, now, that that is what we want, not a return to the 'old order of things.'"

A Lieutenant

I love America, and I have been fighting in order to be able to go home and begin building the kind of land I was only able to dream about before

Source: Charles Bolte, *The New Veteran* (New York, 1945), pp. 1, 97, 173.

Hitler challenged Western civilization. I wanted to challenge most of it, too, not as Hitler has done, but with new ideas and institutions in place of the old ones. I am glad this war came, because I do not think my generation would have had the courage to speak and act for a better world if the bombs and destruction and clear indication of civilization's failure at this date had not awakened us. I am lucky to be alive.

SOURCE 181

> *Willie Lawton, a black veteran of World War II, had only unpleasant and bitter memories when interviewed in 1970:*

"I most certainly think the Negro GI of World War II did play a great part in the changed overt thinking and behavior of the white military because we'd take so much and that was all. But if I had it to do over again I would take off for Canada like many of the fellows have recently done. We were supposedly sent over there to do a job, fighting for our country, when it really added up to traveling half way around the world to endure the same insults from the same people.

. . .

"The war was a thing I wanted to forget. I've never put on my uniform since I took it off. I've never marched in any parade. I have never applied for my citation. It is something I'd rather forget because it was a bad dream, a real nightmare."

Source: Reprinted from *The Invisible Soldier: The Experience of the Black Soldier of World War II,* copyright © 1975 by Mary P. Motley, ed., by permission of The Wayne State University Press. Excerpt is from pp. 103-04.

SOURCE 182

> *Black veterans of Vietnam living in the Jacksonville, Florida, area were asked questions in 1968 designed to sort them out on an "alienation from white American society" spectrum. They were also asked questions about their social background and military experiences, and their responses were then correlated with their degree to alienation:*

Selected Characteristics of 199 Southern Black Veterans of the Vietnam Era Related to Degree of Alienation from White American Society, Fall 1968

CHARACTERISTIC	HIGHLY ALIENATED GROUP		GROUP WITH ONLY SLIGHT DEGREE OF ALIENATION		TOTAL	
	%	NO.	%	NO.	%	NO.
Means of Entry into Military						
Drafted	58%	(63)	42%	(46)	100%	(109)
Enlisted	34	(31)	66	(59)	100	(90)
Number of Close White Friends While in Military						
None	76%	(25)	24%	(8)	100%	(33)
1–4	48.5	(57)	52	(61)	100	(118)
5 or more	25	(12)	75	(36)	100	(48)
Combat?						
Yes	58%	(42)	43%	(31)	100%	(73)
No	41	(52)	59	(74)	100	(126)
Year Discharged						
1963–65	42%	(31)	58%	(43)	100%	(74)
1966–67	46.5	(42)	53.5	(49)	100	(91)
1968	62	(21)	38	(13)	100	(34)
Religious Participation?						
Yes	37%	(32)	63%	(54)	100%	(86)
No	55	(62)	45	(51)	100	(113)

Source: Condensed from two tables compiled by James Fendrich and Michael Pearson, in "Black Veterans Return," in Martin Oppenheimer, ed., *The American Military* (New Brunswick, N.J., 1971), pp. 172, 176.

SOURCE 183

A black infantry veteran of Vietnam with a felony conviction to his name described "the effect" that service in Vietnam had on his life, November 1975:

Source: M— — S— — to Pat Merwin, November 1975. I am indebted to Mr. Merwin and his respondent for this passage.

"The Vietnam experience was a good experience. Don't knock it. It made me politically aware of some of the things that are going on now. Now I question what I'm told. . . . It [opened] my eyes to use my skills [as?/and?] education for open urban guerrilla *warfare* against the power structure."

SOURCE 184

A young man who resisted the draft was also "radicalized" by war; his metamorphosis simply preceded that of those who served:

Although I had been in some sit-ins during the civil rights days, I was hardly political and was strongly dedicated to privatism. It was really the war that woke me up. I knew about the [David] Miller, [David] O'Brien [two of the 1966 resisters who received extensive publicity] and Sheep's Meadow events [draft card burnings in Central Park, April 15, 1967], but I didn't visualize myself doing it. It took a real depression about the war which was rapidly becoming an obsessional thing. I couldn't sleep well and nightmares about the war were frequent when I could sleep. . . . I have a metaphysical bent which can isolate acts through my imagination. If you take the fact of one child or soldier dying 12,000 miles away, it seemed that the distance was arbitrary and it was as if it were happening in my backyard to those I loved. The war became personalized through an extrapolation of the perception of senseless death, steel, and bullets.

Source: Michael Useem, *Conscription and Social Conflict* (New York: John Wiley & Sons, Inc., 1973), p. 181.

SOURCE 185

First Sgt. P. J. Duffy, a combat veteran with over twenty years of service, commented on the same subject:

"My experience in Vietnam was just like the last 2 wars. Hell, this had no effect on my life. I knew what to expect and was ready. However, I can see it would have an effect on an insecure and immature person. Society changes day by day, but I do not feel·the Vietnam War made any lasting effect. . . . Each to his own way of life. . . ."

Source: Duffy to Pat Merwin, late 1975.

4

Homecoming, Adjustment to Civilian Life, and Veteran's Status

SOURCE 186

Revolutionary War veteran Joseph Plumb Martin recalled the moment when his company was disbanded:

I confess, after all, that my anticipation of the happiness I should experience upon such a day as this was not realized; I can assure the reader that there was as much sorrow as joy transfused on the occasion. We had lived together as a family of brothers for several years, setting aside some little family squabbles, like most other families, had shared with each other the hardships, dangers, and sufferings incident to a soldier's life; had sympathized with each other in trouble and sickness; had assisted in bearing each other's burdens or strove to make them lighter by council and advice; had endeavored to conceal each other's faults or make them appear in as good a light as they would bear. In short, the soldiers, each in his particular circle of acquaintance, were as strict a band of brotherhood as Masons and, I believe, as faithful to each other. . . . Ah! it was a serious time.

Source: George Scheer, ed., *Private Yankee Doodle* (Boston: Little, Brown and Co., 1962), p. 203.

SOURCE 187

Cpl. Will Judy recorded a comparable entry in his diary, January 18, 1919:

We talk much of comradeship in the coming civilian life. Like mystics, we are conscious of an association that will bind us into a passionate group different and superior, as we think, to all others.

Source: Will Judy, *A Soldier's Diary* (Chicago, 1931), p. 173.

SOURCE 188

Sgt. Henry Giles entered a similar comment in his journal in late 1945:

What we had together was something awfully damned good, something I don't think we'll ever have again as long as we live. Nobody in his senses wants war, but maybe it takes war to make men feel as close to each other as we have felt. We'll never feel toward anyone else the way we have felt toward each other, for the circumstances will never be the same again. We are all a little homesick for it already.

Source: J. Giles, ed., *The G.I. Journal of Sgt. Giles* (Boston, 1965), p. 377.

SOURCE 189

Sgt. Dominick Yezzo's diary entries for his final week in Vietnam are also comparable:

Aug 10

This is my last day to spend with my unit. God willing, I should be home in a few days. I'm not as excited as I'd like to be. I'm kind of leary about going home.

I leave tomorrow but tonight I'm still here.

Aug 11

I was airlifted to Bien Hoa this morning. Last night we had an incoming ground attack. I almost went crazy my last night out there and BAMB—it was an all night shootout. Charlie fought past the guard bunkers at one position and got into the base camp. There were still enemy inside the barbed wire when I hastily boarded the chopper this morning.

I hated parting with Sergeant So that way. I shall always pray for his welfare. Alabama is traveling home with me.

Aug 12

Bien Hoa.

A couple of rocket rounds landed real close to me. They scared the hell out of me. I'm almost finished processing out.

Source: Dominick Yezzo, *G.I. Diary* (New York, 1974), unpaginated.

Aug 15

Long Bien—hit this morning with mortars. They woke me up. I depart sometime today.

Aug 16

It's all over, my war is finished. I felt real sad about parting with my friends. We went through so much together.

I'm on my way back to the United States right now. Flying on a huge Air Force C-141. I cannot help but look back over all that's happened to me in the past year. All the hurt and suffering, all the stupidity and pity I saw, all the good I remember. There were many wonderful and new experiences in that small foreign land. I shall never forget the Vietnamese.

Now it's all past, the good and the bad, and I'm going home to my family, Jennifer, and school. I pray that my mind and head remain the same and that I build myself into what I want to be.

I'm truly sorry for all the dead young men I leave behind. I made it and they didn't. Why . . . ?

Thank you, Lord, for keeping me.

SOURCE 190

> *Sgt. Will Judy's unit returned from action in Europe to a state-side garrison in June 1919; the men distressed at the "by-the-book" character of garrison life:*

France has bred in us the habit of acting first and asking questions afterward. Here red tape, insolence and much ado about nothing are the order of the day. The camp officials have not learned as did we, on fields of war, where our mistakes wrought their cost first upon us, perhaps at price of our lives. They do not possess our qualities of swift action, daring effort and great labor.

Source: Will Judy, *Soldier's Diary* (Chicago, 1931), p. 211.

SOURCE 191

> *Combat veterans who returned to garrisons in late 1944 had acquired an outlook toward discipline, leave, and officers that was quite different from that of soldiers in such garrisons who had not been overseas:*

Source: S. Stouffer et al., *Studies in Social Psychology in World War II*, 4 vols. (Princeton, N.J.: Princeton University Press, 1949-50), II, p. 509.

Attitudes Toward Aspects of the Garrison Situation, Returnees and Nonreturnees, November 1944

PERCENT WHO SAY THAT:	AIR FORCE		INFANTRY		ENGINEERS		QUARTERMASTER	
	RETURNEES	NONRETURNEES	RETURNEES	NONRETURNEES	RETURNEES	NONRETURNEES	RETURNEES	NONRETURNEES
Military control and discipline at their post is too strict and a lot of it is unnecessary	51	36	47	41	65	41	72	67
Passes are tougher to get than is necessary	22	16	32	31	30	18	40	32
Military Police treat returnees worse than other men who haven't been overseas	33	6	30	9	25	5	22	8
Officers get far too many privileges as compared with enlisted men	52	43	44	35	47	25	54	44
Few or none of their officers try to look out for the welfare of enlisted men	60	47	44	36	54	33	46	41
Number of cases	1,427	893	870	432	800	397	906	361

SOURCE 192

> White GIs attached to integrated units during World War II
> and Korea expressed new opinions on the wisdom of such inte-
> grated units once they were pulled out of the combat zone:

During World War II

Company commander from Tennessee: Good cooperation in combat.
They were treated as soldier to soldier. Now they play ball, joke and box
together. The colored go to company dances—we've had no trouble, but
some of the white boys resent it. In garrison the strain on both parties is
too great.

First sergeant from Georgia: Got along fine in combat. But we don't
like to mix too much now and I think they should be pulled out if we're
going to stay in garrison.

Platoon sergeant from Indiana: They fought and I think more of them
for it, but I still don't want to soldier with them in garrison.

During the Korean War

(Enlisted man):   At jump school I learned to get along with them and I
know that they can be good soldiers. But I still don't want to live with
them. I don't mind fighting, training, and working with them but I sure
wouldn't want them eating and sleeping with me.

Source: S. Stouffer et al., *Studies in Social Psychology in World War II,* 4 vols. (Princeton,
N.J.: Princeton University Press, 1949-50), I, p. 592; Leo Bogart, ed., *Social Research and Desegregation* (Chicago, 1969), p. 207.

SOURCE 193

> *Pfc. Richard Marks confessed to his mother in 1965 that he had
> learned how "out of place" his service friends were in his civilian
> social circle:*

Source: Gloria M. Kramer, ed., *The Letters of Richard Marks, Pfc., USMC* (Philadelphia,
1967), p. 66.

This weekend with——was a sheer pleasure—we were able to talk and discuss, and do it with a mutual respect. . . .

I made the mistake of taking two friends with me on liberty—they were terribly out of place. It was embarrasing for all involved. Now I know what Tony meant when he said your friends from service end when service does. Values and grounds for friendship in service are so different from those in civilian life. It seems that I learn a new lesson about life each day.

Each day I am getting to know a little bit more about myself, and each day I gain more real self-confidence—not the type I use to have (for show only).

SOURCE 194

Sympathy for the Allies declined among GIs between April 1945 (before the German surrender), and August 1945 (after the Japanese surrender and the end of the war):

After the war, some of our Allies will need help in feeding their people. Do you think the United States should send food to these countries even if it meant that we would have to keep on rationing food in our country for a while to do it?

Percentages answering "should":

| April 1945 | 58 |
| August 1945 | 49 |

After the war some of our Allies will need money and materials to help them get back on their feet. Do you think we should let them have money and materials to help them get back on their feet, even if it meant that we should have to pay higher taxes for it?

Percentages answering "should":

| April 1945 | 38 |
| August 1945 | 29 |

Source: S. Stouffer et al., *Studies in Social Psychology in World War II,* 4 vols. (Princeton, N.J.: Princeton University Press, 1949-50), II, p. 592.

SOURCE 195

Changes in Attitudes Toward Germans
(Cross Sections of Soldiers in European Theater,
April 1945 and August 1945) (Numbers Following the Bars = Numbers
of Cases on Which Percentages Are Based)

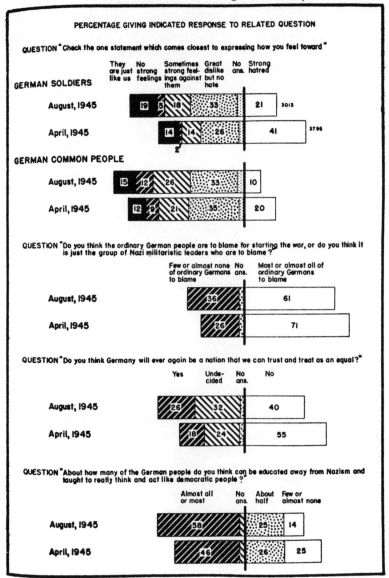

Source: S. Stouffer et al., *Studies in Social Psychology in World War II*, 4 vols. (Princeton, N.J.: Princeton University Press, 1949-50), II, p. 565.

SOURCE 196

Samuel Lubell, a pollster, spoke to a number of Iowa farm families during both the Korean and Vietnam wars. Among them was a man who had been wounded in Korea; his views, and the views of all other members of his family, had changed markedly between 1952 and 1968:

Near Dyersville, Iowa, I reinterviewed ten families I had talked with back in 1952, during the Korean War. I went into this area because it exemplified so well the ethnic nature of much of isolationist feeling in the past. Overwhelmingly Catholic and German-American, this community broke violently with its Democratic heritage in opposition to both world wars. It swung back to vote for Truman in 1948 only to break sharply for Dwight D. Eisenhower in 1952 because of the Korean War.

During the summer of 1968 I found that the war attitudes of these farmers were being shaped this time not by their ethnic background but primarily by each family's vulnerability to the draft and, as a conflicting influence, by economic considerations.

Four of the ten farmers wanted to "pull out." All but one had sons who were in the reserves or who faced being drafted if the war were escalated.

Five other farmers, with no sons of draft age, argued, "If we just walk out, they'll come back in some other place." Three of these, who complained, "This war is bankrupting the country," wanted to "step up the fighting to end it."

The tenth farmer proved to be the angriest of them all. He protested: "My son has just finished high school. He has the brains to go to college but doesn't like school. I can give you the names of farmers around here who put their sons into college just to avoid the draft. Why isn't my son as good as theirs? They should all be taken.

"Either pull out or get out," he stormed. "If we have to, we might as well use the nuclear bomb now as next year."

One of these ten farmers held a special interest for me. In 1952, when I visited the Recker farm, I stumbled onto a family reunion celebrating the return from Korea of one of the six Recker sons.

The father angrily told his son, "Show the man your legs." The boy, still in uniform, lifted his trousers, baring an ugly black scar on each leg.

At that time all of the Reckers wanted to pull out of Korea. In 1968, none of the Reckers wanted to get out of Vietnam.

About forty, the son who had been wounded in Korea still limped as we walked from the pigpen to the house. Several times he seemed to be

---

Source: Samuel Lubell, *The Hidden Crisis in American Politics* (New York, 1971), pp. 258-59.

trying to avoid saying directly what he thought, repeating, "I know how I felt when I was in Korea" or "I wouldn't want to be making the decision."

Finally he said: "I can't see how we can pull out. We've got to do what is needed to win."

SOURCE 197

Difference in Several Self-Reported Beliefs for a Group of 80 Men Between Time of Testing in Vietnam as a Member of an Infantry Battalion and Retesting in the United States Approximately One Year Later

SCALES	TEST GROUP			CONTROL GROUP[a]		
		STANDARD SCORES[c]			STANDARD SCORES	
	T-TEST RESULTS[b]	VIETNAM	US	T-TEST RESULTS	VIETNAM	US
Values Approval from Others	− 2.72***	16	− 14	− 1.81*	− 6	− 26
Prefers Social Interaction	− 3.62***	− 3	− 46	− 1.44	− 6	− 24
Prefers Group Participation	− 1.83*	0	− 23	− 2.19*	24	− 8
Values Status Attainment	+ 2.04*	− 23	− 1	− 0.97	− 6	− 16

[a]Control group consisted of 53 individuals assigned to a relatively safe rear area in Vietnam during the same time period members of the test group were assigned to the rifle companies of an infantry battalion engaged in combat in Vietnam. Both the test group and the control group were retested in the United States approximately one year later via mail.

[b]Computed on the basis of a one-tailed distribution.

* $p < .05$

*** $p < .001$

[c]Average of norm group has been equated to zero and the standard deviation to 100.

[Note:] Zero is the norm for [the table] (pertaining only to the standard scores). This was determined by setting zero in place of the average scores representing over 50 occupational groups in the United States. Theoretically, no particular occupational group exactly fits the norm. The purpose of this norm is to establish a "bench mark" so that the scores different groups of people receive will have relative meaning. It should be recognized that major differences in response may be essential for top performance in different environments. Therefore, the reader should not make a general assumption that "lowest" indicates "worst."

Source: Peter Petersen, Against the Tide (New Rochelle, 1973), pp. 167-73.

SOLDIERS RETURNING FROM VIETNAM:
EXTENT OF THEIR VALUE FOR THE APPROVAL FROM OTHERS

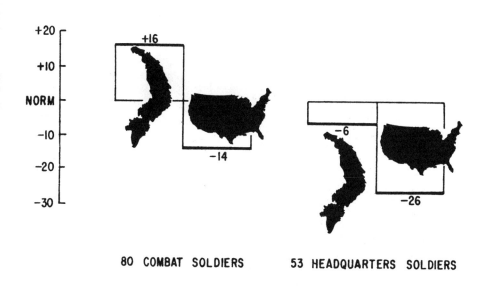

80 COMBAT SOLDIERS   53 HEADQUARTERS SOLDIERS

EXTENT OF THEIR PREFERENCE FOR SOCIAL INTERACTION

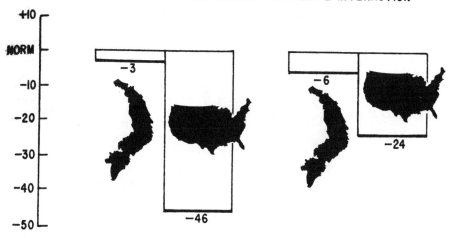

80 COMBAT SOLDIERS   53 HEADQUARTERS SOLDIERS

EXTENT OF THEIR PREFERENCE FOR GROUP PARTICIPATION

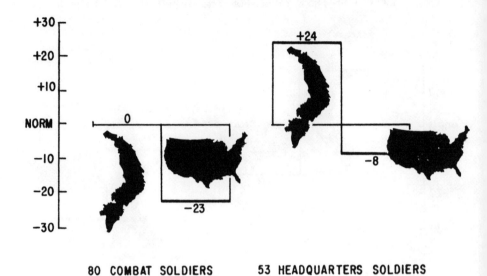

80 COMBAT SOLDIERS   53 HEADQUARTERS SOLDIERS

EXTENT OF THEIR PREFERENCE FOR STATUS

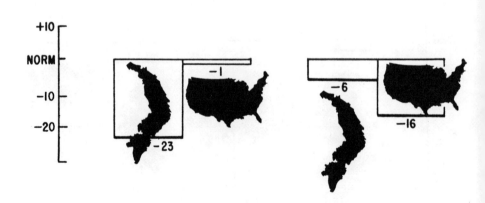

SOURCE 198

> *Charles Bardeen, a fifer in a Union infantry regiment during the Civil War, began an edition of his war diary in 1879 with a caveat: veterans sometimes tell "tall tales." Later in the book he related an incident that occurred in New York, May 1865, as he was being mustered out of the service:*

I have heard old soldiers say that as they talked about war it seemed in a way as if they were telling legends that they had heard rather than experiences they had undergone, and I have something of this feeling. . . .

I went into French's hotel to have my hair cut and the barber observed a scar on the left side of my head about where the part would usually be, caused in my infancy by my jumping from my mother's arms in a fit of anger and striking upon the edge of a hot stove.

"Get this in the army?" he queried.

The temptation was too great. "Yes," I replied indifferently, "at Chancellorsville. Our color-bearer fell, and just as I seized the flag a rebel cavalry officer cut my head open with his sword. Fortunately one of our boys shot him and we got way with our colors."

The barber was interested and wanted particulars. I could supply them for I really had the correct background, and soon there was a gathering about my chair. Who could fail to take advantage of a credulous and sympathetic audience? I turned my early dreams of valor into the past tense, and really felt to be the hero I had represented myself.

Source: Charles Bardeen, *A Little Fifer's War Diary* (Syracuse, N.Y., 1910), pp. 6, 312-13.

SOURCE 199

> *Sgt. Will Judy's final entries in his diary of military life during World War I dealt with the same phenomenon as Bardeen's (Source 198):*

3 June 1919

Supervised the sorting and packing of the division's records for shipment to the Adjutant General of the Army at Washington for permanent file.

We hear much about ourselves as heroes. A thousand questions are asked of us and we know now the answers they wish us to make. We must

Source: Will Judy, *A Soldier's Diary* (Chicago, 1931), pp. 211-12, 216.

say that the enemy were fiends, that they butchered prisoners, that they quaked in fear as we came upon them in their trenches, that they were not nearly as brave as ourselves, that Americans are the best and bravest fighters of all nations, and that it was only necessary to shout "We are Americans."

We are somewhat surprised but soon we learn that the populace insists upon dubbing us heroes; then we are swept into the pose against our will and wishes. We do not talk about the war unless the civilians ply us with questions and drive us into stories about our life on the battlefield. We have come back hating war, disgusted with the prattle about ideals, disillusioned entirely about the struggles between nations. That is why we are quiet, why we talk little, and why our friends do not understand. But the populace refuses to be disillusioned; they force us to feed their own delusions.

Soon we will take on the pose of brave crusaders who swept the battlefields with a shout and a noble charge. The herd among our own number will be delighted with this unexpected glory and within a few years, a cult will be made of it. An ounce of bravery on the battlefield will become a ton of daring in story as related time and again in the years to come. We as soldiers shall find ourselves made the patriotic guardians of our country, a specially honored class, against our will.

The populace is not to be blamed. They never will get away from the effects of the propaganda in the press. To them every American soldier in France was a fighter, rifle and bayonet in hand, rushing mid shot and shell across No Man's Land, and plunging the knife into the cowering enemy. Indeed, they relate to us tales of our own bravery to our surprise; we subdue our astonishment and then obligingly add little touches of exaggeration to the already dropsied story.

Four-fifths of the American soldiers in France never went over the top and scarcely a tenth of us saw a German soldier, other than a captured one. . . .

19 June 1919

. . . The twenty-two months in the army has taught many things to me. My experiences I would not trade for any ten years of my life. I have learned to like and to hate the army. At first I saluted grudgingly; then, as the spirit of the uniform won me, I took pride in saluting promptly and snappily. It caused me to be chivalrous in the presence of women and the aged; to conduct myself creditably to the flag; and to live up to the traditions of American honor.

I could not forget that I was a civilian first and a soldier second. Perhaps I can tell best my thot of war by saying that it is as a painted woman, more attractive at some distance. I hate war, I am a man of peace; I hope there will never be another war; but if my country fights again, right or wrong, I shall be among the first to have the tailor remodel the old uniform.

SOURCE 200

> *Lt. Leander Stillwell described the matter-of-fact homecoming he experienced after several years of hard combat:*

"I arrived at the little village of Otterville about sundown. It was a very small place in 1865. There was just one store (which also contained the postoffice), a blacksmith shop, the old stone school-house, a church, and perhaps a dozen or so private dwellings. There were no sidewalks, and I stalked up the middle of the one street the town afforded, with my sword poised on my shoulder, musket fashion, and feeling happy and proud.

"I looked eagerly around as I passed along, hoping to see some old friend. As I went by the store, a man who was seated therein on the counter leaned forward and looked at me, but said nothing. A little further up the street a big dog sprang off the porch of a house, ran out to the little gate in front, and standing on his hind legs with his forepaws on the palings, barked at me loudly and persistently—but I attracted no further attention.

"Many of the regiments that were mustered out soon after the close of the war received at home gorgeous receptions. They marched under triumphal arches, decorated with flags and garlands of flowers, while brass bands blared, and thousands of people cheered, and gave them a most enthusiastic 'Welcome Home.' But the poor old 61st Illinois was among the late arrivals. The discharged soldiers were now numerous and common, and no longer a novelty. Personally I didn't care, rather really preferred to come back home modestly and quietly, and without any fuss and feathers whatever. Still, I would have felt better to have met at least one person who would have given me a hearty handshake, and said he was glad to see me home, safe from the war. But it's all right, for many such were met later.

"I now had only two miles to go, and was soon at the dear old boyhood home. My folks were expecting me, so they were not taken by surprise. There was no 'scene' when we met, nor any effusive display, but we all had a feeling of profound contentment and satisfaction which was too deep to be expressed by mere words.

"When I returned home I found that the farm work my father was then

---

Source: Leander Stillwell, *Story of A Common Soldier* (Erie, Kans., 1920); cited in D. Wecter and William Matthews, *Our Soldiers Speak* (Boston, 1943), pp. 236-37.

engaged in was cutting and shocking corn. So, the morning after my arrival, September 29th, I doffed my uniform of first lieutenant, put on
some of my father's old clothes, armed myself with a corn knife, and
proceeded to wage war on the standing corn. The feeling I had while
engaged in this work was sort of queer. It almost seemed, sometimes, as
if I had been away only a day or two, and had just taken up the farm work
where I had left off."

SOURCE 201

> An American Expeditionary Forces (AEF) veteran experienced
> the same "disappointment" as Stillwell's in 1919:

When I came back I had all kinds of stripes on my uniform, service stripes,
wound stripes, and the insignia of the Fighting Sixty-Ninth, Rainbow Division. I thought everyone would look at me, the great hero. I'll never forget
that first ride in the subway. I expected people to show recognition. My
uniform told the story of my acts. Well, everyone was busy reading the
paper and no one even looked up. I was really disappointed. You see I
was with the army of occupation and the war was over for six months
when I came back. We had a parade but it was nothing like we had seen
in the movies. The guys who didn't see action got the great applause. By
the time we got back, the country was fed up with these war heroes. . . .
I remember I met a girl I knew and I thought she would treat me like a hero.
She acted as though she had seen me the day before.

Source: W. Waller, *The Veteran Comes Back* (New York, 1944), p. 178.

SOURCE 202

> Samuel Stouffer and his associates described the feelings that
> veterans of the combat theaters expressed upon returning to
> the United States in 1944:

Many psychiatrists have noted that even men who had served arduously
were likely to feel a certain amount of guilt when they returned to the
United States. Besides this feeling that they were deserting their buddies,
returnees often had a feeling of being psychologically deserted themselves

Source: S. Stouffer et al., *Studies in Social Psychology in World War II,* 4 vols. (Princeton,
N.J.: Princeton University Press, 1949-50), II, p. 464.

once they were separated from the close group with whom they had lived and worked for so long and from whom they had drawn psychological support. Among the newly arrived returnees sampled in the summer of 1944, three fifths said they missed being with their old outfit. Moreover, many returnees found all sorts of vague disappointments in their long-dreamt-of return home. In spring 1944, two fifths of a sample of 810 returnees said being back in the United States did not seem as good as they expected it to be—perhaps in part because of these feelings of guilt and desertion and in part because the actuality did not correspond with the overidealized picture of home they had built up for themselves.

*The question was "On the whole, how does it feel to be back in the United States?"

It seems better than I expected it to be	24%
It seems just about the way I expected it to be	33
It does not seem as good as I expected it to be	43
	100%
	N = 810

SOURCE 203

A working-class white Vietnam veteran complained about the disturbance that his military service had made in his "social life":

"My life as it was going, it interrupted it, and put me back like it was a whole new scene when I came back, and all the people that didn't go I was two years behind as far as my social life was concerned. I always seemed to be looking for a crowd that was in the same situation as me, and there weren't too many people around like that. For the first three year period, I was into heroin, and LSD, or whatever you wanted to give me, I would take. It took me about three or four years to catch up to what I had before I went in, and I will never catch up all the way."

Source: Interviews with "Leadertown" vets, 1975, conducted by Tom Conley.

SOURCE 204

An inner-city black veteran of Vietnam was distressed by the homecoming experience for an entirely different reason:

Source: Stanley Friedlander, *Unemployment in the Urban Core* (New York, 1972), p. 172.

I didn't want to come back. I was real scared coming back on that plane.
You know everyone else was happy. Some had wives or girls they were
dying to see and they couldn't wait to land. I wished we didn't land. I was
quiet and alone. When the plane landed and we came to the discharge
desk I nearly felt like running way on back to the plane. I didn't know
what to do, I was so confused. Something tell me stay another six months—
re-enlist. But like I just went along with the crowd. . . . I took a cab all the
way from the airport to right here and, just like I thought, nothing changed.
It was early morning, five o'clock, and quiet. The door, the house, the
street was all the same. I felt kind of sick. I pulled out my things and just
stood there. Everything was the same.

SOURCE 205

*"You soldiers just don't seem to understand
our problems."*

Source: Bill Mauldin, *Back Home* (New York, 1947), p. 65. Drawings copyrighted 1944, renewed 1972, Bill Mauldin; reproduced by courtesy of Bill Mauldin.

SOURCE 206

> *A World War II veteran from "Midwest" wondered whether his military service had helped him to see beyond the town:*

"The service made me see that this is rather a small-minded town. . . . Here they don't count on a person's ability. All they are interested in here is what's gone before—what the person, or people with him, have done in the past. I found this in the service, that it was the man's intelligence and ability which decided he would go ahead, and how far he would go. There's no prejudice because of your name—Romero or Smith or Brown. But here if you don't have a perfect background, it's no good. In the service a man gets ahead maybe by playing politics a bit. But there your past doesn't count a damn thing. It is your present that counts, and what you can do in the future. In this town I know I could do lots of jobs as well as perhaps half of the people here, but I wouldn't even have a chance, simply because of my [unpopular father].

I like to be left alone and do what I please, without someone forever forming a criticism of whatever I do. In a big city you get lost—or a fairly big city. But even if I hadn't been in service, I doubt if I'd ever have stayed in Midwest. I always realized that there were very few opportunities here for me. I've got a lot of ambition and so on, and even though I don't know whether my plans will come through or not, if they don't it will be simply because I'm not working. I'm not going to let this town of Midwest stop me from working them out."

Source: Robert Havighurst, *The American Veteran Back Home* (New York, 1951), pp. 119-20.

SOURCE 207

> *"John Nez," a Rimrock Reservation Navajo, could speak English and had been to school for ten years before being drafted in 1941. When he returned after the war, he was unwilling to be a traditional "reservation Indian":*

I was glad at first to get back and see the folks. Then I got too lonely. It was too lonesome. I didn't like the country too well. Not only around here, but the whole New Mexico. I didn't like the people. Not only the Indians but also the Mexicans and the white people. It just seems that I didn't get along here. It was especially the Indians around here; too much government control, don't have as much freedom. I felt after being in the

Source: Egon Vogt, *Navajo Veterans,* Papers of the Peabody Museum, Harvard University, vol. 41, no. 1 (1951), pp. 53-54, 183-84.

army and being told to do this and that, that when I got back I could
make a living the way I wanted to instead of being told what to do. . . .
When I was away from the reservation, I felt that I had more freedom
and I can go anyplace where a white man goes like bars and places that
are restricted to Indians on the reservation. I went around with white boys
a lot of places where I can't do it here in New Mexico. . . . I wanted to put
up some kind of business. I started thinking about it while I was in France
in the hospital. Ever since they talk about getting GI loans, I thought
anybody could get it. I didn't know it was so difficult. I was thinking about
a small trading post. I was thinking about going to school and getting
commercial training first. Eddie and I start going around asking people in
government administration about it, but it didn't turn out right.

. . .

[The former headman of his community talked to an anthropologist about
"John's" behavior after returning from the service:]

I heard John say that he wants to be in big cities, be with white people
all the time, and keep clean like he did in the army. But that's what he
said when he first got back and still had some money. Now he's broke,
and I haven't heard him say it any more. And he's still living out here
with the rest of us. . . . I don't know how he was acting before he go to
army, but people just been telling me he came back from army and he
got a little bit smart among his people when he came home. He told his
people that he been to army and he got wounded over there, and white
doctors got him well. And he says he's brave, he says, nobody could kill
him. That's why he's drinking all the time, he says, he wants to fight with
his people. He says he knows how to fight and was trained for it. That's
when he's drinking he says that. . . . He thought he had lots of money, and
he could drink all he wanted. Then he got broke pretty soon and lose all
that money. He thought he had plenty of money to do anything, and nobody would bother him.

. . .

["John" was asked to look at some "Veteran's Apperception Test" pictures of vague, shadowy forms and to construct a story to accompany them:]

5. This veteran just got back from overseas. The other fellow is a white
man. He is trying to get him behind a house because he is a bootlegger
and he knows the GI has a lot of money and he is trying to sell him some
liquor at a high price. But the soldier refused to listen to him. He's got a
lot of experience. He was a corporal in the army and so he went home. He
is a good soldier.

2. This soldier has been away for quite a long time and he's finally got
home. He came home to the reservation and found everything about the
same as when he left. He stayed around home for a few months — then he

re-enlists. He went back to Europe to Germany on occupation duties. [Why did he go back into the army?] For several reasons. Because he doesn't like to stay around home and it's too lonesome and he couldn't find a job that would suit him.

1. This soldier came home a second time. First he came home and then he re-enlist again but this time he came home for good. He came home with sergeant stripes. A lot of people were waiting for him when he came home. This time he learned mechanics job. So he got himself a job downtown. [And then what happens?] And that's where he is.

6. (Laughs) The two brothers from somewhere in the reservation came back from the armed service. They were both in the Marine Corps in the same division. They were fighting Japs in the South Pacific. They were doing special duties in the Signal Corps. They came home after the Jap defeat. They came home and found folks and everything were the same. And they don't know just what to do yet. But they don't want to stay around home [Why?] They got a hard time getting readjusted back to civilian life. They been away too long. [Tell me a little about why they have a hard time.] They just don't feel right around home, they feel that they should go outside the reservation where they can become free. . . .

SOURCE 208

> "John Nez" (Source 207) found it very difficult to live on the reservation after army service. "Yazi Begay," who knew no English and had never been away from Rimrock before being drafted, found the postservice readjustment to reservation life easier, albeit he had changed some of his ways:

When I came back from the army, came back home, I don't like it here very well. It's kind of quiet. Where I been there's lots of noise, lots of noise, lots of things to see. Out here there's nothing to see, just woods. Nothing going on. Just sleep on the ground, not on a bed. Long ways to go to town too. I don't like to stay around here. I felt that way for about a month. Kind of lonesome to go back over to the camps. Also the whole Rimrock area here, it seems a whole lot changed around. But now I don't feel that way. Now I'm all right. . . .

Source: Egon Vogt, Navajo Veterans, Papers of the Peabody Museum, Harvard University, vol. 41, no. 1 (1951), pp. 158, 160-61. Compare E. Vogt and J. Adair, "Navajo and Zuni Veterans," American Anthropologist (1949): 547 ff.

Well, when I came back from the army, my home was the same as it was when I left. But when I came back I said, "I'm going to change it a little bit different." They were living the old way when I came home. It's a whole lot different now. I made a new house and some hogans. It's a whole lot better now. The time I left, they made a fire right on the ground inside the hogan. They had it that way when I came home too. But now I don't do that. I just get hold of a big cook stove. That's what I'm using now. When I came back I said to my wife and her folks, "How come you still living the old way? You should build a hogan the new way and make it nice inside." Now I make it a whole lot different; got a new stove and everything. The old way what people used to do, they didn't put any stove in hogan. The fire made it all black inside hogan. I want it like the white people's way. Keep the hogan nice and clean. That's the way I like it.

[The headman in "Yazi's" community talked about "Yazi" with an anthropologist, Egon Vogt:]

Yazi Begay was telling me about himself. When he first went to the army, he says he know just a few words of English and it was hard when he got into the army, especially when he don't understand English. After he got used to it and learned a few words of English it wasn't so hard. First he said he was with some Mexican who taught him some English words. He got along like that. And he seen lots of things that were hard for him to do. He stay down there three years. He says he learned a lot of white people's things. Lots of different kinds of things. Machine guns, bombs, everything. He would rather be in that way he says. He wish he could understand English just as well as white people. He just wish that but he don't understand English. He says the white people are a long way ahead of us. Way ahead. We will never catch up. They are making a lot of things. Airplanes. Machine guns. And they sure know how to handle soldiers. He says he learned that when he was down there. He says he is glad that he seen all that, and he's glad he's been over the ocean. First when he start, he never did like it. But after all he liked it. He says he wish he knew more education like them other boys do. When he first came back, he says he had a little money ahead. He could have built up a little store or something else, so as to make a good living—if he only knew how to read, he says he could do that. But he can't do it now he says. He likes white ways just as much as he knows English. He would go on if he knew more English.

[The wife of the Rimrock trader talked about "Yazi" too:]

There has been more change in Yazi Begay than anybody else. He kept himself clean when he got back, and he knew a few words of English. He was a regular old Navaho when he left, but now he's not so bashful. He comes right up to the counter and tells me what he wants. When he first got back, he bought a toothbrush, toothpaste, towel, washrag, bar of soap, shaving cream—everything to keep himself clean.

SOURCE 209

"Honey, I've only worn it a week."

Source: Bill Mauldin, *Back Home* (New York, 1947), p. 45. Drawings copyrighted 1944, renewed 1972, Bill Mauldin; reproduced by courtesy of Bill Mauldin.

SOURCE 210

Bill Mauldin's veterans were annoyed by the assumption many civilians made after World War II that they had become psychotic or uncontrollable:

"There's a small item on page 17 about a triple ax murder.
No veterans involved."

Source: Bill Mauldin, *Back Home* (New York, 1947), p. 54. Drawings copyrighted 1944, renewed 1972, Bill Mauldin; reproduced by courtesy of Bill Mauldin.

SOURCE 211

Three Vietnam veterans rhymed about their readjustment experiences:

The Longest War
The longest war is over
Or so they say
Again
But I can still hear the gunfire
Every night
From
My bed.

The longest nightmare
Never seems to
Ever
Quite come
To
An end.

                    —Jan Barry

Personal

I have found
that I am still what
I was.
The myth of war
has not eradicated
my weaknesses,
but it has
shown me
the cloven-eyed sport of men.
I am against the strength of war
and that has made
me stronger.
My name
has not changed.

                    — Don Receveur

Source: Larry Rothman et al., eds., *Winning Hearts and Minds* (New York, 1972), pp. 106, 110, 111.

A Visit

"You don't look bitter,"
   she said.
   He thought,
"Bitter is a taste,"
   feeling her words
   scrape across
   memory's slow healing
   like a slow knife.
   Did she think she could see
   how he felt?
"It don't matter,"
   he said, and heard
   outside—voices
   in the wind
   in humming tires
   voices running against
   the window in a heavy rain.

                    —Basil T. Paquet

SOURCE 212

Two combat veterans of Vietnam talked about the difficulty of adjusting to civilian life after a year of violence:

When I came back to the United States in 1967, I knew that some of the things I did in Vietnam I wouldn't have done prior to going over there. At least I don't think I would have done it. But I knew something was wrong because I could still do those things now that I was back here. I had 30 minutes of debriefing, a steak dinner, and a guy patted me on the back and said, "Well, you did a good job in Vietnam. Now you're back home, forget it." It just didn't work that way, because when I was on leave I would get uptight; I'd get very irritable. If someone says something to me, I get real excited sometimes and I can't answer a person. Maybe we'll get into an argument or something, and I can't give them the answer that they want. They start to, you know, like, really pressure me for an answer. I'll get uptight, and I might swing at them. I won't think twice about it 'cause I was taught it's better to give than to receive. A chaplain told me that—"Do unto others before they do unto you."

Source: Vietnam Veterans Against the War (VVAW), *The "Winter Soldier" Investigation* (Boston, 1971), p. 161. Copyright © 1972 by Vietnam Veterans Against the War. Reprinted by permission of Beacon Press.

. . . You're just different. You are. Not because you want to be. And then you come back. And within a matter of two to ten days you're supposed to be a human being again. You know, civilized. After living like an animal for so long. And right away you're supposed to come back and change. I couldn't do it.

Source: Charles Levy, *Spoils of War* (New York, 1973), p. 85.

SOURCE 213

Two wives of World War II veterans commented on their husbands' social habits in the year after they had returned:

"The veterans all want to drink. The ones that didn't drink before, now they say, 'Oh, let's go get a hooker of whiskey and a glass of beer'—a lot of them do. Some of them drank occasionally before, but they drink more now. My husband, he wouldn't sit at a table—he'd sit at a bar, because he hadn't got over his war-jitters or whatever you call it, and at a table the drinks didn't come fast enough."

"They seem to want to go out with their buddies a lot. In preference to wanting to go out with me, my husband seems to want to go out with the boys. He seems to have more fun that way, and he likes it better. The trouble is that when a lot of his friends come home from service, why, all he'll be doing is running around with them all the time."

Source: Robert Havighurst et al., *The American Veteran Back Home* (New York, 1951), p. 72.

SOURCE 214

A Californian, W. G. Morris, veteran of the Civil War, spoke in 1866 to a meeting of the Society of California Volunteers and complained of job discrimination and the heartlessness of San Francisco's elite:

Source: Aurora Hunt, *Major General J. H. Carleton, 1814-1873* (Glendale, Calif., 1958), p. 341.

The results, however, of our services may be far greater than is generally attributed to us and *some day meet with a just reward.* At the present time, however, it must be confessed that to have served faithfully during the war, is the surest way to defeat an application for employment at the hands of the San Francisco merchants and capitalists who have stayed at home, coined money out of the war and lustily shouted freedom, shed huge crocodile tears at the fate of intelligent contraband and the oppressed freed men.

. . . If there has been a single instance of public recognition, I am not aware of it. No! brother officers, the lip-loyalty men of California have turned upon you the cold shoulder and after years of toil, privation and hardship, you are turned out to graze on short feed like a broken down mustang.

. . . It is next to impossible for a veteran to obtain a job. Item men and penny liners of the city paper have taken a fiendish delight in chronicling the shortcomings of the soldier. "A dog before a soldier!"

SOURCE 215

A "GI Bill" veteran complained in 1948 of the effect his military service had on his career:

"The worst effect the war had on me, it chopped me out of four years—it put me behind in age. I'll be 31 when I get out of school and people will say, 'We don't want this old man around here.' And it's cut me out of a lot of other jobs, too. Most airlines chop you off at 26, 29—that's what I wanted to do, fly airlines . . . but I was too old. . . . My wife and I had it a lot rougher after the war than during the war, I think. . . . As soon as the war's over you've got just as many blocks as you ever had. You still gotta get a job and grub like the devil and work like the dickens and maybe then you don't get everything you want. And you change jobs a dozen times and then end up in business school."

Source: Lois and Herbert Stolz, *Father Relations of War-Born Children* (Stanford, Calif., 1951), p. 29.

SOURCE 216

One-half of the Blacks and One-third of the Whites Separating from the Armed Services in 1970 Were in Military Occupations Not Readily Transferable to Civilian Life

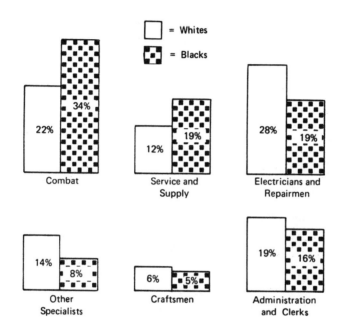

Source: Eli S. Flyer, "Profile of DOD First-Term Enlisted Personnel Separating from Active Service During 1970," *Manpower Research Note,* Office of the Assistant Secretary of Defense, October 1971, Table II; reprinted in Sar Levitan and Karen Cleary, *Old Wars Remain Unfinished* (Baltimore: Johns Hopkins University Press, 1973), p. 112. Reprinted with the permission of Johns Hopkins University Press.

SOURCE 217

Educational Level and Earned Income in 1964 of Retiree
Job Holders (In Percentages)

EARNED INCOME	EDUCATIONAL LEVEL				TOTAL
	NOT HIGH SCHOOL GRADUATE	HIGH SCHOOL GRADUATE	SOME COLLEGE	COLLEGE GRADUATE	
Officers:	(N = 24)	(N = 43)	(N = 183)	(N = 145)	(N = 395)[a]
Under $3,000	12	2	3	2	3
$3,000—$3,999	4	9	9	1	6
$4,000—$4,999	21	19	17	6	14
$5,000—$7,499	38	25	26	23	25
$7,500—$9,999	4	19	14	22	17
$10,000—$14,000	4	5	10	22	13
$15,000 or more		2	3	14	7
Commission only	17	19	18	10	15
Total	100	100	100	100	100
Median income	$5,830	$6,930	$6,995	$9,490	$7.785
Enlisted men:	(N = 373)	(N = 608)	(N = 192)	(N = 14)	(N = 1,187)
Under $3,000	19	11	8	14	13
$3,000—$3,999	27	17	16	1	20
$4,000—$4,999	21	27	18	14	24
$5,000—$7,499	25	34	41	44	32
$7,500—$9,999	3	4	8	7	4
$10,000 or more	1	1	3	7	1
Commission only	4	6	6	14	6
Total	100	100	100	100	100
Median income	$4,185	$4,815	$5,500	$6,250	$4,730

[a]Excludes (45) unknown.

Source: A. Biderman and L. Sharp, "The Convergence of Military and Civilian Occupation Structures," American Journal of Sociology 73 (January 1968): 393.

SOURCE 218

A World War II veteran who had made good use of the "GI Bill's" provisions, acquired a degree in business administration after the war, and become a successful businessman, talked about the shortcomings of the present generation of Americans, 1974:

Source: Personal interview with A., 1974.

"They want everything on a platter. Not willing to put their shoulder into anything. They expect the Government to give them this, give them that. When we got out [of the army in 1945-46], we went back to school and *worked*. You could sit around and loaf or you could work. After 3 years in the Army I *wanted* to work."

INTERVIEWER: "Wasn't the 'G.I. Bill' a Government aid program?"

VETERAN: "Sure."

INTERVIEWER: "Did everyone make equal use of it?"

VETERAN: "Of course not. You [went to] college if you wanted to get ahead. Not everyone wanted to as hard or as much as others. But those who did worked *hard*. I've heard educators say that the World War II G.I.s were the hardest working students they'd ever seen."

SOURCE 219

The Most Deficiently Educated Veterans Tended Not to Enroll in GI Bill Programs
(Cumulative to June 1972)

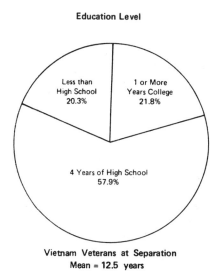

Education Level

Less than High School 20.3%

1 or More Years College 21.8%

4 Years of High School 57.9%

Vietnam Veterans at Separation
Mean = 12.5 years

Source: The figure appears in S. Levitan and Karen Cleary, *Old Wars Remain Unfinished* (Baltimore: Johns Hopkins University Press, 1973), p. 142. © Reprinted with the permission of the Johns Hopkins University Press.

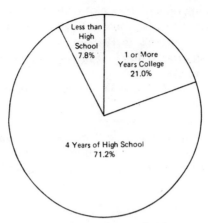

Vietnam Trainees before Training
Mean = 12.6 years

Source: Figures for All Vietnam Veterans: U.S. Veterans Administration, Reports and Statistics Service, *Data on Vietnam Era Veterans,* June 1972, p. 7. Figures for Vietnam Trainees: U.S. Veterans Administration, *Veterans Benefits Under Current Educational Programs,* Department of Veterans Benefits Information Bulletin 24-72-6, June 1972, p. 32.

SOURCE 220

Decomposition of Mean Differences Between Veteran and Nonveteran Income in Specific Occupational Groups in 1971 for Men Aged 25–50

OCCUPATIONAL GROUP	MEAN VETERAN INCOME	DIFFERENCE IN VETERAN, NONVETERAN INCOME	DIFFERENCE ATTRIBUTABLE TO EDUCATION	DIFFERENCE NET OF EDUCATION
		MEXICAN AMERICANS		
Professionals	$7175.	$207.	$134.	$73.
Managers	6533.	175.	274.	− 99.
Clerical	5089.	967.	142.	825.
Sales	6001.	1222.	367.	855.
Craftsman	5355.	131.	158.	− 27.
Operatives	4807.	490.	151.	339.
Service	4471.	1133.	323.	810.
Laborers	4891.	1225.	287.	938.
Total		711.	324.	387.

Source: H. Browning, S. Lopreato, and D. Poston, "Income and Veteran Status," *American Sociological Review* 38 (1973): 81.

	BLACKS		
Clerical	4831.	648.	482.	166.
Craftsman	4492.	57.	− 14.	71.
Operatives	4025.	191.	128.	63.
Service	3492.	364.	64.	300.
Laborers	3994.	434.	218.	216.
Total		344.	181.	163.

	ANGLOS		
Professionals	8892.	453.	143.	310.
Managers	8762.	−716.	408.	−1125.
Clerical	5956.	− 62.	44.	− 106.
Sales	7502.	74.	269.	− 195.
Craftsman	6421.	6.	87.	− 81.
Operatives	5797.	178.	95.	83.
Service	5584.	185.	157.	28.
Laborers	5075.	238.	114.	124.
Total		122.	289.	− 167.

SOURCE 221

Vietnam Era Membership in Service Organizations, 1971

GROUP	TOTAL[a] MEMBERS JUNE 30, 1971 (000s)	NUMBER OF VIETNAM ERA MEMBERS (000s)	VIETNAM ERA AS PERCENT OF TOTAL MEMBERS	VIETNAM ERA MEMBERS AS PERCENT OF ALL ELIGIBLES[b]
American Legion	2,700	300	11.1	5.7
VFW	1,700	450	26.5	15.0
Amvets	250	50	20.0	—
Disabled American Veterans	352	30	8.3	—
Marine Corps League	30	3.5	11.0	—
VVAW	20	20	100.0	0.4

[a]"Vietnam Era" veterans include *all* service veterans from 1963 to 1971 for the purposes of this table—*not* simply veterans of Vietnam.

[b]Computed only for the Legion, VFW, and VVAW. Eligibility requirements differ for each group: the first requires only military service with honorable discharge; the second, military service in a theater of war; the third, military service under any condition of discharge.

Source: John Helmer, *Bringing the War Home* (New York, 1973), p. 68. Compare William Gellermann, *The American Legion as Educator* (New York, 1938); and Rodney Minott, *Peerless Patriots* (Washington, D.C., 1962), for figures for the 1920s, 1930s, and 1940s.

SOURCE 222

Veterans may initially be slow in associating with veterans'
organizations, but, as time passes, the impact of military service
stands out more clearly in their memories. Harold Bond, a vet-
eran of the war in Italy, took his family back to the scene in the
early 1960s to share with them his reminiscences:

Monte Cassino has haunted my mind for the past twenty years. The last
time I saw the abbey and the town was on a cold, wet afternoon in late
February 1944, when I was being evacuated to an army field hospital. I
had been an infantry soldier engaged in the bitter fighting on the German
Gustav Line. This was the worst combat of the entire war for me, and during the long years of peace that followed, memories of it came back again.
Scenes and incidents which I would have been happy to forget remained
disconcertingly vivid. They were troublesome memories, and sometimes
I brooded over them.

Like other ex-soldiers after the war, I was caught up in the business of
starting a career in the workaday world and raising a family. There is
little connection between a great battle and the ordinary rounds of life in
peacetime, and as the war slipped further into the past I rarely heard
mention of Monte Cassino and almost never had occasion to talk about
it. Yet I found myself now and again reflecting on the terrible fighting.
With experiences such as those I had had so deeply branded on my mind,
I could not help wondering what they finally did mean to me and to the
others with whom I had shared them. Had they consisted, after all, merely
of senseless suffering without meaning, or was there a significance in them
that I had been unable to discover?

Source: Harold Bond, *Return to Cassino* (New York, 1964), p. 1.

SOURCE 223

Fredric Keffer, a World War II veteran of the 6th Armored Divi-
sion, made a different kind of trip with his son Tom, to the
thirtieth reunion of the survivors of Buchenwald; he had been
a part of the first Allied unit to reach the camp. Keffer described
the reunion for his "Super-Sixer" comrades, and commented on
the meaning to him of what had transpired a generation before:

Source: The Super-Sixer [6th Armored Newsletter] 26 (January 1976): 3-6.

On April 11, 1945, HERBERT GOTTSCHALK and I crossed through a hole in a twelve-foot-high double barbed wire enclosure and were suddenly swarmed upon and cheered and tossed up and down and madly jostled, embraced, and crushed by the 21,000 political prisoners of Buchenwald Concentration Camp. We had arrived in an M-8 scout car, just four of us, HARRY WARD and JAMES HOYT (radio operator and driver, both of whom remained with the scout car) and HERB and myself, on a side trip several kilometers away from the main body of Combat Team 9. We had come—the first American soldiers—minutes after the brutal SS guards had fled. We had come, in fact, because many of the guards had been picked up by our main body, and we wanted to find out just what it was they were fleeing. And those wonderful prisoners, those emaciated and battered skeletons of men, had somehow summoned-up a last bit of adrenalin for joyous welcome. There was little else left in them, and it didn't seem likely that any could survive another year, even in a hospital.

Yet here we were, HERB and I, over thirty years later, on September 20, 1975, being honored by nearly a hundred healthy and hearty Belgian survivors of Buchenwald, members of an organization very much like our Association, called the Amicale de Buchenwald. And we were assured that they were in close touch with many survivors from France, Netherlands, Denmark, Poland, Czechoslovakia, indeed from all over Europe—even from West and East Germany; and in fact we met one German anti-Nazi who had spent ten years, from 1935 to 1945, in various Nazi prisons. It was the first time we had seen Buchenwalders since 1945, and we were amazed and delighted by their tenacity of body and exuberence of spirit. Our Belgian hosts, together with their wives and a few fellow prisoners from outside Belgium, were assembled in the sumptuous new Congress Palace in Liège. Any Super-Sixer who had seen the crumbling town of Liège in 1945 would hardly have been prepared for the bustling, sky-scrapered, traffic-choked, steel-mill-smoked, river-polluted metropolis of 1975, complete with Holiday Inn right next door to the Congress Palace. I had trouble adjusting to the reality of today, just as my son TOM, who came with me, had trouble adjusting to a past which had produced concentration camps.

TOM and I began our journey into present and past with a drive around Bastogne, through northern Luxembourg, and across the Our River into Germany. We had to look hard to see any evidence of those awful days of 1944-45 in the cold snow. We were able, with real effort, to find one miserable little pile of rocks that looked like it might once have been part of the massive Sigfried Line. Here and there in Luxembourg one finds a German tank, an 88, or an American tank, but only because some local group has carefully maintained these relics like stuffed animals in a museum. And in Clervaux there even is a museum, yes Sir, a genuine museum, where you pay admission to look at such rare old specimens as GI helmets and OD shirts, and carbines and M1 rifles, and K rations (and even German counterparts) which were carefully collected from all that good old American (and German) litter that was left on Luxembourg battlefields. We stared in disbelief. Somehow none of this seemed to be real anymore. . . .

On Sunday noon there was a formal meeting, with speeches. [Maurice] Bolle chaired. A fiery speech with pounding on the rostrum was presented by a Frenchman who was introduced as head of the International Congress of ex-Concentration Camp Prisoners. A non-fiery, 40-minute speech in soporific French was given by the president of the Belgian group. Bolle read a "wish I could be with you" telegram from a comrade in Moscow, in French, but broken with several "STOP"s in English. I was moved to give a short speech, in English of course, to thank them all on behalf of my fellow soldiers and to say that the liberation of Buchenwald and indeed of the European continent was what World War II was all about. I didn't say so, but if I had ever had any doubts that our participation in that war was right and just, those doubts had been completely dispelled on greeting and being greeted by these wonderful men of Buchenwald. . . .

There was one little session in Liège that I have saved mention until last. Bolle brought a small group together, gave each American a handsome pewter plate memento, and then read a speech (in English, followed by translation into German by BONNIE ELDER). This Speech which expressed his worries about the future, was directed to us Americans and most specifically to TOM and to his generation. How easy it is, he said, to forget the terrors of fascism, and how hard it is to prevent fascism from arising. The principal reason he spends his time and energy keeping the Amicale de Buchenwald functioning is to educate the public and make people aware of the brutalities that might come again. He cannot rest, even at age 85. How can he get more publicity, he kept asking.

The question has no simple answer. I had already given a portion of my own answer by inviting TOM to accompany me to Liège. Another portion of my answer has been to write this account. I hope that many Super-Sixers will pass this on to their sons and daughters. Memories of evil get erased, for life must go on, and new generations cannot be locked into the past. But they would do well to remember the past.

SOURCE 224

Many veterans feel called upon to honor those who did not return. A leader of the United Spanish [-American] War Veterans in Newburyport, Massachusetts, explained a Memorial Day

Source: W. Lloyd Warner, The Living and the Dead (New Haven, Conn., 1959), p. 261.

ceremony in the late 1930s to those who had gathered to honor
the memory and sacrifices of Newburyport men who had died
in the service:

The purpose of this ceremony is to honor those who preceded us to the
land of the dead. This is the true patriotic day of the nation when the
children of these men honor their fathers, the flag, and all for which the
flag stands—bravery, glory, courage of people. It is fitting that the men
who sleep beneath the flag of the Union should have graves decked with
flowers in remembrance of this trying period of suffering and sorrow
which molded this nation. This was in the cause of liberty and of God. It
is only right that we quicken the memories of the dead. It is our purpose
to preserve and protect Memorial Day. In times of peace it is the duty of
us citizens to defend the flag and fulfill the patriotism of those who preceded us.

SOURCE 225

Jim Knickman, the correspondent for a tank unit attached to
the 6th Armored Division, wrote this note to his comrades in an
issue of the Division's newsletter:

I wrote this column the day before Memorial Day. By the time you read
this the holiday will be long gone and the summer will have us in its grip.
But, I just can't let this day, May 26th 1975, go by without a thought and
a prayer for our buddies we left behind. Without getting morbid, let me
remind you that at the reunion we always have a memorial service. It is a
sad reminder of what it is all about. This is why membership in the association and attendance at the reunion should take on an added significance
for all of us. When you read this article won't you please say a prayer for
the guys we can't see at the reunion? I know they will be there in spirit
but only you can be there in person. In their name I exhort you to attend
the reunion and devote that brief portion of time set aside from fun and
pleasure to remember them all. I know I can't forget them. You can't
either and you know it.

Source: Jim Knickman, in The Super-Sixer [6th Armored Newsletter] 28 (June 1975): 8.

SOURCE 226

> *Another editor (unnamed) of* The Super-Sixer *commented on the value of the 6th Armored Division Association:*

We have arrived at that age in the life of our Association when we seem to constantly be experiencing sadness on the loss of more and more of our fellow members. We know that all Super Sixers everywhere are joined in their expressions of sympathy to the families of our departed friends and buddies.

We feel that they always were proud of their Association and somehow we are sure they still are. They know that there are a lot of good things going on in their old outfit. They know that their buddies are in the process of writing and publishing their very own history. They know there is a top-level committee of dedicated and interested members at work on a recommendation that will effect the future of the Scholarship Project. They know there is another equally top-level committee at work towards coming up with a recommendation for reunion sites for future reunions. They know that hundreds of their fellow members continue to enjoy each other's friendship and companionship thru the many task forces across the country.

If brotherhood could be practiced everywhere as it is in the Sixth Armored Division Association, the world would have no problems, no suspicions, no investigations, no shortages. You, as an important part of this Association, have every right to stand tall and shout aloud the pride you have in being a Super Sixer.

Source: The Super-Sixer [6th Armored Newsletter] 27 (January 1974): 4.

SOURCE 227

> *A veteran wrote to Jim McNicol, the editor of* The Badge, *newsletter of the 222nd Infantry Regiment, "Rainbow" Division:*

April 14, 1975

DEAR JIM:

I am always thinking of the Rainbow.
I wish I was able to come to the Re-Union.

Source: The Badge (October 1975): 26.

I am totally disabled. I hope the Rainbow will never die. I have met several boys and to see them made me feel real good.

God Bless America as we are in a bad stage of times.

A. G. Gaines
Nicholson, Ga.
30565
M-222nd. Infantry

[*Badge*] EDITOR'S NOTE—Glad to hear from you Buddy. I have sent your dues to Col. Davis. Keep your chin up. Hang tough. Your friends in Rainbow think of you often.

SOURCE 228

During the Vietnam War, the "Legislative Officer" of the Pennsylvania Department of the Catholic War Veterans of the United States, George McGovern, called upon veterans to take certain political actions:

There is one other thing I would like to point out and I think as veterans, especially Catholic War Veterans, that we should take a stand on a lot of things; one of them is the things that are going on today, things that are going on on the college campuses this past spring. It was all brought out more or less by one organization, that is the SDS. I had heard one delegate make a remark that that was on the way out—but it is on the way in.

Now, when big business takes time out to study it, because they have threatened to go in the streets and disrupt the production lines and they're taking that action and taking the time out for men who they pay good salaries to take time out and study this thing, I think that we as Catholic War Veterans should keep an eye out so that if it takes place in our area we can notify the State Department so that they can be exposed for what they are. . . .

Another thing I want to bring out is that we should take a stand on this, and at the last State Board meeting the Adjutant stated the same thing and I think it should be done. I was greatly disappointed that Memorial Day, that the State Department did not come out and take a stand against the stores that were open for business as a normal day. It was a day that

Source: Report of the Proceedings of the 29th Convention of the Catholic War Veterans of the U.S., Dept. of Pa., June 1969, pp. 24-25.

was laid aside by the Federal Government to have memorial services for those fellows that died and are dying, but for big business it is a chance to make money.

Now, it is up to us to take the stand because once we have lost our heritage — and also if we lose that, you can say we have lost everything — when they forget to remember, then it is time that we once again start acting to make them remember.

Thank you. (Applause.)

SOURCE 229

The past commander in chief of the Pennsylvania department of the Veterans of Foreign Wars (VFW), Louis Feldmann, offered similar views to a VFW convention in July 1968:

We should say that people who loot places are burglars and robbers. We should speak up on these things, speak up on the draft. Speak up on our military stand. We want to win in Vietnam, and we should say to the State Department, "Your job is politics. War is the antithesis of politics. Let the military men win in Vietnam and then you come in and see what you can do about straightening the peace." But let's say in this convention here that we are not just a bunch of flag-waving patriots. We are a rip-roaring bunch of fellows who fought for this country, and we intend to continue to fight even though all the uniform is missing except the cap. We intend to fight for the United States. We intend to make sure that what Lenin said is not going to come true. We want better schools, better hospitals, better housing. We want work for everybody, but we are going to get it in the old-fashioned, American way. The good, old-fashioned American way comes from the Bible. "Man shall earn his bread by the sweat of his brow." The Government can't keep us forever because somebody has to produce. Let's say with feeling and finality that the most important election in the history of this country is probably in November. Forget whether you are a Republican or a Democrat or whatever else you might be. Listen to what these men say. The devil with the political bosses trying to get us to go a certain way. Vote for the man that you think will win the Vietnam war. Now, I am not talking about a wholesale slaughter. I am talking about winning, and there are many ways to win. Vote for the man you think has the courage, who has come before the VFW and has expressed

---

Source: VFW, Department of Pennsylvania, *Proceedings of the 49th Annual Convention, Annual Convention, July, 1968,* pp. 52-53.

his opinion. There are at least two of them who have done that. Vote for the man that you think is going to make the best President of the United States, and forget about whether he is a Republican or a Democrat, whether you like the way he appears on television or you like his sister or the car he drives. Vote for the man that you think will be the best President of the United States, because the Lord knows we need the best man that is possibly available. We must save ourselves, because nobody else wants to see us saved, and it has to start here with the Veterans of Foreign Wars in the Department of Pennsylvania. Charge out to Detroit in the third week in August and make sure that the thing you say in resolutions here will appear in resolutions out there. Have a floor fight. Stand up. Don't be afraid to be contradicted. Stand up and fight for what we believe in. Get into the fighting spirit we were in in 1946, and, damn it, we are going to win this thing. (Great applause.)

[He was seconded by Comrade William Tepsic, a past department commander:]

. . . I think we ought to again become a militant organization and stand up as the Veterans of Foreign Wars to be counted. I think many people feel that the Veterans of Foreign Wars are sound asleep, but may I say that in the Pittsburgh area we are not sound asleep. I think we ought to spread this all around the United States and talk about America. I have been speaking on the Vietnam situation. I don't know too much about it, but I think it must be talked about and we must start in our own back yard.

Here in Philadelphia, in the City of Brotherly Love, when I picked up the newspaper and looked on the front page of the edition on Wednesday, July 10th, the Evening Bulletin, what did I see? Not a darned thing about the Veterans of Foreign Wars, but apparently again the Students for Democratic Action are again at work. What are they doing? They are taking the statues in this city, the statues of national heroes, and they are gagging them. I think we in the Veterans of Foreign Wars ought to stand up at this convention and be counted against these kinds of people. I think, too, that we ought to enact laws whereby the kids who are under eighteen years of age must be held responsible through their parents, because today as we take these kids into the courts, you know what happens. The judges are dismissing the cases and the end result is they are getting out with some of these Pinkoes who are proliferating over the United States, while we can't do a darned thing about it. I think, too, that we have got to get behind our police. We ought to stand solidly with them to bring back law and order. From this convention we all ought to get up on the floor and talk about America and tell the news media that we don't give a darn whether they give us bad or good publicity, we want publicity to bring America back on the right road. We can do it if all of us get up here and talk about America and the problems that confront us. Let's bring our economy back to the place where the dollar means something. Let's send ships into North Korea and bring the crew of the PUEBLO back tomorrow morning.

I think Lou Feldmann is right when he says we must have guts. Out of this convention there should be a mandate to National to get those eighty-two guys on that PUEBLO out tomorrow morning. We shouldn't bicker back and forth. They were within the 12-mile limit. We have lost something when we say, "Sure, they are right." But let's get those kids out and from this convention let's get up and resolve to so mandate our National Organization and all of our veterans' posts to send communications to your Representatives in the Congress of the United States, telling them to get off their fannies and do something about these kids, wherever they may be.

SOURCE 230

Gary Wood, a Vietnam veteran, talked about the differences between World War II veterans and Vietnam veterans:

"I would rather deal with a nonvet than a World War II vet.

"World War II vets are the lifers. They are the biggest obstacle to Vietnam vets making it.

"They grew up in the depression, and they came back to victory parades and prosperity. They saw World War II as a means of getting out of the bad times.

"We grew up in prosperity, and we came back to no jobs, lousy bennies, and civilian contempt. We see the Vietnam War as a means of getting out of the good times.

"World War II was a team effort. You went into it with units made up largely of guys from your own geographical area. You came home with the same guys. Pennsylvania still calls Route 322 the '28th Division Highway' because the 28th was basically guys from the state.

"We went to 'Nam by ourselves. We survived it by ourselves. We came back by ourselves. I only knew one guy who went through Basic and Advanced and then went to my first post and then to 'Nam with me.

"The 'World War II Generation' came out with this attitude: The way to take care of yourself is to fit in with the team. It's worked good for us. It should work for you. If you don't want to *fit in,* there's something wrong with you. If you don't want to loud enough, we'll cut your water off.

Source: C. Noell and G. Wood, *We Are All POWs* (Philadelphia, 1975), pp. 55-57.

"That's what they did in the McCarthy period. They purged all the guys who didn't fit in. That's why we didn't hear any criticism about the country when we went to school in the fifties. Everybody was a team player.

"The Vietnam Vets Against the War held this demonstration in 1971. They stood outside Congress and threw away their medals. Those medals were the symbols of being good team players in 'Nam.

"I wasn't a Vietnam vet against the war, and I didn't like demonstrations. But I thought that one was cool. It showed that Vietnam vets aren't buying into the team mechanism.

"We've seen the team in action.

"When I was in Pleiku, the warrant officer in charge of my unit put every E-6 and up in for a Bronze Star. That way he could put himself in for a Legion of Merit because his unit had fought so hard. They hadn't fought worth shit. But everybody moved up the ladder anyway.

"Look at the institutions that are supposed to help vets. Most of the big shots in the VA are American Legion. And most of the bureaucrats who run the State Employment Service programs for vets are VFW.

"And most of them spend most of their time worrying about their seniority and their pensions and their civil service bennies. Their priority is keeping up the institution, not helping vets.

"The World War II Generation runs every hierarchy you can think of, the same way the Legion runs the VA, because there are so many of them. They are the heart of the vested interests in this country. They are the people who managed Vietnam.

"Vietnam vets prefer to operate through networks of communication among individuals. We are sometimes joiners. We get together to do specific things at specific times. But each time has to be a separate decision of each vet. . . ."

PART II

The effects that war and the military have on those not in the military itself

5

The GI's Family

SOURCE 231

Mrs. James Hoyt of South Carolina recalls the Civil War and its effect on her life, 1902:

". . . . while my young life was somewhat shadowed, and I was cut off from the privileges of an education, . . . still I am glad to have lived through a period like this, and believed that what there is in me of womanliness and strength of character and endurance is greatly due to the lessons of self-confidence . . . taught me during the war."

Source: Sallie E. Taylor, ed., *South Carolina Women in the Confederacy,* I (Columbia, S.C., 1902), p. 371; quoted in Anne Firor Scott, *The Southern Lady* (Chicago, 1970), p. 98.

SOURCE 232

When an anonymous male machinist penned a sarcastic poem about female machinists employed during World War I, an anonymous female machinist responded with revealing zest:

The Man's Poem:

The Reason Why

The shop girls had a meeting
They came from far and near
Some came from Bryant's, J and L
And some from Fellows Gear.

But before inside the hall
They were allowed to look
They had to take their bloomers off,
And hang 'em on a hook.

Then into the hall they went at once,
With courage ever higher
But hardly were they seated
When someone shouted "Fire."

Then out they ran all in a bunch,
They had no time to look,
And each one grabbed a bloomer
At random from the hook.

They got their bloomers all mixed up,
And they were mighty sore,
To think they couldn't have the one
They had always had before.
And that's the reason that you see
As you go 'round the streets,
Each one will stop and take a look
At every girl she meets.

And hence the reason that the girls
Who are not so very stout,
Have had to take 'em in a bit,
And the fat ones, let 'em out.

The Woman's Response:

She Hands Him a Lemon

My man, you're really out of date
And now before it is too late,
I'll try to set you right;
We never mixed our bloomers, clown,
They fit just like a Paris gown,
They're neither loose nor tight.
The simple, tender, clinging vine,
That once around the oak did twine,
Is something of the past;
We stand erect now by your side,

Source: Wayne Broehl, Jr., *Precision Valley: The Machine Tool Companies of Springfield, Vermont* (1959), pp. 98-99. I thank Maurine Greenwald for bringing these to my attention.

And surmount obstacles with pride,
We're equal, free, at last.

We're independent now you see,
Your bald head don't appeal to me,
I love my overalls;
And I would rather polish steel,
Than get you up a tasty meal,
Or go with you to balls.
Now, only premiums good and big,
Will tempt us maids to change our rig,
And put our aprons on;
And cook up all the dainty things,
That so delighted men and kings
In days now past and gone.

Now in your talk of shouting "fire,"
You really did arouse my ire,
I tell you, sir, with pride,
That you would be the one to run
While we would stay and see the fun,
And lend a hand beside.
To sit by your machine and chew
And dream of lovely Irish stew,
Won't work today you'll find.
Now, we're the ones who set the pace,
You'll have to bustle in the race
Or you'll get left behind.

We're truly glad we got the chance
To work like men and wear men's pants,
And proved that we made good.
My suit a badge of honor is.
Now, will you kindly mind your "biz"
Just as you know you should.

SOURCE 233

The wife of a man from Illinois who had served during World
War II was no less "cosmopolitanized" by her stay on the West
Coast than were many of the GIs themselves:

Source: Robert Havighurst et al., The American Veteran Back Home (New York, 1951), p. 42.

"I went to camp with Johnny after we were married and stayed there until just before he shipped out. I liked it a lot there. Since I've come back here I feel cramped. After having all that space around us, with mountains in the distance, it makes me feel cooped up to come back to this town."

SOURCE 234

> Florence Woolston described the effect of World War I mobi-
> lization in America upon her nephew Billy:

Billy, my nephew, is twelve years old. With the possible exception of the beef profiteers and a few superpatriots to whom life has been a prolonged Fourth of July oration, no one has got quite so much fun out of the war as Billy and his inseparable companions, Fritters, George and Bean-Pole Ross.

Clad in the khaki uniform of the Boy Scouts, with United War Campaign, Red Cross, War Saving, first, second, third and fourth Liberty Loan buttons, small American flags and service pins spread across their chests, they have lived the war from morning until night. I did not understand Billy's passionate allegiance to the Scout uniform until I discovered the great game of hailing automobiles bearing the sign, "Men in Uniform Welcome." Billy has never been willing to accompany his family on automobile rides but the pleasure of this boulevard game has been never ending.

They call the suburb in which Billy lives one hundred per cent patriotic. Everybody is in war work. Even the children under five years have an organization known as the Khaki Babes. These infants in uniform assemble, kindergarten fashion and solemnly snip for the Red Cross. Billy's crowd is indefatigable in its labors. With the other Scouts, the boys usher at meetings, assist in parades, deliver bundles and run errands. They are tireless collectors of nutshells, peach pits and tinsel paper. As Victory Boys they are pledged to earn five dollars for the United War Workers. Since most of them expect to do this shovelling snow they are praying for a severe winter.

One bit of voluntary war work was carried on through the periods of gasolineless Sundays when the four boys took positions on Common-wealth Avenue in such a way as to obstruct passing vehicles. If a car did not carry a doctor's or military sign, they threw pebbles and yelled "O you Slacker!" It was exciting work because guilty drivers put on full speed ahead and Billy admitted that he was almost run over, but he added that the cause was worth it.

In my school days history was a rather dull subject.

Source: Florence Woolston, "Billy and the World War," New Republic (January 25, 1919), pp. 369-71.

. . . It is not so with Billy. Modern history is unfolding to him as a great drama. Kings and tsars and presidents are live human beings. War has nothing to do with books. It is a perpetual moving picture with reels furnished twice a day by the newspapers. Wars were as unreal as pictorial combats with painted soldiers and stationary warships. Even the Civil War belonged to historical fiction. Once a year, on the 30th of May, a veteran in navy blue came to school and in a quavering voice told stories of his war days. Thrilling as they might have been, they always seemed to lack reality. . . .

. . . Billy and his chums . . . know what boundaries mean; they pore over war maps and glibly recite the positions of the Allied troops. Billy has a familiarity with principal cities, rivers and towns that never could have been learned in lesson form. The war has created a new cosmopolitanism. The children of Billy's generation will never have the provincial idea that Boston is the centre of the world. They will see the universe as a great circle, perhaps, but all the Allies will occupy the centre.

I must confess, however, that Billy, Fritters, George and Bean-Pole Ross have a rather vague idea of what the war is about, but then so do others with more years to their credit. I asked Billy what caused the war originally, and he replied in a rather large and lofty way, "You see, the French took Alsace and Lorraine away from the Germans a long time ago and Germany wanted it back. She thought it would be nice to get hold of Paris, too, and conquer the French people, then they would have to pay taxes and indemnities to support Germany. So they started to march to Paris and then all the other countries decided to stop them."

When I compare the anemic stereopticon travel talks of my school days with Billy's moving picture shows, I have the sense of a cheated childhood. We had nothing in our young lives like Crashing Through to Berlin, The Hounds of Hunland, Wolves of Kultur and the Brass Bullet. Billy's mental images have been built by such pictures as these with the additional and more educational films of the Committee on Public Information and the Pathé weekly where actual battle scenes, aeroplane conflicts and real naval encounters are portrayed.

In the matter of books, too, Billy has had high revel. I sowed a few wild oats with Oliver Optic and Horatio Alger wherein poor lads were conducted from prairie huts to the Executive mansion. Of course we had Scott and Cooper to make medieval times or Indian days vivid. But think of reading Over the Top and going to shake hands with the author, a live, red-blooded officer in the army! Billy revels in Private Peat, Hunting the Hun, Out of the Jaws of Hunland, From Base Ball to Boches, and With the Flying Corps. I'm afraid he will never have a Walter Scott period and I am sure it will be years before contemplative literature can hold his attention.

Of course, the war has given us all an enlarged vocabulary. Billy calls his school "the trench"; he and Fritters go "over the top," "carry on," play in dug-outs, move in units, carry kits, eat mess and have elaborate systems of wig-wagging and passwords. When he is unsuccessful in a parental encounter, Billy throws up his hands and cries "I surrender!" Hun, Boche and Bolshevik are terms of terrible opprobrium. There was a bloody fist fight at recess recently, when Henry Earl was called "O you Kaiser!" The mere suggestion of a German name brings forth expressions of loud disgust and none of the boys would use a toy made in Germany.

At present it is in fashion to collect war posters. Billy has a remarkable collection of Food, Red Cross, Marine, War Savings, Navy and United War Work Campaign posters. He has trudged miles and spent much ingenuity in getting them. His room is papered with them and it is a matter of deep regret that the family is unwilling to have the entire house so placarded. A thriving business goes on in poster trading and a steady stream of small boys passes the house carrying large rolls of posters. From Billy's room, after a visitation, come delighted exclamations, "Gee! what a bute!" "Say, I'll give you a Join the Gas Hounds for a Beat Back the Huns." "Fritters has two Teufelhunden and he's going to swap it for a Clear the Way and a Tell That to the Marines."

Billy came to me with an ethical problem connected with his poster campaign. "I've got," he declared, "five Joan of Arcs, three Must Children Starves, five Blot it Outs, a Britisher and a big Y. I can sell them and make lots of money. Would that be profiteering?" I thought it might be so considered by taxpayers. "Well," he demanded, "If I sell them and buy Thrift Stamps that would be profiteering to help the war, and that would be all right, wouldn't it?"

When a campaign is on, the boys find it hard to wait until the posters have done their work as propaganda. Sometimes a lucky boy gets a whole new set. Recently, there had been much buying and selling of addresses where posters may be obtained, five cents for a plain address, ten for a "guaranteed." I mailed a postal card for Billy addressed to the Secretary of the Navy which read, "Kindly send me a full set of your Marine and Navy posters. I will display them if you wish." Billy's collection numbers about two hundred but he knows boys who have a thousand posters. As evidence of his great delight in them, he made the following statement: "If the last comes to the last, and we couldn't get coal and we had to burn all the furniture, I'd give up one set of my duplicates, but only if the last comes to the last."

Billy is a kind-hearted lad with humane instincts toward all creatures except flies. He feels, however, that the Kaiser can neither claim the protection of the S.P.C.A. nor demand the consideration usually afforded a human being. He loves to tell what he would do to the Kaiser. It is a matter of bitter disappointment that Mr. Hohenzollern is in Holland instead of in Billy's hands. At breakfast he issues bulletins of carnage. Some days he plans simple tortures like beheading, skinning, hanging, burning. At other times he concocts a more elaborate scheme such as splitting open the Kaiser's arms and putting salt on the wound, cutting his legs off at the knee and hanging his feet around his neck, or gouging out his eyes. A favorite idea is that of inoculating him with all the diseases of the world or to starve him for months and then eat a big Thanksgiving dinner in his presence.

Billy has had a full course in atrocities and is keen for reprisals. He longs to fly with an aviation unit, dropping bombs on Berlin, he aches to destroy a few cathedrals and palaces, burn all the German villages and poison the reservoirs. His description of what he would do to the Huns makes the Allied armistice sound like a presentation speech with a bunch of laurel.

There is a marked absence of patriotic sentiment with Billy and his chums. To them patriotism is action; they do not enjoy talking about it. When a Liberty Loan orator gushes about the starry banner, they roll their eyes expressively and murmur "Cut it out." Of course, some of this is the self-conscious stoicism of the small boy. But there is a matter of fact attitude toward suffering and pain which is new and due to familiarity with the idea. Boys discuss the kinds of wounds, operations and war accidents as a group of medical students might refer to a clinic.

Death seems to give them no sense of mystery and awe. "Gee! a thousand killed today," "That Ace has got his," "Say, John Bowers was gassed and he's gone now." They look over the casualty lists as grown-ups might read lists of guests at a reception. It may be because youth cannot understand the tragedy and heartache back of the golden stars on the service flags, but I think it goes deeper than that. These boys have a sense of courage and gallantry that makes the risking of life an everyday affair. Self-sacrifice is not a matter of poems and sermons and history, it is the daily news. Billy's attitude is that going to war is part of the game; when you're a little boy you have to go to school; when you're older, you draw your number and are called to camp—it's all in a day's work. . . .

SOURCE 235

The destitute wife of a volunteer in the Continental Line appealed to the Revolutionary government in Connecticut for relief, September 1777:

On the representation of Mary Vose, resident in Colchester, wife of Henry Vose of Nova Scotia, now a soldier in one of the continental battalions from the State of Rhode Island, that she is destitute of the means of sub-

---

Source: C. Hoadly, ed., *Records of the State of Connecticut,* I (1894), p. 398.

sistence, having with her three sons born at one birth aged about nine months, *viz:* John Hancock, George Washington and Charles Lee,—a letter was sent to the selectmen of Colchester to provide for her subsistence what may be necessary more than her earnings and what her husband may supply her with, and lay their account before his Excellency the Governor and his Council.

SOURCE 236

This folk song, of a distressed Irish-American woman whose husband had enlisted, was popular during the war of 1812:

Johnny Has Gone for a Soldier

Oh, Johnny dear has gone away,
He has gone afar across the bay,
Oh, my heart is sad and weary today,
Since Johnny has gone for a soldier.

Chorus:

Schule, schule, schule agrah,
Time can only ease my woe,
Since the lad of my heart from me did go,
Oh, Johnny has gone for a soldier.

I'll dye my dress, I'll dye it red,
And through the streets I'll beg my bread,
Oh, how I wish that I were dead.
Since Johnny has gone for a soldier.

SOURCE 237

The destitute wife of a Michigan volunteer during the Civil War complained of the inadequacy of her husband's pay and the county's relief system:

"Soldiers will regret leaving their families to such heartless wretches [as Calhoun County's relief supervisors]. Such feelings [among soldiers] have caused a great many desertions and will cause many more if continued."

Source: George Herdman, "The Impact of the Civil War on Calhoun County, Michigan," unpublished Ph.D. dissertation, University of Maryland, 1972, p. 93.

SOURCE 238

Families surveyed during World War II indicated that a number of problems remained unsolved when the husband left to serve:

UNSOLVED PROBLEMS AT INDUCTION	NUMBER OF FAMILIES REPORTING
Jealousy	32
Handling money	31
Sickness and need for medical care	26
Mounting expenses	24
In-laws	22
Drinking	20
Housing	19
Child discipline	17
Recreation	15
Troubles on the job	14
Number of children	11
Sex satisfactions	10
Clashing temperaments	9
Wife working	5
Religion	5
Use of contraceptives	1
Personal habits	1
Demonstration of affection	1
No problems at induction	14

Source: R. Hill et al., *Families Under Stress* (New York, 1949), p. 39.

SOURCE 239

Sociologists studying American families during World War II reported on the effects that the separation of the soldier-father had on the wife and child:

The H family was a contented, equalitarian one that wisely faced the possibility of induction a whole year before it happened, prepared for it by planning to move in with the in-laws and have Mrs. H go to work. The plans made little impression on Sally, though. All she knew was that the tight

Source: Reuben Hill et al., *Families Under Stress* (New York, 1949), pp. 62-63.

little family group within which all her world and her joys lay was suddenly disrupted. Father had gone off to war and might be killed. Mother went out to work every day because there wasn't enough money and it helped to keep her mind occupied. They moved from the nice little apartment that had always been home to a big house in a strange neighborhood and there was no one home all day to take care of her except grandmother. All of a sudden the very bottom had dropped out of her happy, secure existence, and she was badly frightened. She began to feel that nobody loved her, and as the comfortless situation continued she lost all confidence in her mother, becoming convinced that she and the whole family hated her and wanted to get rid of her. Evenings spent by Mrs. H with Sally did nothing to dispel her fears, and it was not until father returned and the old three-way companionship was reestablished that she regained her zest for life. . . .

The DS couple had gradually built up a cooperative, equalitarian relationship after an estrangement early in their married life. Mr. DS wanted to enlist and do his part, but for a year his wife wouldn't let him. When she finally gave in, he had a little talk with their eleven-year-old son before he left, in which he told him to be the man of the house while daddy was away and take good care of mother. The son became transformed overnight from a carefree boy who played with the gang all the time and was never home, to a serious-minded little gentleman who stayed home and helped mother in the house. This was what the community admired, but what drove mother wild was that he considered part of his duty to be making a minute check on all mother's activities. She had to account to him for every moment spent away from the house and was scolded when she went out too much. He told her how to do things in the home and was generally bossy in the way that only self-important children can be bossy. She was helpless to assert herself, particularly as the son wrote long letters keeping his father minutely informed about mother as well as about himself.

SOURCE 240

A neurotic child whose father was in the army came to the attention of the New York Bureau of Child Welfare in late 1943:

Source: Amelia Igel, "The Effect of War Separation on Father-Child Relations," *The Family: A Journal of Social Case Work* 26 (1945): 6. Compare C. Seplin, "A Study of the Influence of Father's Absence for Military Service," *Smith College Studies in Social Work* 22 (1952): 123-24.

Tommy, an 8-year-old boy, was referred to the Department of Welfare at the insistence of the school principal, who stated the school had made every possible effort to help the child, but if the child were not placed, he would be expelled from school. They reported that since Tommy's father had been inducted in May, 1943, the child had been having explosive outbursts of temper, had been threatening to kill his mother, was demanding of affection, always wanted to be the center of attention, and was restless and uncontrollable in the classroom. The mother reported that at home the child was threatening, tried to hurt her, refused to eat or to bathe, and had reverted to wetting and soiling both day and night.

During the time the school had been attempting to work with the mother and child, Tommy had been studied at a mental hygiene clinic. The psychiatrist reported that the boy was of above average intelligence. When Tommy saw so many men in soldiers' uniforms on the streets he could not understand why his father had left him and thought that "something was being put over on him." His threats to kill the father were retaliatory because the father had left him, and his threats to kill his mother were because she "made him eat" and he "didn't want to grow big and strong." Much of his behavior—the refusal to eat, the soiling, the rolling on the floor to get dirty—were overt efforts to worry and enrage the mother.

The history revealed significant material of family tensions. Tommy was an out-of-wedlock child whose father had deserted the mother when Tommy was about 18 months old. The mother had never nursed Tommy and the first 18 months of his life were rather precarious because the family moved frequently from one furnished room to another. The mother's husband had first been attracted to her through Tommy and, when he married the mother, was frank in saying he was marrying her because he loved Tommy. Both parents came from broken homes. We know very little about the stepfather except that he was seven years older than the mother and had a rather poor work record (the family had received Home Relief up to the time of his induction in May of 1942). He had taken over the entire management of Tommy and had always been able to discipline him without beating him. When the mother wrote her husband that she had applied for his discharge from the army on a "hardship" basis and if that failed she was going to "put Tommy away," the husband wrote her an angry letter saying he had married her to keep Tommy from going to an institution and he wanted her to stay home and take care of him. Shortly after this he was sent overseas.

The mother was described by the family agency that had tried to help her during the period prior to referral to the Department of Welfare, as of low average intelligence. She was physically debilitated, was unable to plan anything beyond an immediate concrete goal, and was absorbed in keeping her home immaculate and in securing as many material possessions as possible. Her financial position had actually been improved following her husband's induction since she had been able for the first time to move to an unfurnished apartment and buy furniture (on time payments). She was considered rigid, neurotic, and cold. Her relations with both maternal and paternal relatives were poor.

Tommy was placed in January, 1944. The mother, who visits at the request of the worker as often as allowed (three times a month), expresses herself as entirely pleased with Tommy's adjustment there. The worker, however, reports that Tommy is still a very disturbed child. His toilet habits have improved, but he is restless and overdemanding of affection and attention. He begs for his mother to visit him but pays little attention to her once she comes after she "tells me the things that my father writes in the letters about me." He says he doesn't want to go home until his father comes home. He seldom talks about his father, except to say how happy he would be if his father would come home. However, he knows that is not possible until the war is over. He never expresses fear or anxiety about his father.

SOURCE 241

> *The wife of a submariner came to the attention of navy psychiatrists in the mid-1960s when she suffered a nervous breakdown while her husband was at sea:*

Mrs. A., a 32-year-old mother of five, married for 15 years to a chief petty officer, had never previously had psychiatric difficulties. Two weeks before her husband was due home, she experienced a sudden onset of anxiety and was seen in the emergency room that same evening. The anxiety was intense and accompanied by uncontrollable weeping and a persistent, diffuse headache. She felt all would be well if her husband would return "tomorrow." She denied any anger at his being away, but lamented the hardship to her and her family caused by the frequent patrols. On the visit to the psychiatrist the next day, she spoke with considerable anger about the previous years of hardship. "If only I could show him what he's done to us!"

Source: Richard Isay, "The Submariners' Wives Syndrome," *Psychiatric Quarterly* 42 (1968): 648.

SOURCE 242

> One Southern wife wrote to her husband urging him to desert
> the Confederate army, and others wrote to the anticonscription
> governor of North Carolina, Zebulon Vance:

Mary — to Her Husband:

"My dear Edward:—I have always been proud of you, and since your connection with the Confederate Army, I have been prouder of you than ever before. I would not have you do anything wrong for the world, but before God, Edward, unless you come home, we must die. Last night, I was aroused by little Eddie's crying. I called and said 'What is the matter, Eddie?' and he said, 'O mamma! I am so hungry.' and Lucy, Edward, your darling Lucy; she never complains, but she is growing thinner and thinner every day. And before God, Edward, unless you come home, we must die."

Martha Curtis of Homing Creek, N.C., to Governor Vance:

"He is the only man I haf that is able to work. I has won small son that is sickly and is not able to work. All the way that I has to git my living is to keep up my farm and I am not able to tend my farm without help."

Margaret Perrey to Governor Vance:

"If he does not return shortly nothing but starvation, devastation & final ruin to his family will be the consequence. . . . I have to break up house-keeping in a short time if he dont return."

Source: Ella Lonn, *Desertion During the Civil War* (New York, 1924,) p. 13; Francis B. Simkins and James Patton, *The Women of the Confederacy* (Richmond, 1936), p. 226.

SOURCE 243

> A wife and mother wrote to the Army during World War I, hoping
> to obtain a discharge for her husband:

Oak Park, Illinois, November 12, 1917

DEAR GENERAL

I'm going to ask you to help me please be so kind not to refuse me Im a mother with a baby boy 14 months old and cant go out to work so I ask

---

Source: Will Judy, *A Soldier's Diary* (Chicago, 1931), pp. 40-41.

you if you would be so kind as to give my husband . . . his discharge and if
his country will need him very bad then of course he will go again I didnt
think it would be so hard for me but it is very hard for me I have no mother
or father they are both dead and his mother is old she is a widow and is
got to go out to work since he left so if you would be so very kind as to
give my husband his discharge I dont know how I will ever thank you I
pray for you every night so God would look after you and keep you well
to win this war and if it would be necessary for my husband to go and fight
for his country by that time our little boy will be bigger and I will be able
to go to work and make my living but now you know yourself how hard
every thing is and his mother said she will remember you also so please
be so good as to give my husband his discharge do it for the little boy sake
I tell you the truth that some day all I have is tea and dry bread and you
now how it is for a nursing mother so dear sir I ask you with all my harth
to send him hom Ill be waiting for your answer

Yours very truly
Mrs. . . .

SOURCE 244

*A psychiatrist wrote this case history of a boy frightened badly
by the air raid drills of 1942 in Ithaca, New York:*

Boy H.G. (clinic number 1701915), 12 years 7 months, I.Q. 104,101, the
older of two children, was seen in the Out Patient Department of the
Payne Whitney Psychiatric Clinic by two psychiatrists from June 1937 to
May 1941 at frequent intervals for a severe anxiety syndrome with obses-
sive-compulsive features. One conspicuous symptom, which was a great
social handicap, was the fear that his father would die. Consequently, he
refused to go to school, since this involved leaving his father. Both parents
are neurotic individuals, and the mother was also treated in the clinic.
After a period of three years, there was considerable improvement and
the boy was discharged. In March 1942, i.e., 3 months after the onset of
the war, the patient's mother asked that her son be seen again "for a few
times until he gets over his scare." She reported that after his discharge
from the clinic, the boy had been getting along well at home and at school
(substantiated by School Principal's report) "until the war started." He

Source: J. Louise Despert, *Preliminary Report on Children's Reaction to the War* (Ithaca,
N.Y., 1942), pp. 76-77.

was "panicky," feared air-raids and the possible death of his father and mother. When seen briefly at the time of writing, he had a recurrence in a milder form of his previous anxiety. He had also developed religious rituals. There can be no question that, as is generally recognized, the function of these compulsive mechanisms was to relieve the anxiety.

SOURCE 245

Using 1961 Survey Research Center public sample data, an analyst correlated opinions regarding the likelihood of nuclear attack with information derived from respondents about themselves:

ATTACK WORSE "HERE" THAN MOST OF THE U.S.	ATTITUDE TOWARD ARMS CONTROL MEASURES			HAVE OR PLAN TO HAVE A SHELTER
	SUPPORTIVE	MIXED	OPPOSED	
War very likely in 2 years or less	14%	30%	42%	7%
War possible in 2 years or less	19	30	26	15
War unlikely; 5 yrs. away if it happens	67	40	32	—
	100%	100%	100%	—
	N (42)	(26)	(38)	
ATTACK WORSE "ELSE—WHERE" IN THE U.S.				
War very likely in 2 years or less	21%	55%	61%	7%
War possible in 2 years or less	8	18	16	25
War unlikely; 5 yrs. away if it happens	71	27	23	5
	100%	100%	100%	—
	N (28)	(22)	(61)	

Source: Stephen Withey of the University of Michigan's Survey Research Center, in an essay reprinted in Davis Bobrow, ed., *Components of Defense Policy* (Chicago, 1965), pp. 172-74.

	INCOME			EDUCATION		
ATTACK WORSE "HERE" THAN MOST OF THE U.S.	UNDER $4,000	$4,000– $7,500	$7,500 OR MORE	8TH GRADE OR LESS	GRADES 9–12	COLLEGE
War very likely in 2 years or less	64%	25%	11%	45%	28%	21%
War possible in 2 years or less	36	25	17	33	24	21
War unlikely; 5 yrs. away if it happens	a	50	72	22	48	58
	100%	100%	100%	100%	100%	100%
N	(22)	(48)	(36)	(16)	(32)	(46)
ATTACK WORSE "ELSWHERE" IN THE U.S.						
War very likely in 2 years or less	71%	48%	28%	60%	60%	27%
War possible in 2 years or less	24	13	29	7	16	17
War unlikely; 5 yrs. away if it happens	5	39	43	33	24	56
	100%	100%	100%	100%	100%	100%
N	(34)	(46)	(28)	(30)	(50)	(32)

aLess than 0.5 per cent

ATTACK WORSE "HERE" THAN MOST OF THE U.S.	LEVEL OF INFORMATION ABOUT THE WORLD			SEX		MENTIONS "SHELTERS" SPONTANEOUSLY AS SAVING LIVES AFTER AN ATTACK
	LOW	MEDIUM	HIGH	MALE	FEMALE	
War very likely in 2 years or less	38%	37%	17%	18%	45%	30%
War possible in 2 years or less	24	19	26	18	35	30
War unlikely; 5 yrs. away if it happens	38	44	57	64	20	40
N	100% (16)	100% (32)	100% (46)	100% (66)	100% (40)	100% (40)

ATTACK WORSE "ELSEWHERE" IN THE U.S.						
War very likely in 2 years or less	67%	38%	33%	37%	71%	71%
War possible in 2 years or less	22	8	14	17	10	18
War unlikely; 5 yrs. away if it happens	11	54	53	46	19	11
N	100% (36)	100% (26)	100% (30)	100% (70)	100% (42)	100% (54)

SOURCE 246

Some wives of returning GIs were not worried about readjust-
ment or their own careers in the work force:

"When Fred comes home, . . . I know he'll just want to hang around for a
month or two, as he is certainly entitled to a rest. I'll probably work for
this time, to keep things going—longer if necessary; but I don't plan to
keep on."

"I figure when Sam comes home he'll probably just hang around for a
few months. I won't force him to go to work, or even ask him. I'll keep on
a while, until he gets tired of hanging around. I want Sam to take time
and get the kind of job he wants."

[But others were worried:]

"You know, there is gong to be a terrific adjustment to be made when our
husbands come back. My sister and I have talked it over a lot of times.
For instance, take the way I'm handling money now. When my husband
was around, I never had anything to do with money. I didn't even pay the
telephone or electric light bill. He took care of everything. Now I take
care of those bills and pay the insurance on the car and keep everything
going; and it's going to be difficult for me when he comes back because
it'll be so hard for me, after taking care of everything so long, to hand it
all back to him. It's not that I want to continue handling money this way
—I'd much rather he did it. But it's still going to be hard to get used to
having him do it again. And there's going to be another adjustment we
wives will have to make, too. As things are now, I can go out and get the
car whenever I please and go out to dinner with Jackie, or go to Joliet to
the movies, or do pretty much as I please. When my husband comes
home I'll never be able to do that again. This is going to be quite an adjustment, because I've had a year to do as I please, and it may be another
year or even two years before he'll be back."

Source: Robert Havighurst et al., *The American Veteran Back Home* (New York, 1951),
pp. 84, 90.

SOURCE 247

Wives of American prisoners of war indicated a number of anx-
ieties they felt toward the reunion they anticipated upon their
husbands' repatriation in the early 1970s:

Source: Hamilton McCubbin and Barbara Dahl, "Prolonged Family Separation in the
Military," in Ham. McCubbin et al., eds., *Families in the Military System* (Beverly Hills, Calif.,
1976), p. 125.

Wives' Concerns About Repatriation

CONCERN	POSITIVE RESPONSES	PERCENT[a]
Becoming too independent	28	46.0
Not saving more money	13	21.3
Dating	12	20.0
Manner in which children raised	10	16.0
Drinking too much	3	5.0

[a]N = 61

SOURCE 248

Attitude of Veterans and Nonveteran Fathers During World War II Toward Personality Characteristics of First-Born

TRAITS	WAR-SEPARATED	NON-SEPARATED
Criticized		
Highly emotional	7	5
Unhappy	2	—
Stubborn	5	4
Disrespectful	3	—
Selfish	3	1
Demanding	3	—
Unresponsive	7	—
"Sissy"	9	5
Other	16	11
Total	62	29
Approved		
Intelligent	11	17
Verbal	4	5
Creative	1	3
Disciplined	3	5
"Good"	2	8
Self-reliant	2	5
Sense of humor	3	5
Friendly	3	10
Good natured	1	3
Interested	1	5
Other	3	8
Total	34	74

Source: Stolz and Stolz, Father Relations of War-Born Children (Stanford, Calif., 1954), p. 66.

SOURCE 249

The wife of Vietnam veteran talked about the problems that led to her separation from her husband:

You think it's all your fault. There must be thousands of women married or relating to these men who have this awful sense of rejection and loneliness when they can't get close to their guys and who feel this terrible isolation. . . .

He slapped me around maybe three times. Sometimes I'd egg him on — "For God's sake do something" — because I couldn't get close to him. And what he did was hit me — or just walk out. Often he didn't come home for days, and I'd say, "Why can't I do anything right? . . ."

Jack and I had a lot of distance between us after his return. Initially I thought the failure of our relationship was an individual failure, but then, as I started talking with other women who were married to or living with vets, I realized we were all going through shock which resulted from Vietnam. We had to start sharing our pain, just as the men were trying to do, because we were building our own scars and defenses in reaction to them.

After a year, we made our group, "Ourselves," formal. We were all antiwar, so we tried to at least do interviews with women who weren't antiwar. We discovered that most of them felt relieved to learn that other women were going through the same troubles they were. We wanted to do more, but we couldn't raise the money we needed to hire staff or organize programs.

Eventually we could go on only so long reacting to the men before we had to get in touch with ourselves as women. We were brought up to be dependent on *his* career and *his* identity, but now we had to realize our own responsibilities as independent people. It was the only way to make our pain a source of strength rather than a handicap.

By now, all of us have gone through separations. There's guilt because we couldn't stand by our men, but we couldn't stay because our own lives were being destroyed. And yet — I find that I'm learning a whole lot now that I'm apart from Jack that I couldn't learn when we were together. We can see each other now. We're not two dependent souls who are leaning on each other. I don't know if Jack and I will get back together or not, but that isn't the important question. What's important is that we're getting out of being mired in bitterness and blame.

Source: C. Breslin, "Vietnam Vets . . . ," *Redbook* (May 1973), p. 143; Noell and Wood, *We Are All POWs* (Philadelphia, 1975), pp. 82-83.

SOURCE 250

The imminent retirement of one's military spouse can precipitate marriage problems too, inasmuch as it often constitutes a significant adjustment crisis, both economic and psychological. One such crisis was described by a military psychiatrist in the early 1970s:

The 40-year-old wife of an officer was seen in the hospital Family Clinic crying and visibly depressed; she expressed to the examining physician some suicidal ideation. She was referred to the Department of Mental Health for further follow-up, diagnosis, and treatment. Her husband had received a mandatory date for retirement from the service, and likewise he was becoming tense and upset. The wife complained that they no longer seemed to be able to communicate with each other and that her husband was drinking more. He had remarked to her that he believed that her personality was changing. During her husband's military tour, she had been an active member of the Officers' Wives Club and engaged with her husband and their friends in many of the activities available. Upon her husband's retirement, her symptoms became worse. She seemed to be more tearful and upset. She related that her husband either was unable or did not want to seek employment, and merely remained around the house. Although the patient was not a compulsive housekeeper, she enjoyed running her house on a schedule. Her husband's being at home markedly interfered with her functioning.

The husband was also seen at the Mental Health Clinic, and some of the problems that are fairly common in individuals going from active status to retirement were discussed with him. He was encouraged to seek employment actively, but for a while the situation did not change. The retiree occasionally would look for jobs, but he considered these beneath his ability and capability. The wife was encouraged to try to pursue her previous outlets and activities with her friends and to include her husband in these activities. Finally the husband received word that he had been accepted for a job that was to his liking. The marital relationship seemed to improve and the symptomatology that his wife presented some eight months previously began to resolve. The last information received indicated that both were progressing satisfactorily; he was still gainfully employed and she was entering into activities in the community again.

Source: John McNeil, "Retirement from Military Service," in Hamilton McCubbin, ed., *Families in the Military System,* p. 253.

SOURCE 251

The wife of a young officer killed in Vietnam spoke in 1970 of her loss and of the war:

The war came home to me on the 4th of March when I learned that my husband had been killed. I am not bitter about this war. I'm extremely shocked and grieved over his death. He was a professional officer and it seemed inevitable that he would go to war. I am the daughter of a career officer and I've grown up really all over the world. I've always had in the back of my mind that I would want to marry a military man, and while we were stationed in Germany I met my husband. On the morning of Tuesday, March the 4th, my Principal came to my classroom and asked me to go into the office with him. [She was a primary school teacher.] I did, and there were two officers who had been sent to notify me that my husband was missing in Vietnam. Of course, I had many telephone calls to make, to his parents and to the rest of our families, and I stayed at school to make those. I couldn't go home then, and shortly after that a friend came and she took me home. I spent the rest of the day at home sitting and waiting for more news, and also for the first telegram that had been promised to confirm this notification of missing. Since his death I've been surrounded by family and friends and I've also returned to my teaching job where I've been since last September.

Many people do consider this war to be an immoral war, to be unjust. I feel the United States entered this war under an agreement and we must continue there as long as we can fulfill our duty to that country, even though it does mean tremendous sacrifices in manpower for the United States, tremendous suffering for families and a tremendous economic strain on the country. We can't lose the ship halfway at sea. That he did not die in vain—I would never believe that nor would any one who knew him or anybody as dedicated to the military as he was. I've lived with it for two and half years with my husband, at times I've thought maybe I should be a man so that I could also serve my country. I'm an American first and foremost even though I've lived in different countries and enjoyed different countries thoroughly. They've afforded me different experiences, but the United States is my fatherland, and I respect and admire it's Government and it's military force. My husband's death was not a useless death. It was untimely.

Source: Robert Jones, *The War Comes Home* (New Films Co., 1972). I am grateful to Jack Hayes and Robert Jones for permission to print these remarks.

SOURCE 252

> *Alberta Mierun's son may or may not have volunteered. In any event, her views, expressed in a letter to the editor shortly after President Carter announced his pardon of Vietnam-era draft resisters, are comparable to those offered in the preceding source:*

So President Carter is giving pardons. Maybe he will give my son a pardon.
In case he doesn't know where he is, I will give him his address:
Sgt. James Roberts, Calvary Cemetery.
If this cannot be done, then why should the evaders get pardons and come home as if they were heroes?
It's boys like my son who are the heroes, but it's the evaders who are getting the glory for not going into a war that was not declared war. Big deal!
They were nothing but cowards.

Alberta Mierun
Clinton

Source: The Pittsburgh Press, January 29, 1977.

SOURCE 253

> *A Chicana widow of a GI who died in Vietnam sent an open "letter to Chicano G.I.s," printed in* Right on Post, *a GI underground newspaper, in August 1970:*

It is my intention in writing this letter, that I will place some very important questions in your minds. It is also my most sincere hope that I may save your women, and your mothers the heartache and sorrow I have experienced.
It has been almost three years since my husband was killed in Viet Nam, leaving me without a man and my daughter without a father.
Recalling the memory of my husband, I've asked myself many times why he died in a war I knew nothing about. And the truth that I found was not easy to accept. Because I then realized my husband died for nothing.

Source: Larry Waterhouse and Mariann G. Wizard, *Turning the Guns Around* (New York, 1971), p. 99. Compare L. Nielson, "Impact of Permanent Father Loss on . . . Male War Orphans," unpublished Ph.D. dissertation, University of Utah, 1971.

Not only did he die for nothing, but he fought and killed in the name of a government that has shamed and discriminated against our race for over two hundred years. This same government that robbed our land and kept us as slaves to work his fields. The same government that won't allow our children to speak our language in his racist schools. The same government that denied us our rights as human beings.

Every day our chicano brothers are being sent to Viet Nam and every day they're coming home in boxes. Our fight is not in Viet Nam fighting people who are fighting for their land and freedom. Our fight is here in this country; for *our land and our freedom.*

The rich white pig has used us as his slaves enough, I say. Ya Basta to the white pig politician and Ya Basta to the white pig businessman. Ya Basta! I want freedom and justice for myself and my people.

Chicana Sister

6

The Economy

SOURCE 254

Lt. Commander Charles Sigsbee, U.S. Navy, commanding the Blake, received an urgent note from the superintendent of the U.S. Coast Survey Office in April 1878:

SIR:

It is reported to this office by Mr. William Orton, President of the Western Union Telegraph Company, that one of the cables between Key West and Havana is broken, and he requests the services of the *Blake* to pick up the cable and have it spliced.

You will therefore please consult with the agent of the Telegraph Company at Key West, and render every assistance in your power to pick up, splice, and restore communication through that cable. The Company will supply you with such appliances, in addition to those you have onboard, as may be necessary for the purpose. It is important that this work be executed with as little delay as possible.

Yours respectfully,

C. P. Paterson
Supt. Coast Survey

Source: Folder 66, Box III, C. Sigsbee Papers, New York State Library, Albany.

SOURCE 255

*The president of the American Foreign Trade Corporation, a
New York-based export-import firm, wrote the Secretary of the
Navy in March 1921, praising the efforts of Admiral Mark Bristol,
Allied High Commissioner in Istanbul, on behalf of American
traders:*

SIR:

I trust that it will not be presuming on my part in view of my having spent
over eighteen months in the Near East, to take this opportunity to place
before you a few lines in commendation of the phenomenal work that
has been done and is continuing today by your representative, and that
of the State Department, Admiral Mark L. Bristol.

As the largest mercantile organization trying to blaze the way in the
Near East for American merchandise, the success which we have had we
attribute very largely to the great assistance and tireless efforts of Admiral
Bristol and his staff in demanding for us as Americans equal rights and
protection, the welfare and even the lives of many of our employees.

I know that my opinion is shared by all Americans who have had the
good fortune to judge of the position that America has attained in this
part of the world through having a representative who received without
demanding, respect and recognition and whose opinion is valued by every
nation and subject represented in the Near East, and it is hoped that both
your Department and that of the Secretary of State may see its way clear
to recognize the wonderful diplomacy and ability of a true American
working for Americans as a whole, without prejudice, as is always seen in
the leadership of Admiral Bristol.

Respectfully

Mason Day
President

Source: Box 1, Mark Bristol Papers, Manuscript Papers, Library of Congress.

SOURCE 256

Source: Bruce Russett, *What Price Vigilance?* (New York, 1972), p. 150.

The Effect of Defense Spending on Civilian Activities in the United States, 1939–68

	PERCENTAGE OF VARIANCE EXPLAINED (LINEAR REG.)	REGRESSION COEFFICIENT	INDEX OF PROPORTIONATE REDUCTION
Personal Consumption (Total)	84[a]	−.420	*−.041*
Durable Goods	78[a]	−.163	−.123
Nondurable Goods	04	−.071	−.014
Services	55[a]	−.187	−.050
Fixed Investment (Total)	72[a]	−.292	*−.144*
Nonresidential Structures	62[a]	−.068	−.140
Producers' Durable Equipment	71[a]	−.110	−.123
Residential Structures	60[a]	−.114	−.176
Exports	67[a]	−.097	−.115
Imports	19	−.025	−.037
Federal Civil Purchases	38[a]	−.048	−.159
State & Local Gov't Consumption	38[a]	−.128	−.105

[a]Indicates both the percentage of variance and the regression coefficient are in principle statistically significant at the .001 level with a one-tailed test. In fact because of various technical problems (autocorrelation and non-normal distributions) the significance level is somewhat exaggerated here, but it is nevertheless high enough to indicate relationships of real interest. See Russett, "Some Decisions in the Regression Analysis of Time-Series Data." in Bernd, ed., *Mathematical Applications in Political Science, V.*

SOURCE 257

The Effect of Defense Spending on Public Civil Activities in the United States, Fiscal Years 1938–67

	PERCENTAGE OF VARIANCE EXPLAINED (LINEAR REG.)	REGRESSION COEFFICIENT	INDEX OF PROPORTIONATE REDUCTION
Education (Total)	35[a]	−.077	*−.139*
Institutions of Higher Ed.	12	−.013	−.146
Local Schools	34[a]	−.053	−.125
Other Ed.	19	−.014	−.265
Federal Direct to Ed.	16	−.013	−.309
Federal Aid to State & Local Gov'ts for Ed.	08	−.004	−.140
State & Local Gov't for Ed.	24	−.060	−.124

Source: Bruce Russett, *What Price Vigilance?* (New York, 1972), p. 150.

	PERCENTAGE OF VARIANCE EXPLAINED (LINEAR REG.)	REGRESSION COEFFICIENT	INDEX OF PROPORTIONATE REDUCTION
Health & Hospitals (Total)	32[a]	−.017	−.113
Total Hospitals	30	−.014	−.123
Fed. for Hospitals	25	−.004	−.130
State & Local for Hospitals	29	−.011	−.120
Total Other Health	22	−.033	−.087
Fed. for Health	06	−.001	−.101
State & Local for Health	45[a]	−.002	−.078
Welfare (Total)	54[a]	−.019	−.128
Fed. Direct for Welfare	13	−.003	−.493
Fed. Aid to State & Local Gov'ts for Welfare	17	−.005	−.087
State & Local for Welfare	30	−.011	−.134

[a]Both percentage of variance and regression coefficient are statistically significant at the .001 level.

SOURCE 258

Defense-NASA spending accounted for these percentages of the total work force in the states listed in 1968:

STATE:	PERCENT
Alaska	31.6
Hawaii	18.8
District of Columbia	15.6
Virginia	14.1
Maryland	9.9
Utah	9.9
Georgia	9.7
Colorado	9.6
California	9.3
Connecticut	9.2
Arizona	9.0
South Carolina	8.8
Texas	8.4
New Mexico	8.3
Oklahoma	8.1
Washington	8.1
New Hampshire	7.8
Mississippi	7.3

Note: Figures are as of June 30, 1968.

Source: "Economies in Arms Mean Leaner Times for Many Workers," *U.S. News & World Report* (1970); reproduced in Seymour Melman, ed., *The War Economy of the United States* (New York, 1971), p. 231.

SOURCE 259

When the Martin Company cut its work force at its Baltimore area plant in the early 1960s as it retooled for missile production rather than aircraft, a local TV station interviewed some of those affected:

A Worker, Seated with His Wife:

"I've been working at Martin's for ten years and then two years before that. And all at once, the thing drops out. Nothing."

The Wife:

"I don't know, I just know that the bottom can fall out of government work and that's it. I mean, one day it's here and next day it's gone. We came here in 1948. Why, everything was going! And we've seen this place build up. One time here there was one schoolhouse; now there's three elementaries and three junior high. We've seen it come up like that, and [at] one time this Middle River Church was in another building—they have a big church now. And then all at once it's all gone, and we don't know where the people are going to."

Source: Jack Raymond, *Power at the Pentagon* (New York, 1964); quoted in S. Melman, ed., *The War Economy of the United States* (New York, 1971), p. 78.

SOURCE 260

Low per capita defense contracting correlated with population decline during World War II in the South:

War Activity, November 1943 and Civilian Population Change, 1940 to November 1, 1943

	WAR CONTRACTS, DOLLARS PER CAPITA OF CIVILIAN POPULATION, 1940	CIVILIAN POPULATION CHANGE
Virginia	821.08	+ 4.8
Tennessee	630.65	− 3.3
Louisiana	613.88	− 1.8
Alabama	537.88	− 3.9
Georgia	474.60	− 4.1
North Carolina	360.92	− 6.1
Mississippi	279.18	− 8.6
South Carolina	296.24	− 5.4
Arkansas	215.73	−10.9

Source: Rudolph Heberle, *The Impact of the War on Population Redistribution in the South* (Nashville, Tenn., 1945), p. 21.

SOURCE 261

A woman who, with her husband, had changed professions and had moved to Willow Run, Michigan, to work at the Ford bomber plant recorded her thoughts in a diary in 1942:

Monday, November 2:

How war changes everything! As I look back upon the last few weeks I can see how greatly it has altered the pattern of our lives, of John, my husband, of Tommy, our seven-year-old son, and of my own.

We were in business for ourselves back home. John is a masseur by profession and I a teacher. For the past year, however, I had left my teaching profession and became his helper.

We gave steam baths and massages in our home which was a very satisfactory arrangement. Our home was three miles from town. Whenever we were not busy with our patients we would welcome the chance to get in our garden or orchard. A great deal of our food came from our garden. In my "spare time" I managed to can about 400 quarts of fruits and vegetables we had grown on our "5-acre Farm."

Those summer months were short, happy ones. But toward the end of the summer it became apparent that gas rationing would be nationwide. Our customers expressed the desire that we move our business into town in order that they might walk to get their treatments. We realized that we would need to do this in order to maintain a satisfactory business during the winter months. But my husband also realized that our business was a non-essential one and that sooner or later he should get into war work. There were no war industries in our home town, which meant seeking employment elsewhere.

So, here we are at last—all parked and "propped up" in a trailer camp.

Arrived here about eight o'clock this morning in the rain! Drove miles, it seemed, to find a park. Every place had more trailers than the law allows, and every private yard either had its quota or else "didn't want any."

Finally found this place with a vacancy. It is easy to understand why there was a vacancy as we are parked in a water-hole with mud all around. "Muddy Lane," we call it. Surely glad we left son Tommy with my brother until we got settled. I must get used to John and myself tracking in clods of mud before I start scolding Tommy for doing it.

Source: L. J. Carr and J. E. Stermer, *Willow Run* (New York, 1952), p. 97.

SOURCE 262

Older residents of the Willow Run area were disturbed by the influx of bomber plant workers during the war:

Mrs. "Cliff," a Widow:

Before the bomber plant was built, everything was perfect here. . . . People all owned their own homes and kept up their properties with pride. Only one family didn't own its own place, but they were good renters and neighbors. Everybody knew everybody else and all were happy and contented.

Then came that bomber plant and this influx of riffraff, mostly Southerners. But not the educated Southerners. Of course, some are nice, decent people. But I like to walk along the street and greet people. Now they walk along the street without looking at you.

You can't be sure of these people. A little boy from one of those families came into our back yard and picked some pie plant. Of course, the yard is not marked off. One of my neighbors told him to go home. You know what he told her?

"I'm not afraid of the state police or of any of you big shots!"

That's what he said. I guess he meant *because we live in a house.* His parents must have told him that.

Mrs. "Wenborn":

These new people are inferior to the old residents. . . . We expected this when they built the plant. We knew there would be a rush of workers here, and the houses simply weren't here. We didn't have any use for these houses on wheels and decided not to have any on our property. We treated them all alike. But we decided not to make any more improvements till we could see how things would come out. My husband still wants to stay here, but I don't. There are too many dogs and foreigners in the neighborhood. So many septic tanks are being put in, I don't see how the water can help becoming contaminated.

Source: L. J. Carr and J. E. Stermer, *Willow Run* (New York, 1952), p. 240.

SOURCE 263

A black man who moved to the North during the "boom" period in World War I wrote to a friend in Hattiesburg, Mississippi:

Source: Emmett Scott, *Negro Migration During the War* (Carnegie Endowment for International Peace, No. 16, New York, 1920), pp. 34, 156. I am indebted to Marvin Fletcher for the suggestion that I scan this book for relevant passages.

Mike, old boy, I was promoted on the first of the month. I was made first
assistant to the head carpenter. When he is out of place I take everything
in charge and was raised to $95 per month. You know I know my stuff.
What's the news generally around H'burg? I should have been here twenty
years ago. I just begin to feel like a man. It's a great deal of pleasure in
knowing that you have got some privileges. My children are going to the
same school with the whites and I don't have to humble to no one. I have
registered. Will vote the next election and there isn't any "yes sir, and no,
sir." It's all yes and no, and no, Sam, and Bill.

[And another wrote to the Montgomery *Advertiser:*]

And the negro will not come back once he leaves the South.

The World War is bringing many changes and a chance for the negro to
enter broader fields. With the "tempting bait" of higher wages, shorter
hours, better schools and better treatment, all the preachments of the
so-called race leaders will fall on deaf ears.

It is probable that the "well informed negro," who told the Birmingham
editor that it was good schools that were drawing the negro, could have
given other and more potent reasons had he been so minded. He could
have told how deep down in the negro's heart he has no love for proscrip-
tion, segregation, lynchings, the petty persecutions and cruelties against
him, nor for the arresting of "fifty niggers for what three of 'em done,"
even if it takes all of this to uphold the scheme of civilization.

From Savannah alone, three thousand negroes went, from sixteen year
old boys to men of sixty years. There must be something radically wrong
when aged negroes are willing to make the change. There is greater unrest
among negroes than those in high places are aware.

Let the *Advertiser* speak out in the same masterful way, with the same
punch and pep for a square deal for the negro, that it does for democracy
and the right for local self-government.

SOURCE 264

*A nonveteran from a midwestern town talked in 1949 about the
effect that World War II had on his life:*

"Well, yes. You see, I was brought up on a farm. I started out being a farmer,
but even when I was a boy I got the asthma so bad that I couldn't do a
full day's work. You know, the dust and all that. The only right thing to do
seemed to be to come to the city. So I came here and went to work. During
the war I went up and started working at the TNT plant at Lawrence. I

Source: Robert Havighurst et al., *The American Veteran Back Home* (New York, 1951), p. 176.

had some trouble with the asthma there, but I took it easy while I was off duty—eight hours of working there just about wore me out. So I started looking around for something that wouldn't irritate my condition, and I found the filling station where I am now. I had saved some money up at the plant and what with that and a private loan I was able to swing it. I think the experience of being up at Lawrence did a lot for me. You see I was trained to act as a foreman there, and I learned plenty about it. There's a definite art to handling a group of men, and, it's something you have to learn how to do. Up there they put me through a regular training period, and it came in mighty handy while I was working as foreman. I'm mighty glad I had that experience in my present work, too; I don't have many men working under me here, but you have to know how to get the most out of them, and I couldn't do it half as well if I hadn't had that training."

7

Social and Political Values

SOURCE 265

*A Southerner designed an arithmetic book for youngsters during
the Civil War with a second not-too-subtle purpose:*

"(1) A Confederate soldier captured 8 Yankees each day for 9 successive
days; how many did he capture in all? . . . (2) If one Confederate [can]
kill 90 Yankees how many Yankees can 10 Confederate soldiers kill? . . .
(3) If one Confederate soldier can whip 7 Yankees, how many soldiers can
whip 49 Yankees?"

Source: L. M. Johnson, *An Elementary Arithmetic Designed for Beginners* (Raleigh, N.C.,
1864), pp. 34, 38, 44; quoted in Bell Irwin Wiley, *Life of Johnny Reb* (Indianapolis, Ind., 1943),
p. 123.

SOURCE 266

*A black woman reacted to the vigorous resistance put up by
black veterans of World War I during the attacks upon blacks
in Washington, D.C., in 1919:*

The Washington riots gave me the thrill that comes once in a lifetime. I
was alone when I read between the lines of the morning paper that at last
our men had stood like men, struck back, were no longer dumb, driven
cattle. When I could no longer read for my streaming tears, I stood up,

Source: Francis Grimke, *The Race Problem* (Washington, D.C., 1919), p. 8; cited in Arthur
Barbeau and Florette Henri, *The Unknown Soldiers* (Philadelphia, 1974), p. 182.

alone in my room, held both hands high over my head and exclaimed, "Oh, I thank God, thank God!" When I remember anything after this, I was prone on my bed, beating the pillow with both fists, laughing and crying, whimpering like a whipped child, for sheer gladness and madness. The pent-up humiliation, grief and horror of a lifetime—half a century— was being stripped from me.

SOURCE 267

Enthusiastic readers of the World War II comic series "SGT Fury and His Howling Commandos" wrote to the editor in 1971 — the first from Vietnam, the third from a naval station in Scotland:

DEAR EDITOR:

I have been a regular reader of Marvel mags for many years. They have provided me with pleasure throughout my college years and afterwards. It has never occurred to me that one day I might be writing to you. However, something has come to my attention of late and I feel that I must write to you collectively.

At the present time I am serving with the "Free World Forces" in Viet Nam. As an American citizen I too feel like "Nick Fury," ". . . Fact is, the American fightin' man has always been there when the call came. . . . I ain't saying' whether we're right or wrong." I am here doing my duty. I may be opposed but I am doing my job the best way I can.

Now I'm gonna cut all this formal jazz n get to the point, And the point is . . . I've got, as we say here in the Nam, a case. Here's why.

I used to be out in the field. Not as a grunt or a Howling Commando type, but out there close to it doing the job my government trained me to do. Out there you have a lot of time to think. You pick up on things, real easy. Things you never thought about back in the world. Out there I used to pick up your mags at the PX, read em' and think about them. You guys have been saying stuff for a long time. Good things that tell it like it is. Believe me, your audience digs it. I do 'n became a legit KOF [Keeper of the Flame] turning my buddies on to you.

When your Aug. SGT. FURY came out I flipped. I bought all I could without cornering the market. I started leaving them places and passing them on to people. I left them in places where people who normally

Source: Stan Lee and Al Kurzrok, *SGT Fury and His Howling Commandos,* Mag. Management Co., I, no. 88, June 1971.

wouldn't read them would be exposed to it. Any place where guys just pick up something to read while waiting for something to happen. The ish [issue] became a real topic of rap sessions. People who never before were aware sort of got turned on to new ideas. It became sort of a collectors' item in a very short time. A lof of us were waiting for the next ish to arrive. Here's where my "case" comes in.

IT NEVER CAME.

So I figured someone screwed up . . . it is the Army and it does happen. There was nothing to do but wait. Oct ish time came and still no Marvels. I got transfered to another unit cause my old unit was going home. Low and behold I was assigned to Saigon to work. Now Saigon is the New York City, Allice's Resturant, and big PX of Viet Nam. You can get it no matter what you want. N' you know what? There ain't a Marvel Mag in a PX in Nam.

Seems like you guys have stepped on some toes and hit some nerves and the "big wigs" have had you censored. How does that grab you?

It is not because there is not a market. The "other" mags are coming in and being bought. The only difference is the absence of the Marvel line.

Now I don't expect you guys to believe what follows. I have a hard time believing it myself. A couple of weeks ago I had this dream. I didn't really dig it, but you guys should know about it. It wasn't a good trip, but here goes.

I was out in the field humping an M-16 and sweatin like a polar bear in Miami. We came upon this old fort a relic of the French. It was rubble, like somebody had really done a job on the place. You could tell that whoever was hole' up in there had gotten blown away . . . but good. Being hot we dropped our gear an took ten. I went out back to check the place out and found this old fatigue shirt. I was gonna send it to you but it was so old it has fallen apart, so's I'm sending you the name tape which is all that's left . . . "Cpt. AMERIKA."

Like I said, it was a dream and a bad one. I din't like it and I hope it "never happens", God, I really do.

But, right now, I got a real bad *case*.

" . . . you know if you gotta fight, you do . . . but it'd sure be great if we all wised up and decided to chuck all the fighting."

Sgt. Nick Fury, August, 1970.
    RFO, TTV, KOF (in exile) Sp/5 Keith A. Mishne
    275-40-5723, Co. A 519 Sp. Bn. APO S. F. 96307

[From the Editors:] Amen to that, Brother Keith—and we hope you're out of exile soon. That name tape you found sort of worried us, until we realized that it had to be a plant. Guess the Cong don't know how to spell "America."

But, seriously, we've got a stack of letters from Nam complaining that our books disappeared. We don't know what's happened yet, but we've got a guy checking it out with the distributor, and when we know something, we'll pass it on to you guys soonest.

DEAR STAN, GARY, AND JOHN:

How about having Sgt. Nick Fury, Sgt. Bob Jenkins [leader of the "Missouri Marauders"], and Captain Savage on a mission together?

Also, I would like to see the return of all the Marauders and to see the Howlers fighting the Japanese again.

> Tray Turner, 2400 S. Frazier St.
> Phila, Pa. 19143

[From the Editors:] Well, Tray, we're putting it to our assemblage of battle mag buffs. What d'ya say, ya goldbricks?!

DEAR STAN, GARY, AND JOHN:

After reading an old ish last Thursday, I came to the conclusion that you guys deserve the three-star medal for your fine portrayal of our military forces. Too often our country's young criticize and deride the Armed Forces of the United States. Our boys in khaki are fighting for democracy and protecting freedom and liberty.

Your portrait of our unsung heroes is a credit to the future's hopes for our land. I thank you personally and for the men with whom I'll be serving in the ensuing months. Peace

> Usher Dangerfield, 704 Roderick Mayfair House
> Raploch, SCOTLAND

[From the Editors:] We're proud to receive your thanks, Usher. Even though we're not about to say that America's armed forces are always perfect, it's safe to say that we at Marvel can certainly appreciate the heroic part our men played in World War II.

SOURCE 268

> *Random House editor Bennett Cerf reported on his "ten days with the Armed Forces" as a participant in the Joint Orientation Conference in 1950:*

Source: *Saturday Review* (July 22, 1950), pp. 3 ff.

It's become fashionable to remember just where you were or what you were doing when the news broke about Pearl Harbor. Should the invasion of South Korea prove an equally fateful moment in world history, I for one will have no trouble remembering where I heard about it. I was on the hangar deck of the *Midway,* the queen of the U.S. Navy's carriers, steaming to sea for a rendezvous with Task Force 23 and a brief but intensive series of naval operations in the 1950 manner. It was a stunning climax to a session of talks by top Government officials at the Pentagon Building, a display of new weapons and infantry tactics at Fort Benning, Georgia, and an inspiring show of the latest equipment and striking power of the Air Force at Eglin Base, Florida. The program was arranged for the Seventh Joint Orientation Conference, and that I was invited to be a member of it I consider one of the biggest honors and luckiest breaks of my career.

At Fort Benning, Georgia (the population of the post exceeds 30,000; the area comprises 282 square miles), the JOC had its first taste of life in the field, and the sounding of reveille at 5:45 A.M. provoked a stream of reminiscences of World War I which were, unfortunately, listened to by nobody. . . . A display of our remarkable new recoilless weapons (and other arms still considered secret) had the audience gasping. There also were exploded shells with four different colors of smoke (for signaling purposes): red, green, yellow, and violet. "Good heavens," exclaimed one JOC-ing Eye, "They're making war beautiful." The disgust of Archy Alexander, Under Secretary of the Army, was only exceeded by that of the first-year class of West Point (also present at the demonstration) when the regimental band bravely struck up the refrain of the Notre Dame football song. . . . The airborne troops begin their parachute training in a control tower exactly like the one that packed them in at the New York World's Fair and is now operating at Steeplechase Park. The stunt they perform just five weeks later give you goose pimples! . . .

[After parties with military leaders, service secretaries, and his fellow conference participants (industrialists, financiers, educators, churchmen, government officials, professionals, etc.), Cerf was given a ride in an F-80.]

Well, after that jet ride, a tour through the climatic hangar (the temperature there was forty degrees below zero; when I came out my glasses remained frozen over for fifteen minutes) was routine stuff. I even failed to respond when a tailor lost a pair of my sports pants and three colonels were dispatched to look for them. . . . The last thing we saw at Eglin was a B-36 (two and a half times the size of a B-29!) drop a stick of bombs that destroyed a series of targets five miles long. It was an awesome sight—and I only hope some of our potential enemies have seen it. . . . Our best and jolliest meal at Eglin was served at the Non-Com Club (which has just loaned the Officers Club $18,000 to help keep it afloat!). . . .

The next day we boarded the *Midway* and the Navy's famous Captain

Jimmy Flatley told us about the Korean attack as we steamed out to sea. Planes landed on the carrier deck and took off moments later, submarines submerged and snorkeled, a drone was catapulted from the deck and sunk by amazingly accurate ship fire, and night operations were more spectacular still. But how much excitement can you absorb in ten short days?

I came home revitalized and simply busting to shout from the house-tops this deep-felt conviction: when and if a war comes with Russia or anybody else this country is blessed with the basic equipment and leader-ship to knock hell out of them. We need more fighter planes and more carriers. We need more men in the armed forces. Our intelligence and propaganda departments need bolstering most of all. The money already allotted to defense has been, on the whole, wisely spent. In light of day-to-day news developments, increased appropriations are not only a wise investment but an absolute "must." When your life is at stake, you don't haggle over the cost.

SOURCE 269

Workers in southeastern Connecticut were asked questions in 1964 designed to sort them out on a "belligerent" - "concilia-tory" scale of foreign and military policy views. The number of years "on the job" did not appear to be a significant feature of the attitudes of nondefense workers, but defense workers with more years "on the job" gave more "hawkish" responses than those with fewer:

Attitude and Defense Work, by Length of Employment (in Percentages)

	0–5 YEARS AT PRESENT JOB (89)		6–15 YEARS AT PRESENT JOB (141)		16+ YEARS AT PRESENT JOB (151)[a]	
	DEFENSE	NONDEF.	DEFENSE	NONDEF.	DEFENSE	NONDEF.
Belligerent	34	32	44	28	44	23
Intermediate	25	40	27	40	35	46
Conciliatory	41	26	29	26	18	30
No Answer	0	2	0	6	3	1
Total	(32)	(57)	(45)	(96)	(34)	(117)

[a]Difference between defense and nondefense workers (X^2) significant at .05 level of con-fidence.

Source: Nancy Phillips, "Militarism and Grassroots Involvement in the Military-Industrial Complex," *Journal of Conflict Resolution* (December 1973): 622.

SOURCE 270

0(Very Poor) ← 2.0 2.5 3.0 3.5 4.0 4.5 5.0 5.5 → (Very Good)8
U. S. Military   5.50
Colleges and Universities   5.48
Churches and Religious Organizations   5.26
Small Businesses   5.21
Public Schools   4.95
News Media   4.89
U. S. Supreme Court   4.82
Large Corporations   4.72
U.S. Congress   4.59
State Governments   4.47
All Courts, Judicial System   4.35
Local Governments   4.33
Labor Unions   4.26
Federal Government   3.86
President & Administration   3.30

The Public's Rating of American Institutions: How Well They Are Serving the Country

Scale shows overall rating from 0 to 8 (from very poor job to very good job)

Source: Institute for Social Research, *Newsletter* (Winter 1974), p. 8. (The survey was conducted in 1973.)

SOURCE 271

*"I was hoping you'd wear your soldier suit,
so I could be proud of you."*

Source: Bill Mauldin, *Back Home* (New York, 1947), p. 44. Drawings copyrighted 1944, re-newed 1972, Bill Mauldin; reproduced by courtesy of Bill Mauldin.

SOURCE 272

Veterans (40 percent of the male population over twenty-five) were overrepresented in the primaries of the period studied by two political scientists (1950, 1952, and 1954):

Veteran Nominations in Marginal and Safe Districts
A. Marginal Districts

	1950	1952	1954	3 ELECTION TOTALS
Republicans	62%	66%	69%	65%
	(N = 52)	(N = 56)	(N = 54)	(N = 162)
Democrats	46	50	58	52
	(N = 50)	(N = 56)	(N = 53)	(N = 159)

B. Safe Districts

	1950	1952	1954	3 ELECTION TOTALS
Republicans	51%	51%	53%	52%
	(N = 49)	(N = 53)	(N = 57)	(N = 159)
Democrats	54	48	52	51
	(N = 82)	(N = 75)	(N = 75)	(N = 232)

[But if political "Kingmakers" assumed that voters favored veterans, the election results did not sustain that assumption:]

Party (Overall) and Veteran (Vet-Nonvet Races) Performance in Safe and Marginal Races, 1950–1954

	MARGINAL	SAFE
Republican Party	61%	59%
	(N = 179)	(N = 179)
Republican Veterans	62	66
	(N = 52)	(N = 35)
Democratic Party	37	61
	(N = 177)	(N = 253)
Democratic Veterans	42	53
	(N = 26)	(N = 32)

Source: Albert Somit and Joseph Tannenhaus, "The Veteran in the Electoral Process . . . ,"
Journal of Politics (May 1957): 192, 199.

SOURCE 273

A 1967 Harris poll asked questions pertaining to civilian control of the military:

	AGREE (%)	DISAGREE (%)	NOT SURE (%)	TOTAL (%)
1. "When civilians tell the military what to do, too often politics rather than military action results."	73	10	17	100
2. "In Vietnam, the military has been handicapped by civilians who won't let them go all out."	65	10	25	100
3. "The President is the Commander-in-Chief, and all important military orders should come from him."	58	29	13	100

Source: The Washington Post, December 9, 1967.

	AGREE(%)	DISAGREE(%)	NOT SURE(%)	TOTAL(%)
4. "In wartime, civilian government leaders should let the military take over running the war."	52	34	14	100
5. "If left unchecked by civilian control, the military could take over the whole government from civilian hands."	46	30	24	100
6. "Military men know how to start wars and fight them, but civilians have to end wars."	33	44	23	100

8

The "Enemy Within"

SOURCE 274

Walter Bates, a young Loyalist from Darien, Connecticut, whose family was active in its support of the British, was sixteen years of age in 1776 when he was seized by rebels and tortured in the hope that he would inform on other Loyalists:

At length the thing I greatly feared came upon me. A small boat was discovered by the American guard, in one of these coves, by night; in which they suspected that one of my brothers, with some others, had come from the British. They supposed them concealed in the neighborhood and that I must be acquainted with it.

At this time I had just entered my sixteenth year. I was taken and confined in the Guard House; next day examined before a Committee and threatened with sundry deaths if I did not confess what I knew not of. They threatened among other things to confine me at low water and let the tide drown me if I did not expose these honest farmers. At length I was sent back to the Guard House until ten o'clock at night, when I was taken out by an armed mob, conveyed through the field gate one mile from the town to back Creek, then having been stripped my body was exposed to the mosquitoes, my hands and feet being confined to a tree near the Salt Marsh, in which situation for two hours time every drop of blood would be drawn from my body; when soon after two of the committee said that if I would tell them all I knew, they would release me, if not they would leave me to these men who, perhaps, would kill me.

Source: From *The Price of Loyalty* by Cathrine Crary, ed. Copyright © 1973 by McGraw-Hill. Used with permission of McGraw-Hill Book Company. Excerpt is from pages 81-82.

I told them that I knew nothing that would save my life.

They left me, and the Guard came to me and said they were ordered to give me, if I did not confess, one hundred stripes, and if that did not kill me I would be sentenced to be hanged. Twenty stripes was then executed with severity, after which they sent me again to the Guard House. No "Tory" was allowed to speak to me, but I was insulted and abused by all.

The next day the committee proposed many means to extort a confession from me, the most terrifying was that of confining me to a log on the carriage in the Saw mill and let the saw cut me in two if I did not expose "those Torys." Finally they sentenced me to appear before Col. Davenport, in order that he should send me to head quarters, where all the Torys he sent were surely hanged. Accordingly next day I was brought before Davenport—one of the descendants of the old apostate Davenport, who fled from old England—who, after he had examined me, said with great severity of countenance, "I think you could have exposed those Tories."

I said to him "You might rather think I would have exposed my own father sooner than suffer what I have suffered." Upon which the old judge could not help acknowledging he never knew any one who had withstood more without exposing confederates, and he finally discharged me the third day. It was a grievous misfortune to be in such a situation, but the fear of God animated me not to fear man. My resolution compelled mine enemies to show their pity that I had been so causelessly afflicted, and my life was spared. I was, however, obliged to seek refuge from the malice of my persecutors in the mountains and forests until their frenzy might be somewhat abated.

SOURCE 275

Samuel Townsend, a farm laborer from Kingston, New York, found himself in "hot water" after he spoke critically, while "in his cups," of a Committee of Safety's orders to all communities to pursue men who had gone to enlist in Loyalist regiments:

Kingston Jail, April 30, 1777

TO THE HONORABLE THE REPRESENTATIVES
OF THE STATE OF NEW YORK IN CONVENTION ASSEMBLED:

The petition of Samuel Townsend humbly sheweth

That ye petitioner is at present confined in the common jail of Kingston for being thought unfriendly to the American States. That ye petitioner

Source: From *The Price of Loyalty.* Cathrine Crary, ed. Copyright © 1973 by McGraw-Hill. Used with permission of McGraw-Hill Book Company. Excerpt is from pp. 151-52.

some few days ago went from home upon some business and happened to get a little intoxicated in liquor, and upon his return home inadvertantly fell in company upon the road with a person unknown to yr petitioner and discoursing and joking about the Tories passing through there and escaping, this person says to yr petitioner that if he had been with the Whigs, [they] should not have escaped so. . . . To which your petitioner, being merry in liquor, wantonly and in a bantering manner told him that in the lane through which they were then riding five and twenty Whigs would not beat five and twenty Tories and, joking together, they parted, and yr petitioner thought no more of it. Since, he has been taken up and confined and he supposes on the above joke.

Being conscious to himself of his not committing any crime or of being unfriendly to the American cause worthy of punishment . . . That yr petitioner is extremely sorry for what he may have said and hopes his intoxication and looseness of tongue will be forgiven by this honorable convention as it would not have been expressed by him in his sober hours. That yr petitioner has a wife and two children and a helpless mother all which must be supported by his labor and should he be kept confined in this time his family must unavoidably suffer through want, as yr petitioner is but of indigent circumstances and fully conceives it is extremely hard to keep him confined to the great distress of his family as well as grief of yr petitioner. Yr petitioner therefore humbly prays that this honorable convention be favorably pleased to take the premises under their serious consideration so as that yr petitioner may be relieved and discharged from his confinement or [granted] such relief as to the honorable house shall seem meet and ye petitioner shall ever pray.

Samuel Townsend

SOURCE 276

Lt. Anthony Allaire, a North Carolina Tory, reported on the retaliatory treatment meted out to captured Loyalist "traitors" after their defeat at King's Mountain:

October 14, 1780

The morning after the action [King's Mountain, October 7] we were marched sixteen miles, previous to which orders were given by the Rebel Col. [William] Campbell (whom the command devolved on) *that should they be attacked on their march, they were to fire on and destroy their prisoners.* The party

Source: From *The Price of Loyalty,* Cathrine Crary, ed. Copyright © 1973 by McGraw-Hill. Used with permission of McGraw-Hill Book Company. Excerpt is from pp. 238-39.

was kept marching two days without any provisions. The officers' baggage, on the third day's march, was all divided among the Rebel officers.

Shortly after we were marched to Bickerstaff's settlement, where we arrived on the thirteenth. On the fourteenth, a court martial composed of twelve field officers was held for the trial of the militia prisoners; when, after a short hearing, they condemned thirty of the most principal and respectable characters, whom they considered to be the most inimical to them, to be executed; and at six o'clock in the evening of the same day executed Col. [Ambrose] Mills, Capt. [James] Chitwood, Capt. Wilson, and six privates, obliging every one of their officers to attend at the death of those brave, but unfortunate Loyalists, who all, with their last breath and blood, held the Rebels and their cause as infamous and base, and as they were turning off extolled their King and the British Government.

On the morning of the fifteenth, Col. Campbell had intelligence that Col. Tarleton was approaching him, when he gave orders to his men that should Col. Tarleton come up with them, they were immideately to fire on Capt. [Abraham] DePeyster and his officers, who were in the front, and then a second volley on the men. During this day's march the men were obliged to give thirty-five Continental dollars for a single ear of Indian corn and forty for a drink of water, they not being allowed to drink when fording a river; in short, the whole of the Rebels' conduct from the surrender of the party into their hands is incredible to relate. Several of the militia that were worn out with fatigue, and not being able to keep up, were cut down and trodden to death in the mire. . . . Dr. [Uzal] Johnson was . . . knocked down and treated in the basest manner for endeavoring to dress a man whom they had cut on the march. The Rebel officers would often go in amongst the prisoners, draw their swords, cut down and wound those whom their wicked and savage minds prompted.

This is a specimen of Rebel lenity—you may report it without the least equivocation, for upon the word and honor of a gentleman, this description is not equal to their barbarity.

SOURCE 277

William Moorhead reported his misfortune to the Royal Commission on the Losses and Services of American Loyalists in 1784:

Memorial of Willm Moorhead

Jany the 30th 1784.

Source: Hugh E. Egerton, ed., *Royal Commission . . ., 1783-85, Being the Notes of Mr Daniel Parker Coke, M.P. . . .* (London, 1915), p. 66.

Willm Moorhead — the Claimant — sworn.

He went from Ireland to Philadelphia in 1773 & took his family with him viz.a Wife & two Children. He carried out more than   £ 100 in Cash & Cloaths. He sold a Lease which he held under Lord Mountcashel. In 1774 He purchas'd 180 or 190 Acres of Land about 100 Miles from Philadelphia he paid near   £ 100S. for the Land. When he bought it about 18 Acres were cultivated. He continued in possession more than four Years. Then he was driven away by the Inhabitants of the Country because he would not take up arms ag^t the Crown. They seiz'd him & everything he had. He made his Escape & fled down to the English Lines. He would have taken arms for the British if his health had permitted but he remain'd sick for six Months & then came to Ireland. He left Philadelphia in April 1778 & has been in Ireland ever since. He does not know whether his property is confiscated or not as he has never enquired after it since.

SOURCE 278

Scipio Handley, a black fisherman, told the Royal Commission his story, which was corroborated by another witness:

Memorial of Scipio Handley — a Black

13th of Septr 1784.

Scipio Handley — the Claimant — sworn.

He has been Christen'd here about a Year ago & knows the Nature of an Oath. He lived in Charlestown & was free born. He was carrying on trade for himself as a fisherman. He never carried Arms or took any Oath for the Americans. He was taken by the rebels when he was carrying things to Lord Wm Campbell on board. They took his Boat. He was put in Irons & confined for this six weeks. He left the province at that time & never returned. He came to Georgia with the British Troops.
Property.

He had no Land. He Lost some furniture & a few other Articles which are contain'd in the Schedule which he values at   £ 97 9s. He kept his House with his Mother but says the furniture was his own.   £ 28 Cash left in the House. Two Trunks valued at   £ 15. He had 7 Hogs Valued at 8 Gās. He has rec^d   £ 5 in full from the Treasury.
Ellenor Listor — Widow — sworn.

Knew Scipio Handley at Charlestown. Knows his Mother to have been a free Woman. The Mother sold Gingerbread. Knows that he carried things

---

Source: Hugh E. Egerton, ed., *Royal Commission . . . , 1783-85, Being the Notes of Mr Daniel Parker Coke, M.P. . . .* (London, 1915), p. 198.

to Lord W[m] Campbell & the Americans confined him for it. She believes him to have been loyal. There was some furniture used both by the Mother & the Son but she does not know to whom it belonged. She never saw any Mahogony furniture. She left Charlestown in Easter 1782 & she believes the Mother is in poss[n] of the furniture.

SOURCE 279

> *A young Nisei man living in the California interior in 1941 went through a stressful period of his life in the days after Pearl Harbor, and he began to look upon the world very differently:*

The beginning of the war caused a great change in my life. I was studying for [exams] that Sunday of December 7, 1941. I happened to be reading a book that morning and I idly turned on the radio to relax for a few minutes. When I first heard the news of the Pearl Harbor bombings, it didn't sink home at all. I thought that the report was false. However, I began to have some disturbing thoughts in my mind so I went outside to ask the other fellows what they thought about it. At that moment another Nisei fellow came dashing down the walk saying that the Japs had attacked America. Suddenly it dawned upon me that it was the real thing and I had a terrific reaction. I felt, "Oh, those damn fools, why are they attacking America?" I didn't conceive of it in terms of right or wrong. I thought that the Japanese Army was doing a hell of a stupid thing and I couldn't see how they had a chance.

A group of us got together to talk about this stunning news. We began to crystallize our thoughts on how it would affect us as individuals. I got in a depressed mood. My whole reaction then was to withdraw into myself as I usually do when confronted with a crisis. I didn't want to talk to the other Nisei fellows any longer. I went out and I became greatly upset. I had immediate fears that I would attract attention as a treacherous Jap. I realized that I would not be able to finish college. The thought occurred to me very selfishly, "Why couldn't they have waited until after the finals before attacking Pearl Harbor?" I knew I wouldn't be drafted immediately as I had been classified 4-F. Everyone in [town] was excited by that time so I thought it was better for me to get off the streets. I went right home and locked myself in my room. I hovered over the radio all the rest of the day and I forgot about my finals. I had a dejected sort of feeling for the

Source: Dorothy Swaine Thomas with Charles Kikuchi and James Sakoda, *The Japanese-American Evacuation and Resettlement: II: The Salvage* (Berkeley, Calif., 1952), pp. 163-65. Copyright © 1952 by The Regents of the University of California; reprinted by permission of the University of California Press.

rest of the day. We Nisei didn't know whether to go home immediately or not. Toward evening I thought I would go out for a moment but I felt all eyes were staring at me so I didn't go very far. I expected somebody to jump on me and attempt to beat me up at any moment. That evening I was worried sick and I didn't sleep very well.

The following day I had to go to school and I really did hate to go. I had the feeling that everyone would accuse me for the treachery of the Japanese military forces. I knew that I would be immediately tabbed as a Jap. Most of us Nisei had always been led to believe that we were Japs and I knew that most of the Caucasian people would look upon me that way. I was afraid that my classmates would regard me as one of the enemies. When I got on the campus, I was amazed when the fellows spoke to me as an American and we talked about how the war would affect us as Americans. I couldn't get over this reception as I had not been prepared for it. There was only one instructor who spoke of Japan as if it were my fatherland. He spoke to me as if he pitied me because Japan would be whipped in two months. I resented that because I wanted him to understand that Japan was not my homeland.

That afternoon I went to do my work at the ice plant and I had a lot of misgivings. One of the Caucasian fellows that I met by the gate started to talk to me and he was rather apologetic that the United States was going to whip Japan's ass off. He thought that this would hurt my feelings. I tried to explain to him that I did not know a thing about Japan and that I had never been there. I told him that I was a part of this country and I didn't give a damn about Japan. I appeared a little too eager in my efforts to convince him and I was forced to wave the flag. I think that all of the Nisei did the same thing during this period. Our thinking was all confused for weeks and weeks. The rest of the employees at the ice plant and my boss all went out of their way to show that they did not hold anything against me. I was very surprised at this as I had been expecting the worst. I didn't lose my job at all.

My finals suddenly became very insignificant to me. I wasn't in any mood to concentrate entirely upon them but I managed to come out okay in my grades. I stayed around [college] during the Christmas holidays and I only went home for a three-day visit. My parents were quite worried as my father's bank account had been frozen. We had a heck of a problem in trying to figure out how to feed the family when all the money was tied up. My brother S. took charge of family affairs as he was oldest of the children at home and my parents depended upon him for everything as they were frightened. My parents were not concerned about who would win the war as the emphasis was upon our immediate family needs. There were no Issei picked up in our area as far as I know so the community did not have this fear of [the Issei] being suddenly snatched away like in some of the Japanese communities where many fathers had been taken without any notice.

My parents, at first, wanted me to drop out of school but I thought that I should stay on as long as possible. I told them that nothing would happen to me so that they reluctantly gave in. After that I went back and started a new semester. I carried a very heavy load of classwork as I wanted to complete as many courses as possible. Life began to take on a new significance for me. It was at this time that I ceased making myself miserable by worrying excessively over social activities. I realized how insignificant that limited Nisei world was and it had all crashed after December 7. At the same time I got a closer feeling to the other Nisei as we were all in a common predicament. We were simply all Nisei together in a common problem and many of us were stunned for weeks.

Prior to Pearl Harbor, I never gave politics very much thought except where it pertained to race relationships. I began to wake up to the fact that something could be done about race discrimination if the various minority groups could work together. I developed a new sympathy for the Negroes and other minority groups as I began to realize the conflicts that they had to go through before being accepted in any sort of decent way. I had rebelled against Japanese ways all along in my family circle. There was no doubt in my mind as to where I stood. However, since I was a Nisei, I had some sentimental attachments to Japan. I think that this feeling was much stronger among Nisei who came from the rural communities or from a Buddhist background. After the war broke, I could no longer sit on a fence and let my sentiments control my thinking. I wanted to break all ties with Japan as there had to be a choice immediately.

When all of those Army restrictions started to come in I had another terrific reaction. I suffered all sorts of depressions when the evacuation orders were announced. I began to think of how that would affect the Nisei. I still felt a little different from the rest of the Nisei since my home was in the Free Zone and my family was in no danger of being uprooted since General DeWitt had announced in the papers that the people who went into the Free Zone voluntarily would not be moved again. Most of the Nisei students on the campus had homes in the restricted areas along the coast so that they had to quit school and join their families.

SOURCE 280

Nathaniel Jones and sixteen other Farmington men were jailed in 1777 for refusing to serve the Revolutionary cause. After a time, they recanted, were examined, and were released, upon

Source: *Public Records of the State of Connecticut*, I, pp. 259-60. John Shy's reference to this passage in an essay of his led me to it. See Shy, "The American Revolution: The Military Conflict as a Revolutionary Conflict," in Stephen Kurtz and James Hutson, eds., *Essays on the American Revolution* (Chapel Hill, N.C., 1973), pp. 121-156.

> satisfying the Revolutionary government in Connecticut that "there was no such thing as remaining neuters":

On report of the committee appointed by this Assembly to take into consideration the subject matter of the memorial of Nathl Jones, Simon Tuttle, Joel Tuttle, Nathaniel Mathews, John Mathews, Riverius Carrington, Lemuel Carrington, Zerubbabel Jerom jun^r, Chauncey Jerom, Ezra Dormer, Nehemiah Royce, Abel Royce, George Beckwith, Abel Frisbee, Levi Frisbey, Jared Peck, and Abraham Waters, all of Farmington, shewing that they are imprisoned on suspicion of their being inimical to America; that they are ready and willing to join with their country and to do their utmost for its defence; and praying to be examined and set at liberty, as per said memorial on file, reporting that the said committee caused the authority &c. of Farmington to be duly notifyed, that they convened the memorialists before them at the house of Mr. David Bull on the 22^d of instant May and examined them separately touching their unfriendliness to the American States, and heard the evidences produced by the parties; that they found said persons were committed for being highly inimical to the United States, and for refusing to assist in the defence of the country; that on examination it appeared they had been much under the influence of one [James] Nichols, a designing church clergyman who had instilled into them principles opposite to the good of the States; that under the influence of such principles they had pursued a course of conduct tending to the ruin of the country and highly displeasing to those who are friends to the freedom and independence of the United States; that under various pretences they had refused to go in the expedition to Danbury; that said Nathaniel Jones and Simon Tuttle have as they suppose each of them a son gone over to the enemy; that there was, however, no particular positive fact that sufficiently appeared to have been committed by them of an atrocious nature against the States, and that they were indeed grossly ignorant of the true grounds of the present war with Great Britain; that they appeared to be penitent of their former conduct, professed themselves convinced since the Danbury alarm that there was no such thing as remaining neuters; that the destruction made there by the tories was matter of conviction to them; that since their imprisonment upon serious reflexion they are convinced that the States are right in their claim, and that it is their duty to submit to their authority, and that they will to the utmost of their power defend the country against the British army; and that the said committee think it advisable that the said persons be liberated from their imprisonment on their taking an oath of fidelity to the United States: Resolved by this Assembly, that the said persons be liberated from their said imprisonment on their taking an oath of fidelity to this State and paying costs, taxed at £22 7 10; and the keeper of the goal in Hartford is hereby directed to liberate said persons accordingly.

SOURCE 281

Two young Nisei interned in Manzanar angrily explained to government officials their refusal to attest to their loyalty to a country that had ignored their civil liberties in the passion of war:

First Nisei

A. Here is the thing. I'm supposed to be a citizen of the United States. At the time of registration, I asked them how far my citizenship went. I don't know if there is such a thing as restricted citizenship in this country. I refused to answer because if there is such a thing as restricted citizenship, I have the right to refuse to answer. What security have we? If this can happen now, why can't the same thing happen in five years?

Q. What has happened is unfortunate. But other minorities have had to face discrimination too. In my part of the country the Germans are probably treated worse than Japanese.

A. It's all right to be of a minority as long as you're of the same race.

Q. I can't see that. If you're discriminated against because you belong to a minority group, it's as bad whatever race you happen to belong to.

A. This is the reason you look at it differently; you are a white man. At the end of the war, animosities will be high. There will be high feelings against us. There will be a boycott of us if we start in business. At the end of the last war, the bad feeling didn't continue against the Germans. But you can't tell a German from an Englishman when he walks down the street. But when I go down the street they say, "There goes a Jap." Perhaps it will be 15 years before this feeling will die down. I disagree with you when you say that 100,000 Japanese can be assimilated now. I know the [government is] doing what [it] can. But the one hundred thirty millions in this country are hostile. (After additional discussion of this same topic) Well, you'd better write me a ticket to Tule Lake. . . .

Q. Your record doesn't show any interest in Japan and you haven't said anything that would indicate that you want to go to Japan. Why is it then that you object so strongly to question 28 [Loyalty to the United States]?

A. I have not been given citizenship rights so I don't have to answer questions like that.

Second Nisei

Q. Don't you feel that whatever has happened you should express your loyalty to the only country in which you now hold citizenship?

Source: Dorothy Swaine Thomas and Richard Nishimoto, *Japanese-American Evacuation and Resettlement: I: The Spoilage* (Berkeley, Calif., 1946), p. 97. Copyright © 1946 by The Regents of the University of California; reprinted by permission of the University of California Press.

A. At the time of the draft I was deferred because of my dependents. At that time I said I'd die for this country in the event of war. That's the way I felt. But since I lost my business when I was young and just starting up I've changed my mind. You Caucasian Americans should realize that I got a raw deal.

Q. But things like these happen in a time of war. Evacuation was a war measure, an emergency measure.

A. They shouldn't happen to citizens. What did a war with Japan have to do with evacuating me? You've got to realize that I am an American citizen just as much as you. Maybe my dad is not, because of Congress. He couldn't naturalize. But my associates in school and college were Caucasians. It's been a hard road to take.

SOURCE 282

> A first-generation (Issei) man and a second-generation (Nisei) woman who was married to an Issei responded to questions put to them by government officials regarding their negative responses on the loyalty questionnaire:

The Man (via a Translator)

A. He didn't register because of the rumor that those who registered would be forced to leave [Tule Lake] and he had no place to go.

Q. Does he understand now that that isn't so?

A. I guess he does.

Q. He can't understand or speak English?

A. Very little.

Q. Does he plan to return to Japan after the war?

A. Yes.

Q. Does he feel more sympathy to Japan than to the United States?

A. His sympathy lies with Japan.

Q. Why?

A. He was a law abiding citizen, worked hard, respected law, and yet he was placed here. He can't stand it any longer.

The Woman

Q. Are you disloyal?

A. Yes.

Source: Dorothy Swaine Thomas and Richard Nishimoto, *Japanese-American Evacuation and Resettlement: I: The Spoilage* (Berkeley, Calif., 1946), p. 90. Copyright © 1946 by The Regents of the University of California; reprinted by permission of the University of California Press.

Q. Why?

A. Well — no reason. If I say "loyal" will they take me or leave me here?

Q. We don't split families. If one member is on the segregation list the others in the family are given their choice of leaving or remaining. We don't want you to answer a certain way just because your husband does. This hearing is just to determine your loyalty.

A. Then it doesn't have anything to do with staying?

Q. No, you'll just be given the choice of following your husband or not.

A. Then I'm loyal.

SOURCE 283

Renunciation of U.S. citizenship tended to be an "all or none" affair in Japanese-American families, as the renunciation of citizenship by one member of the family led others to renounce as well, often solely to avoid forced separation of the renouncing member from the family unit:

Frequency Distribution per 1,000 of 4,390 Families Having Citizen Members Eligible to Renounce by Possible and Actual Renunciants

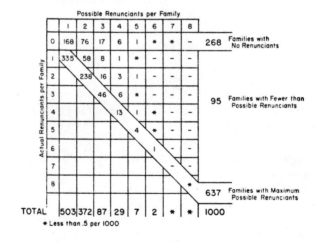

Source: Dorothy Swaine Thomas and Richard Nishimoto, *Japanese-American Evacuation and Resettlement: I: The Spoilage* (Berkeley, Calif., 1946), p. 358. Copyright © 1946 by The Regents of the University of California; reprinted by permission of the University of California Press.

SOURCE 284

A Nisei young woman explained to U.S. officials in September 1945 the family pressures that had led her to renounce her citizenship during the war:

I am a Nisei girl, age 20, born and raised in Alameda, California, until the time of evacuation in Feb. 1942. My father passed away in May 1940. So there is my mother . . . 56 years old, and my brother [now] 18 years old. We were living a normal American life until we were uprooted from our beloved home. It was the home and security my father and mother worked so hard for when they came to America. This America was strange to them but they wanted to make their home here and raise us as good American citizens. Not knowing the language they had a hard time. . . . My mother was especially taken back by [evacuation] since my father passed away, so you can imagine her bitterness. Being pushed from one WRA camp to another (Pleasanton, Turlock Assembly Center, Gila Center and Tule Center) only hardened her bitterness and I myself got pretty disgusted being shoved around but I reasoned that this would not happen under normal conditions. Life was not too hard up to Gila Center, but since segregation and coming here it has been a life of turmoil, anxiety and fear. My brother and I did not want to come here but we could not go against the wishes of our mother. She isn't young anymore so this life of moving about hasn't been easy for her so we obeyed her, thinking it was the only way to make up to all her unhappiness. We had life before us but mother's life is closer to end . . . so we couldn't hurt her with any more worries. Since coming here I found out it was wrong in coming here. There are too many pro-Japanese organizations with too much influence. Naturally mother in the state of mind she was in would be greatly taken in by them. She had the family name in one of the organizations but we (my brother and I) absolutely refused to acknowledge it so she reluctantly withdrew our name. . . . When the renunciation citizenship came mother again wanted us to renounce. My brother luckily was under age but I could not fight against her this time. One [thing] that put a scare into me was that families would

---

Source: Dorothy Swaine Thomas and Richard Nishimoto, *Japanese-American Evacuation and Resettlement: I: The Spoilage* (Berkeley, Calif., 1946), p. 352. Copyright © 1946 by The Regents of the University of California; reprinted by permission of the University of California Press.

be separated. To me, I just had to sign on that paper, so I piled lies upon lies at the renunciation hearing. All horrid and untruthful lies they were. I didn't mean anything I said at that time, but fear and anxiety was too strong. I have regretted that I took such a drastic step—in fact I knew I would regret it before I went into it but I was afraid if I was torn away from the family I would never see them again in this uncertain world. I should have had more confidence in America but being torn away from my home and all made things so uncertain. I would never have renounced if the Administration made it clear that there would be no family separation. But the Administration could not assure us there would be no separation.

Appendix

Sources Regrouped Chronologically

1775–1783 (American Revolution)	1, 2, 44, 186, 235, 274, 275, 276, 277, 278, 280
1784–1860	3, 4, 67, 85, 101, 236
1861–1865 (Civil War)	5, 6, 9, 10, 12, 13, 15, 45, 72, 81, 86, 87, 88, 89, 114, 116, 117, 136, 138, 140, 168, 176, 198, 200, 214, 231, 237, 242, 265
1866–1916	82, 153, 254
1917–1918 (World War I)	7, 11, 16, 43, 69, 83, 91, 92, 93, 105, 118, 141, 179, 187, 190, 199, 201, 232, 234, 243, 263
1919–1940	30, 32, 46, 224, 255, 266
1941–1945 (World War II)	17, 18, 19, 35, 36, 37, 38, 53, 65, 66, 68, 70, 73, 74, 75, 79, 80, 95, 96, 97, 98, 99, 100, 102, 106, 107, 108, 109, 110, 115, 119, 122, 123, 124, 125, 126, 127, 128, 129, 130, 133, 134, 135, 142, 143, 144, 151, 152, 154, 155, 159, 161, 162, 163, 174, 180, 181, 188, 191, 192, 194, 195, 202, 205, 206, 207, 208, 209, 210, 213, 215, 218, 222, 223, 225, 226, 227, 228, 229, 233, 238, 239, 240, 244, 246, 248, 260, 261, 262, 264, 279, 281, 282, 283, 284
1946–1964 (Including Korean War)	31, 33, 33a, 34, 39, 40, 41, 47, 57, 58, 59, 62, 63, 90, 94, 103, 104, 112, 147, 150, 156, 157, 158, 164, 217, 220, 241, 245, 256, 257, 259, 268, 269, 271, 272
1965–present	8, 14, 20, 21, 22, 23, 24, 25, 26, 27, 28, 29, 42, 48, 49, 50, 51, 52, 54, 55, 56, 60, 61, 64, 71, 76, 77, 78, 84, 111, 113, 120, 121, 131, 132, 137, 139, 145, 146, 148, 149, 160, 165, 166, 167, 169, 170, 171, 172, 173, 175, 177, 178, 182, 183, 184, 185, 189, 193, 196, 197, 203, 204, 211, 212, 216, 219, 221, 230, 247, 249, 250, 251, 252, 253, 258, 267, 270, 273

Index

ABOUT THE AUTHOR

Peter Karsten, Professor of History at the University of Pittsburgh, is the author of *The Naval Aristocracy, Patriot Heroes in England and America,* and *Law, Soldiers, and Combat* (Greenwood Press, 1978). He has written articles for such journals as *Military Affairs, Foreign Policy,* and *American Quarterly.* He is a consultant to the Hudson Institute and other centers of policy analysis, and often serves as a guest lecturer.